# Hope 365

## Daily Meditations for the Grieving Heart

CLARA HINTON

ISBN: 1539991539
ISBN-13: 978-1539991533

*To Grandmom who introduced me to pork chops, mashed potatoes and gravy, and most importantly to listen for the sounds of the whippoorwill. I miss you forever and always.*

## ACKNOWLEDGMENTS

To caffeine and chocolate, my best friends through countless all-nighters. You kept me awake through those long nights and gave me five extra pounds as a bonus that I really didn't need.

A most special thank you to the one who kept me on task meeting deadlines, spent many late nights correcting my grammar and hideously long run on sentences, and who was the quiet voice of inspiration whispering to me, "You can do it. You're almost there. You can do it, Mom!"

I love you, Alex. I seriously could not have written this book without you. I, along with all those who will read this book and receive daily nourishment of the soul, thank you from the depths of our very being. You truly are a one-in-a-million. You have been my main source of hope and inspiration throughout the many months of writing this book!

# INTRODUCTION

If your life has been touched by loss, then *Hope 365* is a book written just for you!

My life was shattered by loss at an early age when my young sister tragically died. Following her death, I've suffered through several miscarriages, a stillborn son, and most recently my heart has been shattered by the death of my adult son. Grief and despair have been my companions many times over.

Several years ago, I began to notice that every time loss entered my life, there was an unexplainable emptiness that lingered for a long time. The nights became unbearably lonely, and the days were clouded by the pain and grief of loss. It felt as though the world had been turned inside out and upside down and nothing at all made sense anymore.

But, in the midst of this agonizing pain, there was always a stirring deep within my soul that I just couldn't stop. Time and time again, that feeling led me to a place of a new, deeper appreciation of life and a place of quiet inner peace.

Hope is much greater than any grief we will ever bear! As Rumi has stated so well in his ancient writings, "There is a candle in your heart, ready to be kindled. There is a void in your soul, ready to be filled."

I wrote this book of daily meditations to gently guide you from a place of deep, inconsolable grief to a place of inner peace and hope. Your grieving soul will be filled with the assurances of hope found in the simplicity and beauty of nature, and these meditations will guide you through the hard questions we ask during grief to a place where the embers of your inner flame of hope will be ignited!

Hope is endlessly alive and lives within you! It is my prayer that *Hope 365: Daily Meditations for the Grieving Heart* will not only sustain you through the dark days of grief but will guide you to a place of life-giving hope and inner joy.

With love and endless hope,

Clara Hinton

## Day 1

*Never be afraid to trust an unknown future to an all-knowing God.*

We know this journey of grief all too well. It's long. It's exhausting. It hurts. Others don't understand. We don't even understand. We question. We ask why a thousand times and more, full well knowing we'll never get an answer. Some questions never have answers. So, we are left with the one thing that we must do. TRUST. We can trust that we will get through. We can trust that the sun will shine again. We can trust that others have made it and we will, too.

**Today I will place my faith in trust. I will get through today. That's all I have to do. Just get through today with trust that tomorrow is a new day.**

## Day 2

*Each new day bursts forth with the promise of new hope.*

Do you feel like no one understands your pain? This grief you're carrying is so heavy that sometimes it weighs you down to a point of total despair. Everywhere you look is tainted by dark clouds of sorrow and tears. When will the pain end? When will there be a day when life feels good again?

Deep inside of us is an inner strength pushing to make its way out. Close your eyes and picture your life in a peaceful state. Listen for sounds of nature and allow these sounds calm your spirit and soothe your soul. Remember that today is just one day of your life. Tomorrow is full of expectancy and hope. Cling to that thought and make it your strength—just for today.

**Just when the sky looks the darkest a star appears to brighten the way.**

## Day 3

*If it can be verified, we don't need faith. Faith is for that which lies on the other side of reason. Faith is what makes life bearable, with all its tragedies. Faith holds us up when nothing makes sense.*

Why do bad things happen to good people? Why do the innocent have to suffer? Why is there sickness and death? Why are young children afflicted with sorrow and pain? Why does life have so much tragedy? These are valid questions. This is real life in the trenches.

The truth is we live in a world where sickness and evil exist. From the beginning of time, innocent ones have suffered. No, it's not fair! Life isn't fair in so many different ways. But, we must remind ourselves over and over again that even in the darkest of times we can find blessings.

Look to this day for the rainbow and not the storm. Just for today focus on your blessings. You can do it! Allow that blessing to hold you steady when you are on shaky ground.

**The strength of a ship is only fully demonstrated when it faces a hurricane. Call on your inner reserves to guide your ship full of burdens and grief safely ashore.**

## Day 4

*"I will refresh the weary and satisfy the faint."* Jeremiah 31:25

Grief causes us to shed so many tears. Our hearts literally weep when we experience loss in our lives. We spend sleepless nights soaking our pillows with the grief pouring from our hearts in the form of tears. We want nothing more than for dawn to appear and to bring us new hope.

Is your grief born of the loss of a loved one? Is your heart breaking because of discouragement and endless trials here on earth? Do you feel as though no one understands you and all of your friends have abandoned you? Don't allow these feelings to overtake you. You are never alone!

Say a prayer. Call a friend. Look for your guardian angel sitting by your side. Take several deep breaths and allow your spirit to be comforted and your soul to be calmed. Practice taking slow, meditative breaths today as you say, "I am not alone in this. When I call on help, I am comforted."

**A teardrop on earth summons the King of heaven.**

## Day 5

*"In Thy presence is fullness of joy." Psalm 16:11*

When a new year arrives there are so many different emotions. For many, this is an exciting time of setting new goals and looking forward to the coming year with enthusiasm and the anticipation of having the best year ever!

Reality often settles in very shortly after the New Year, though, serving as a reminder that last year's bills are still unpaid, the health diagnosis has not changed, and the broken relationship has not been restored. Unresolved grief issues loom heavily on the heart, and the joy of the New Year quickly disappears, ushering in waves of loneliness, discouragement, and fear.

Rather than thinking in big terms such as an entire year, it helps to chunk life down into measurable moments that are not so overwhelming. We can be joyful for one hour. We can be filled with hopeful anticipation for one day. We can be thankful for our blessings this moment.

Thinking in smaller segments of time helps the grieving heart to cope with today's pain and gives enough energy to wake up feeling ready to tackle one more day. A grieving heart needs time to find the rainbow. A heart that feels lost needs time to catch the shimmering star shining through the dark night. A heart that is lonely needs time to change focus in order to see the miracle found in the daily sunrise. Be patient with yourself, and approach every new year one day at a time.

**It only takes one tiny flicker of hope to spread sunbeams across the endless sky.**

## Day 6

*In the darkest night there is light. In the deepest grief there is hope.*

Did you ever feel so alone in your grief and pain that you felt there was never going to be a day when life would get better? I think every grieving person has had situations like that when life felt utterly hopeless. Your dearest, most cherished relationship has been broken. You've experienced the death of a child. Your body has been stricken by cancer. Or, an accident has left you paralyzed. Where is the hope? Where is the light? You cry out in pain that life isn't worth living any more!

Hold on! The morning is a critical time of day. That is when the sun rises. I'm convinced that God designed it that way. With every new sunrise comes a new ray of hope. Today practice looking for your one ray of sunshine—even if you're in the middle of a torrential downpour. Remind yourself over and over again that the morning brings with it a freshness—a time when you can begin a new day. Your circumstances might not change, but you can change your thoughts and that will give you the hope you need to carry you through this day!

**For this moment, I will let go of all questions about my life and simply be still.**

## Day 7

*My grief will someday ebb like the tide, but for today grief is my constant companion.*

Why are we so hard on ourselves when we grieve? Do you know that tears were given to us as part of our human makeup for a reason? Tears are cleansing. Tears relieve stress that is unhealthy for us. Tears allow us to vent held in anger and pain.

We know that time allows the pain of grief and loss to settle and we'll eventually be able to manage our grief more easily. But, sometimes it's helpful to have a friend pull up a chair, sit by our side and, without saying a word, allow us to grieve. No questions asked.

**I will push forward in my grief, but just for today I have a need to release my tears and have a listening ear.**

## Day 8

*Anxiety does not empty tomorrow of its sorrows, but only empties today of its strength.*

Why is it that grief magnifies our anxiety? We worry about everything when we're grieving. We can't seem to focus on even the tiniest of things because our anxiety overtakes our thinking. Anxious thoughts are so overpowering that they can rob us of any joy that might come our way.

Just for one day try tossing all anxious thoughts aside and see what happens. Our headache leaves us. We feel full of new energy. Our thoughts are clearer. We can even find the cloud with the silver lining!

**It's important to calm my anxious thoughts so that I can enjoy the blessings of today.**

## Day 9

*Laughter is a thing of the past when grief is dwelling in my heart.*

One of the first things that ends when we lose a loved one is our ability to laugh. It's almost as though we believe that laughter is some kind of betrayal. We tell ourselves that if we enjoy laughter we are no longer putting our loved one at the front of our thoughts. We convince ourselves that it is wrong to laugh because that means we're being disrespectful. We're afraid to laugh because if we do, we'll know that we are finding joy in living once again.

Do you know that laughter is a wonderful gift? When we grow to the point of giving ourselves permission to laugh again, we will know that we are moving forward in this difficult journey of loss and grief.

**To be able to laugh without guilt is a beautiful gift to give myself—healing to the heart and soul.**

## Day 10

*The weather changes from hour to hour and so does our grief.*

We're forever checking the weather. We know that storm clouds can appear one hour, followed by rainbows and sunshine the next. We debate taking an umbrella to work or taking a chance that the storm will pass over.

That's how it is with grief. We never know from hour to hour what kind of mood we'll be in. Will a trigger come along that will send us back to deep, raw grief? Will this be a calm, reflective day where we are able to smile and be productive?

Our emotions are on one wild roller coaster ride when we're grieving, and we never know what to expect. Keep in mind that eventually our emotional weather evens out. There will be more predictable days of sunshine than rain. There will be greater spans of time between the storms. In time we will not be so concerned about our emotional setbacks because we will experience fewer and fewer of these days. Pack your tissues, but know that you won't always need them!

**The emotional roller coaster of grief is to be expected, but the ride eventually evens out and slows down.**

## Day 11

*Faith sees the invisible, believes the incredible, and receives the impossible.*

Grief is such a tricky thing. It surprises us by appearing at all hours of the day and night, and just when we think we've gotten beyond our grief, it comes back again to bite us and leave us in pain. This is especially true when we've had a loved one die. We try to move forward in life, but that five-letter word grief clings to us and doesn't want to let go.

We need our faith more now than ever before. Faith that we will one day see joy in life again. Belief that there is still more good in life than bad. We need to practice looking for the sun that is hidden beyond the storm clouds and really, really believe that there will be a day when that hovering darkness will move beyond us and we will see more sunshine than clouds.

Can we truly do this? Yes! Time has a way of allowing our hearts to manage our pain and to remove the filter of tears that has clouded our daily lives. Be patient. Believe. Trust. Look ahead. Your day of joy is coming!

**I know it can't be forced, but my day of sunshine is coming if I keep looking ahead in belief!**

## Day 12

*"The Lord lifts the burdens of those bent beneath their loads." Psalm 146:8*

When we are grieving, our smiles disappear. In fact, one of the most common ways we can know a person is in deep grief is by their inability to smile. It's so hard to see joy through our tears. When a heart is broken by loss, we find it almost impossible to see beyond our hour of pain and distress. We hurt from the inside out and we find no relief. Day and night our tears cry out asking for this pain to go away, but we find that the darkness remains.

Have you noticed, though, that smiles are contagious? There is something gentle and peaceful about a smile. Smiles are like rays of sunshine in a dark, dreary room. A smile can lift our heart and brighten our darkest hours. Can you smile when you're in deep, unrelenting grief?

Everyone can smile, but it sometimes takes lots of practice. Why not begin today by looking in the mirror and forcing a smile? Look at the image of yourself softening. Feel the tension begin to be released.

Give yourself permission to smile every day about something. Think of something that has made you smile in the past, and just for that minute smile. You will find light entering your world of grief!

**Every smile brings light into a world of darkness.**

## Day 13

*Joy can be found in the simple pleasures of nature. A flower in bloom. The cool summer breeze. The sunlight dancing over the ocean waves. The moonlit sky on a starry night.*

Our sadness from loss will be with us forever. We know that because we realize that nothing can fill that empty space left by the passing of our loved one. It's so important to take little mini grief breaks in order to replenish our souls.

Just for a few minutes each day lay aside your grieving and soak up the joy found in the small pleasures of life. Pick up a kitten and lay its furry face against your cheek and listen to it purring. Go outside and splash your bare feet in a puddle. Sit under the shade of a tall tree and sip on some homemade lemonade.

Allow the earth to embrace you and shower you with blessings. When we take these small breaks from our grief, we give our heart some much-needed hugs of comfort and joy!

**When I give myself permission to experience small everyday joys, I'm also giving myself new courage, new strength, and new hope!**

## Day 14

*"Cast your burden upon the Lord and He will sustain you."*
*Psalm 55:22*

Children are wonderful teachers of prayer. They can pray about anything. Their list of thanks at mealtime covers blades of grass, tiny ants, scampering rabbits, singing birds, and the brightly colored dandelions. It's so refreshing to hear the prayers of children because they are never at a loss for words.

When we are grieving a loss, we often feel like praying, but we don't know what to say. We find it so hard to honestly express our thanks during times of deep inner pain. We need help, but we don't know how to ask. We want to talk about our grief in our prayers, but the words just won't come.

Do you know that God tells us he knows our thoughts already? Do you know that we don't even have to say a word for a prayer to be a prayer? God knows the pain of a broken heart and is listening even when we can't talk. He is there to help us. Eventually the words for our prayers will come, but until then don't worry. Let your thoughts be your prayers.

**I know there is strength in prayer, but sometimes I can't find the words needed to pray.**

## Day 15

*A sunrise is nature's way of telling us there is hope.*

If you're like me, you never grow weary of watching the majestic beauty of sunrises. Every day, right at the appointed time, the sun appears over the horizon dressed in radiant beauty. That gives me hope in the master plan of life.

When our hearts have been broken by grief, we lose track of our days and nights. Time blends into one enormous span of chaos and nothingness. Nothing in our life seems to make sense any more and we long for some normalcy. We long for something that is consistent. Something that will give us the hope that our lives will not always feel chaotic and out of sync.

Take time this week to watch an early morning sunrise. Savor the moments right before the breaking of dawn. Bask in the sunshine of this new day knowing that there is a rhythm to life. Give it some time. When your grief begins to settle, you will find your way back into the flow of life again.

**Life will never be the same again after loss, but I can eventually learn to enjoy the sunshine of each day.**

## Day 16

*Every winter comes to an end making way for a beautiful spring.*

Winters where I live are harsh. For five months the harsh winds blow, snow falls, the temperatures never rise above freezing, and the sky remains gray. Every year I mark on my calendar how many days until spring because I know, without doubt, that nature never fails me. Spring will arrive and with spring will come beautiful flowers, green grass, and warm sunshine.

Grief settles in on our hearts like the cold winter. We sometimes feel like spring will never arrive to give us relief from the storms of life. Hold on. Remember the lessons that nature teaches us. Just as spring arrives on time each new season, so will your day of replenishment and hope.

**All suffering must somewhere stop; all grief holds the seeds of new hope.**

## Day 17

*"Do not fret." Psalm 37:1*

It's human nature for most of us to worry. This is especially true when grief has knocked us down. When a loved one dies, we worry about so many things. How will we survive even a day without the one we love so much?

If this tragedy can happen, what is next? What if our health goes and we have no way of paying the bills? What if our relationship ends and we're left all alone? We worry about work. We worry about finances. We worry about our children. We worry about the future. We worry about every detail in life.

The truth is that worry never helps us. Worry stresses us. Worry creates added pressure in our lives. Worry is such a waste of time and energy. Grief has already depleted us of energy and emotional resources. Worry drains us completely to the point of not being able to enjoy anything.

Practice one hour every day of ridding your mind of all worries and cares. Close your eyes and envision yourself in a place where you can toss aside every worry and care. For me, that place is sitting on the sandy shores of a beach watching the ebb and flow of the tide as sunbeams dance upon the sparkling water.

Breathe deeply and slowly, freeing your mind of all worries. As you do, you will relax and find that the circumstances in your life haven't changed, but you are in a much better place emotionally and physically to handle the grief that is in your life.

**Worry is the biggest joy robber of all.**

## Day 18

*A kind word rings throughout all eternity.*

For whatever reason, when we're experiencing grief in our lives, we distance ourselves from many of the bigger things in life such as international happenings. It's almost as if our world has shrunk and the only things that are pressing to us are the immediate.

We know what it's like to hurt on a personal scale, and we become intensely concerned with the small things. We watch the birds soaring through the sky. We closely examine the petals in a rose. We pick up a leaf and study the veins running through it as if we understood every connection between the earth, leaf, and tree. The little things count.

Maybe that's why it means so much to us when someone gives us a kind word during our moments of grief. We don't need lengthy, eloquent speeches about how one day our hearts will heal and we will see some kind of good out of the ashes of our life. It's the little, ordinary words that mean so much: "I care."; "I'm here with you."; "I'll be back tomorrow with some food."; "I think of you every day."; "I'm here to listen."; "I'm your friend for life."

**A kind word can lift a broken spirit and help bring hope to the hopeless.**

## Day 19

*Real grief is not healed by time. If time does anything, it deepens our grief. —Henri Nouwen*

We don't want to hear things like time deepens our grief! That's too hard for us to think about when our pain already feels unbearable. How can our pain feel any worse?

The truth is that our grief does deepen with time. Time allows us to really examine the true meaning of the life that is no longer with us. After my son died, I thought of so many wonderful character traits about him that I hadn't thought about while he was alive. Why did it take his death for me to realize how much inner strength he had? Why didn't I see all of the facets of his creative mind at work? Why didn't I understand how resilient he was when life threw hard knocks at him?

Time opens up new avenues of insight. We see deeper and more fully, and at first that hurts because we grieve deeper. We miss our loved one even more. We sorrow in the fact that we didn't see more of the miracle of life that we were given.

Yes, time deepens our grief. But, time also allows us to appreciate those around us more fully. Let us focus on that and learn from our grief.

**My loved one is with me forever, and through my grief I can learn to love even more. My eyes are opened to an entirely new side of life that can be seen only through death.**

## Day 20

*Grief can weaken even the strongest mind and cause it to question.*

I never understood what grief did to the mind until I was flattened by grief when my son died. I couldn't make the simplest decision of what to eat for breakfast. I would lay in bed for over an hour trying to decide if I should make coffee or tea. Next on the list was what to wear. It got to the point that I had to write down a list the night before and then I would toss and turn in bed wondering if I had made the right decision.

When loss occurs and grief enters our hearts, our minds are confused. We no longer have normalcy as our everyday thermometer. Chaos is the norm, and even the simplest of things don't make any sense. Tomatoes and cheese or tomatoes and cucumbers? It's frustrating, and it's frightening. It's a wonder that we remember how to breathe in and breathe out. Truth be known, sometimes we don't remember. That's how grief affects the mind!

It gets better, but it takes time and patience. We get so frustrated with ourselves because we realize how disorganized our world has become but we simply don't have the strength or the ability to make a simple decision.

Baby steps...remember to take baby steps. Accomplish one thing today. Make one decision today. And, another one tomorrow. In time, you will be walking once again.

**Even small decisions seem like mountains in the early days of grief. Be patient. It won't be like this forever. One step, one decision at a time.**

## Day 21

*We must let go of the life we planned in order to accept the life that is now waiting for us.*

Life rarely goes as planned. In fact, I don't know too many people who have set out in a direction and have stayed the course achieving all of the goals that were set before them.

Instead, life is full of all kinds of highs and lows and unexpected twists and turns. There are unforeseen tragedies that come into our lives, leaving us wondering why we even took the time to set goals. This is especially true when the grief of loss enters into our lives. We never plan on losing a loved one, especially a child. No parent ever thinks about burying their child, and yet this happens more often than we'd like to think.

Life is full of changes and when tragedy strikes we must learn to eventually let go of the plans we once made and learn how to live within the new life that is now ours. Is this easy? Absolutely not! But, we draw strength from seeing others who have gone before us. They have forged the way for us and have shown us that it can be done. The inner will to survive amid life's greatest tragedies is stronger than we think!

**I cannot always choose the path that is before me, but I can choose the attitude I will have about the journey.**

## Day 22

*"Your heavenly Father knows your needs. He will always give you all you need from day to day." Luke 12:30*

When grief enters our lives, we begin to think about all of the things we will miss in the future. Our minds run wild thinking about all of the additional losses we will encounter. This is especially true if a child has died. We think about the entire loss of the future such as graduations, weddings, grandbabies, and vacations spent together. We grieve so much harder because the future is too much for us to think about without our child.

Why do we think we have to think about all of our losses at once? There is only so much the heart and mind can handle, and the future is far too much of a span of time to grieve. Just for today, let's think of life one day at a time. That's enough for a heart that has been broken. We need time to digest the minutes and not try to project into the wide expanse of the future. We know we can handle anything for just one day, so let's keep our mind focused on today.

**I will not look to the future, but will think only about today.**

## Day 23

*The days of winter seem to drag on and on. My soul needs the freshness of springtime and the blossoming of summer.*

Grief seems like it will never end. No matter how hard we try to look for the bright spots in the day, there always seems to be that dark cloud hovering above us reminding us that there is sorrow in our heart. A broken heart carries within it a deep hole that nothing can ever fill.

Yet we know that life must be lived even though we're carrying this heavy load of grief in the very soul of our heart. Deep inside we realize that we can make choices that will help lift some of the heavy grief. Sometimes it helps to act out our joy.

Pretend that you can reach up and lift that dark cloud and move it aside. When you do this, envision light streaming around you showering you with soft rose petals, dancing sunbeams, and fluttering butterflies. Breathe slowly and take in the peacefulness of the moment. Feel the tension floating away and savor every precious moment. Summer has arrived, if only in your dreams, for you to enjoy.

**I can make choices that help move the mountain of grief that is stored within my heart.**

## Day 24

*Since grief has made its dwelling place in my heart, this earth doesn't seem like home to me.*

When we grieve the loss of a loved one, our hearts are consumed day and night with grief. We sometimes struggle with life on this earth because we want to go where our loved one has gone. All of the familiarity that we once knew is gone. It feels like we're a stranger in a foreign land. It's lonely and frightening to be here.

Thankfully, these moments of desperation and loneliness pass and we know that we must stay here until it is our time to leave. Until then, we will hold close to us those memories that are so precious, and we will begin to make new memories as we learn to live within our brokenness. We understand that nothing will ever be as it once was, but we can keep those things that comfort us and make us feel safe as we begin to explore life as a new person.

**I will not be afraid of the changes that are happening to me. I will accept the new me and learn to love me just as I am.**

## Day 25

*The grief of losing a loved one never ends, but we can learn to be thankful for the blessings that have remained by our side.*

Many people will tell you that there is good that comes out of everything including the death of a loved one. There's no guarantee that comes with that statement. Some people become very angry and embittered. Others are all-consumed by their grief and never leave that place of desolation and loneliness.

What makes the difference, then, in the ones who can survive such a blow to the heart? When we surround our lives by loving family, friends, and our faith community and seek out the blessings found in nature, we can make it through this storm. In time, we will learn how to see the small, meaningful blessings that touch our lives every day, and we will feel the warmth of the sun shining on our face.

**I will look for the gifts that life sends my way and practice being thankful.**

## Day 26

*There is never a good time for a loved one to die, but it is always the right time to cherish the joy our loved one brought into our life.*

Death really does sting. When we lose a loved one, the pain is worse than anything we've ever felt before. In our pain, we cry out that this isn't fair. Our loved one's life wasn't supposed to end this way. The one we loved with all of our heart was supposed to be here with us and not be taken away so soon.

When we move beyond the initial raw days of grief, we will come to realize that we were so blessed to be given the opportunity to have someone to love with all of our heart. Even when our pain is so severe that we think we can't go on another minute, we realize that there are some people who never have this opportunity to feel this kind of pain. Why? Because they never had the blessing of someone so wonderful to love. It is then we become aware of what a wonderful gift we had been given.

**I will always be thankful and humbled because I was given the gift of someone wonderful to love.**

## Day 27

*"Weeping may linger for the night, but joy comes in the morning." Psalm 30:5*

Have you ever noticed how grief seems to grow worse during the night? Maybe it's the stillness of the evening that brings our sorrow to the surface. Or perhaps nighttime is when our thoughts cannot be quieted because we must be alone with them. We toss and turn, and our thoughts grow out of control. Grief engulfs us and the tears flow like a swollen river.

Most people do their crying at night when they are alone. That's when our hearts seem to open up and pour out all of the pain we've been holding in during the day. Nighttime seems to be the most appropriate time for us to cry.

When the sky begins to lighten and the sun peeks out from behind the darkness, something happens. We are still sad and our pain is still living within our heart, but we feel different in the morning. Less afraid.

Maybe it's because of the familiar sounds of birds singing outside our bedroom window. The smell of freshly brewed coffee and cinnamon rolls hot out of the oven. The familiar sight of the sunshine and blue sky help carry away the tears of the night and allow us to start over again.

**Every sunrise is God's announcement of a brand new day.**

## Day 28

*"Have no anxiety at all, but in everything, by prayer and petition, with thanksgiving make your requests known to God. Then the peace of God that surpasses all understanding will guard your hearts and minds."*
*Philippians 4:6-7*

Losing a loved one does something to our trust in life. We become fearful of so many things. Our minds race with anxious thoughts. We're so afraid of what might come our way. In our human reasoning we think if the loss of a loved one can happen then anything can happen. We might fall down the steps and break both of our legs. While on vacation, we might have a heart attack and there won't be any doctor available to help.

On and on our fearful thoughts go. Why? Because our trust has now been broken by the loss of the life of someone we loved dearly. We somehow thought that death would never take the one we loved. Not this way. Not this suddenly. Not when it was least expected.

When fear overrides your trust, it helps to pause and silently meditate. Think of all of the many things that have gone right today. You're 're alive. You were able to breathe. You saw the rising and setting of the sun. You were given the promise of a brand new day with countless possibilities.

Rest your head upon your pillow tonight and say some words of thankfulness. Force the words if you're not feeling them. As you fall asleep feel your anxiety decrease as your trust in the goodness of life fills your heart. Feel the gentle peace replacing your fear.

**Allow God to calm your anxious heart and to give you peace.**

## Day 29

*"The Lord has sent me to give them flowers in place of their sorrow, olive oil in place of their mourning." Isaiah 61:2-3*

When our grief is fresh and raw, all we can remember is that it happened. We remember every detail of that day when our heart broke in two. We can tell each detail with clarity. Our thoughts are consumed day and night with the pain of that moment when we lost part of our heart.

It doesn't happen quickly, but over time our thoughts begin to change. We start remembering different things. We remember happy moments. We recall times with our loved one and catch ourselves smiling. We can look at pictures with delight as we remember those special times spent together.

The winter thaw takes time, but it will come. One day at a time we will draw nearer to our spring until we see that first sign of the daffodil pushing up through the once-frozen ground. As you stare at those first buds of spring in awe, remember that your grief is also giving way to spring. Your day will come when joy will be more abundant than your sadness.

**Somewhere hidden beneath my grief is the hope that spring will return.**

## Day 30

*When we're lost in the dark without a flashlight, we cry out, "Get me home! Get me to safety now!" There's nobody around to listen, and we keep digging ourselves deeper into the forest. It would be better to find a safe place to sit until the morning sunlight arrives to guide us home.*

We want to run away. We don't have a clue where, but we know we want to get away from all of the pain of grief. If we could just climb to the top of a mountain or hide in a cave away from everyone we'd be okay.

If we could squeeze our eyes shut and sleep we will forget. If we never mention this day again it will vanish from our thoughts. If we drink enough, we can numb our pain.

The problem is we can't run away because we have nowhere to go. We eventually have to open our eyes because we can't sleep forever. Drinking will only cause more pain. Sooner or later we will have to face our loss. And, when we do we will find that we are much stronger than we thought. The wider we open our eyes to what has happened, the less power that day has over us.

**We have to do it, so we might as well begin today. It's better to face our grief today. In the end, it will be much easier on us.**

## Day 31

*To resist change is to resist life.*

We all do it. We fight change. It's uncomfortable. We don't like to leave our places where we feel safe, and who can blame us for that? But, often it's the changes that bring about the emergence of the real person we have been holding back.

Grief pushes us into a place of discomfort and brings about changes that we don't like at first. But, when we look back we can feel good about stepping out in faith as we have learned how to put one foot forward, then another, and then another. We display courage through change!

We will never feel good about the losses that have touched our lives, but we can feel happy about the positive changes that came about when we were pushed out of our comfort zone.

The widow who can now drive a car and pay her bills. The newly single mom who is taking care of the finances, the kids, and managing a job. The dad who has taken over the skills in the kitchen and has learned how to communicate so well with his children.

Give yourself a pat on the back. You deserve it. You've displayed courage in the face of fear, and you've harnessed change into something positive.

**I will keep looking for some good that emerges from the bad. I know it's there, and I trust that one day my eyes will see it.**

## Day 32

*If you stare at the blade of grass long enough you will soon see the plush green field before you.*

In the face of disaster and despair, what gives you hope? What makes you hold on? Have you ever thought about what keeps you going? Is it seeing the sunrise every morning and thinking about the possibilities of a better day? Is it the twinkling of the stars at night that remind you that no night is completely dark? Is it hearing the birds singing their early morning songs of praise? Listen carefully, and you will hear them!

The beauty in all of nature gives me hope. My flowers keep me holding on when life closes in around me. I'm reminded of the harsh, cold winter with the ground covered in snow. I know with full assurance that, right on time, the earth knows when to begin its spring thaw so that the first flowers of the new season can emerge. When I see the very first daffodil burst forth in all of its glory, my spirit is renewed with new hope. I know that no matter what, I can hold on until the spring thaw.

**No winter lasts forever. Spring is on its way and will arrive at the appointed moment, and oh how glorious it will be!**

## Day 33

*"And there appeared to him an angel from heaven, strengthening him." Luke 22:43*

When loss occurs leaving us in deep grief we often ask what happened to our friends. They seem to disappear after a few weeks. Life goes on rather quickly for them and we are left sitting in the ashes of our mourning and pain.

It's kind of strange, yet wonderful, how life works during our moments of greatest need. People we don't even know enter our lives with love and encouragement. They show up in the supermarket. They gift us with smiles when we're walking across the street. We glance up from our seat in the waiting room at the doctor's office and the person next to us asks how we're doing. The mailman brings us a card from "someone who cares."

Our old friends may vanish, but new ones appear. Maybe there is truth in angels visiting us while we're unaware. Yes, I'm sure of it. This world has angels walking among us and they are the ones who tenderly come at just the right moment to give our heart a hug.

**We meet people who leave imprints on our heart not by chance but by divine appointment.**

## Day 34

*My tears are simply the outpouring of my inner grief.*

Why do we try to hide our tears in front of others? We feel embarrassed. We feel weak. We feel uncomfortable. And, we struggle trying so hard to fight back our tears because we're afraid that those who see us will turn away.

Fortunate are we when we find a friend who gives us permission to shed our tears without shame. We long for someone who will let us be ourselves. We want them to somehow share in our grief even if it's just a little bit.

We need to know that someone is feeling part of the pain we're feeling. No, we would never wish this on them, but it helps so much to know that they understand a little bit of what we're going through. We need our grief to be validated.

**Listen to me in my grief and allow my tears to fall without shame. You will be counted among my most cherished friends and support on all the earth!**

## Day 35

*Friends are like sunshine to the soul and a soothing balm to the grieving heart.*

Plants can't thrive without sunshine, and neither can we. We need the vitamins from the sunshine in order to survive.

We also need the love that others can give us when we are grieving. Love is our nourishment. Love is our source of vitamins for the soul. We want to isolate ourselves from others when we're grieving because it's much easier than reaching out. Isolation won't help us in our healing, nor will being shut off from others give us the soul nourishment that we need.

It's a mutual thing. We all need each other in order to survive. Love is the glue that holds us together when we feel like we're falling apart. Love nurtures and nourishes the hurting heart.

**Today I will not let my grief push me away from those I love. Instead, I will draw them near and allow their love to pour nourishment into my weary, malnourished soul.**

## Day 36

*"Come to me, all you who are weary and burdened, and I will give you rest." Matt. 11:28*

Sometimes we feel trapped by the cares and worries of this world. We are overworked, discouraged, and our hearts feel so burdened with the weight of grief. We are often left feeling like life is spinning hopelessly out of control.

During those times of feeling tired and lost, we need reminders of hope to keep us going. When we are tempted to quit, we need reminders that God is still in control. Watch each new morning being ushered in by the glorious sunrise. Gaze at the evening sky and watch the stars light a path through the darkness. Listen to the far away sounds of the songbird whistling a happy tune. Hope is everywhere when we are listening for it!

God hasn't left us alone in our fears. He stays right by our side and tenderly reminds us that He is always near. God's love is everywhere. He will take us through this day and gently guide us through tomorrow.

**When you least expect it hope comes knocking at your door.**

## Day 37

*"Fear not, for I am with you; be not dismayed, for I am your God." Isaiah 41:10*

Have you been perplexed by the happenings in your life? Do you feel the need to know the answers today? Why does crushing pain continue to touch your life? Why do friends around you prosper while you continue to feel the heavy weight of financial setbacks and broken relationships? Why did your loved one have to die?

Sometimes God doesn't choose to give us answers. Instead, He wants us to greet each new day with a confidence that we trust God to know what He's doing in our lives. Look at the mighty ocean and see His power. View the expanse of the sky and feel His unlimited might. Watch the butterfly emerge and understand His ability to perform miracles.

What is God going to do in your life? Often, He will never tell you. Instead, He reveals to you who He is. God is the God you know every time you watch the magnificence of a sunrise. Don't be surprised when God can take the darkest hour of your life and turn it into a bright and glorious day. The same God of miracles can place joy back into your empty heart when you continue to patiently wait on Him.

**When we allow God to be the pilot, we will never find ourselves stranded alone in the dark.**

## Day 38

*"He is my defender: I will not be defeated." Psalm 62:6*

It's so easy to feel lost and afraid when we are facing hard issues in life. We're left wondering what the future holds, and we question whether we will be able to make it through another day.

It takes great courage to look above the darkness of our pain to a place where there is enough light shining to direct our unknown pathway.

When we fix our eyes on the expanse of the sky, we are reminded of the unending love of the Shepherd. As we watch the brilliance of a sunrise, we are reminded of the gift of a brand new day. As we take in the beauty of a rainbow, we are assured of the promises of God to restore our soul, revive our broken spirit, and take us to a place of inner peace and rest.

As we remind ourselves of the many miracles that unfold before our very eyes each and every day our souls begin to fill up with the blessing of new hope!

**No matter how steep the mountain or how rocky the road, you will never be left to climb alone.**

## Day 39

*"Why are you downcast, O my soul? Why so disturbed within me? Put your hope in God, for I will yet praise Him, my Savior and my God." Psalm 43:5*

Hope is not pretending there is no grief or pain in your life. It is knowing that tomorrow will bring a new day with new beginnings and new promises. Hope is knowing that you will find the inner strength to go on. Hope is waiting for God to reveal Himself in the everyday things of life. Hope is believing that no matter what happens, you will be given the strength it takes to make it through.

**No matter how great our sorrow, hope is always greater.**

## Day 40

*"The Lord will be your everlasting light, and your God will be your glory. Your sun will never set again, and your moon will wane no more: the Lord will be your everlasting light, and your days of sorrow will end."*
*Isaiah 60: 19-20*

There are times when nothing in life seems to make sense. You pray for good health, and the illness progresses. You are so thankful for your job but instead of a promotion, you are given a notice that your job is ending. You treasure your friends only to hear that your trust has been broken. Life feels as though it is crumbling all around you.

During dark moments of questioning and despair, step back and take a look at all of the constant reminders of new hope. Watch the sun come up faithfully each morning to usher in a new day. Be reassured when buds appear on the trees following the harshest of winters. Watch the brilliant rainbow color the sky following every storm.

Be filled with new hope as you are reminded that each day brings the promise of new beginnings. Rest in the fact that God is still in control. Be filled with peace knowing that behind every cloud is a ray of sunshine waiting to brighten up the way. Trust always and anchor your trust to the hope for a brighter tomorrow.

**When all of life seems dark, continue to trust. God has a much bigger plan for you even if you don't yet understand.**

## Day 41

*"May the God of hope fill you with all joy and peace."*
*Romans 15:13*

Life can be running along smoothly, everything going just right, and the next thing you know it takes a sudden turn. All of your plans and dreams come to a screeching halt, and you are faced with difficulties and pain like you've never known before.

Each of us handles these difficult situations in a unique way, and it's important to give one another the opportunity to work through losses at their own personal pace.

Remember that just as suddenly as life took a turn for the worse, it can make an unexpected turn in a positive direction again. Just when you least expect it, a new door is opened, an answer to a major problem becomes clear, and help appears when it is needed the most.

Even though it feels like things will never be normal again, hope provides a way of seeing through the darkness into the light of day. Never give up! Your ray of sunshine is ready to break through the clouds and deliver joy back into your heart once again!

**Hope carries you through life's darkest hour into the light of a brand new day.**

## Day 42

*"My flesh and my heart may fail, but God is the strength of my heart and my portion forever." Psalm 73:26*

Wouldn't it be great if we could fast forward our way through grief? We're told that there is a day when we will sing again. Others who have traveled the difficult road of loss remind us that one day the deep sadness will lessen and we will begin to enjoy life again. But, for today grief must have its voice.

While living in that difficult place of not knowing how to move forward yet wanting so much to be rid of the pain, be gentle with yourself. Don't expect the cloak of grief to be lifted from you all at once. The walk towards hope is often slow and unsteady with many detours along the way.

While waiting for your day of new hope to appear, watch the beauty of the rainbow paint bright colors across the sky. Marvel at the miracle of spring's first flowers pushing through the frozen soil of winter. Watch the splendor of the sunrise ushering in a brand new day. Be filled with hope as you are reminded that new beginnings are part of every new day!

**Hope allows us to experience an unexpected delight in our time of need.**

## Day 43

*"In this world you will have trouble. But take heart! I have overcome the world." John 16:33*

It's so easy to allow the problems of life to get us down. We worry about the big stack of bills. There are daily issues to deal with at work. Even home is no longer a happy haven because of the constant intrusions of all of the outside stresses of daily life.

When our hearts hurt and we feel weary, it's time to take a mental break away from life's problems and look for sunbeams instead. Watch the magnificent sun ushering in a new day across the horizon. Savor the delicious aroma of a freshly baked apple pie. Touch the soft fur of a playful puppy. Gaze into the night sky and look at the twinkling stars lighting up the evening darkness.

Allow the small blessings of each day to warm your heart and chase away worry and fear. When you look for little sunbeams, you'll often find a bright shining ray of hope that was meant just for you!

**Every day has just the right amount of sunshine to light the path of hope.**

## Day 44

*"Hope deferred makes the heart sick, but desire fulfilled is a tree of life." Proverbs 13:12*

Life can become overwhelmingly painful at times. Problem after problem comes knocking at our door until finally we become so discouraged that we think we've reached the breaking point. Our heart fills with a painful emptiness that is a constant reminder of all that has been lost.

During these moments of deep questions and feelings of isolation, make a constant effort to look for signs of new hope. Watch the stars lighting up the evening sky and know that your darkness won't last forever. Listen to the constant chirping of the birds and begin to hear the melody hidden deep within your heart. Watch the ebb and flow of the tide and let it remind you that blessings of joy surely will return to your aching, empty heart.

Hope has incredible power to motivate us to go on when all logic says to quit. Hope gives us a reason to look forward to each new day with anticipation. Hope gives all of life new meaning.

**Hope sees each day as a new beginning.**

## Day 45

*"In the day of my trouble I will call to you, for you will answer me." Psalm 86:7*

Many times we just can't seem to understand why life has gone so differently than we planned. No matter how hard we try, our finances just don't add up. We work and work to build up relationships only to be misunderstood. Our health gives us problem after problem even though we've taken every healthy precaution.

Twists and turns in the road of life can present us with challenges that we never thought we would have to face. Things we used to count on don't seem certain any more. Our hearts fill with doubt, fear, and so many questions.

During moments like this, only God Himself can put our hearts at rest. He has given us the promise of hope found in the beauty of a rainbow. We experience the majesty of a new day with the dawning of every bright sunrise. We see the faithfulness of His love found in the stars that light up the evening sky.

The events in our life might not make sense to us, but our Maker knows every detail of our lives and He will be with us every step of the way. He loves us, and that is our hope and our understanding!

**Every smile plants a seed of hope.**

## Day 46

*"Hear my cry, O God; listen to my prayer. From the ends of the earth I call to you, I call as my heart grows faint; lead me to the rock that is higher than I. For you have been my refuge, a strong tower against the foe." Psalm 61:1-3*

There are times when the problems and losses in life keep piling up and it seems like there will never come a day when we will feel joy again. We feel so tired that we can barely get out of bed. In exasperation we want to cry out, "What's the use of trying? Things will never get any better!"

When you feel like letting go, hold on! What seems like the end is often a brand new beginning. A cheerful voice on the phone says the words you needed to hear: "I'm sorry. Forgive me." A card arrives in the mail with an unexpected gift of a hundred dollars. You see a crocus that has managed to push its way through the snow-covered ground, and you are reminded that spring is on its way.

Hope helps us to leave our place of brokenness. Hope helps us to see the sunshine behind the clouds. Hope helps us to have positive thoughts of a brighter tomorrow. Hope helps us to breathe and continue to hold on!

**Every new morning plants seeds of living hope.**

## Day 47

*"Be still and know that I am God." Psalm 46:10*

When the storms of life hit hard, it's difficult to see beyond the clouds. Job loss. Failing health. Depression. Fatigue from daily stresses. The rain seems to keep pouring down without ever giving you enough time to find a warm, dry place of peace and comfort.

When you feel pressed in on all sides, pause for a moment and reflect on the many small blessings that come your way each day. Relief from the harsh elements often comes disguised in small packages right when you least expect it, but always when it's needed the most. A phone call from a friend of long ago. The far-off sound of the whippoorwill giving a reminder that nature is alive. A warm, caring smile from a stranger passing by on the street. The fresh smell of the rain ushering in a new season.

God's signature can be found all around you, and His signature is always colored with the promise of the miracle of new hope!

**Hope gives us the courage to see the possibility of a new beginning from what seems like the end.**

## Day 48

*"Even to your old age and gray hairs I am He, I am He who will sustain you. I have made you and I will carry you; I will sustain you and I will rescue you." Isaiah 46:4*

Have you ever noticed that all of life is balanced by change? The sun shines by day and then disappears into the horizon each night. Trees bud and grow new leaves, then the leaves fall to the earth and winter quickly follows. The barren winter soil thaws and comes alive with the arrival of spring.

The same is true in our lives. Nothing lasts forever, and this, too, will pass. What a wonderful promise of hope to know that our pain is only temporary! No matter how heavy your heart is or how dark the moment might be, remind yourself often that the darkness will fade and morning will surely come.

Nothing in life can defeat you when you know that there is no night without dawning, no tears without the hope of returned happiness. Just as sure as the sunshine follows the rain, joy will return to your broken heart. Rest in the calm assurance of the hope that is found in every new day!

**Nature is God's invitation to experience hope.**

## Day 49

*"Though I walk in the midst of trouble, you preserve my life." Psalm 138:7*

Trying to maneuver through the fog is a frightening experience. We cannot see the road before us, and we often lose sight of the fact that if we take time to stop and rest, eventually the fog will lift.

Life gets foggy at times. Clouds of grief and despair hang ominously overhead. Financial struggles plunge us into a fog of unknown territory. Broken relationships and the loss of a loved one toss us into a wilderness of anxiety and sorrow where we cannot see the rays of hope breaking through the dense clouds.

God knows just when to send along the gentle breezes to push away the heavy clouds of sorrow and tears. The fog suddenly lifts just as quickly as it arrived. An eagle appears, soaring high above the clouds. The buds forming on the barren branches of the tree following winter's storms are ready to break out into new growth. A friend unexpectedly appears with a smile and an encouraging word.

When the fog finally lifts, new hope appears! It was there all of the time waiting to be discovered!

**Whether we see Him, feel Him, or hear Him, God is near. When we look, He can be found.**

## Day 50

*"Cast all your anxiety on Him because He cares for you." I Peter 5:7*

Every day is a gift to be treasured. Some days that's really hard to accept! When our hearts and minds become heavy with grief, we often wonder about the very existence of our heavenly Father.

Just as the frozen earth will change seasons and eventually warm up to spring forth new life, so will your heart change seasons and enter a time of joy. In due time, blessings will again come to you in abundance, and your season of hope will spill over into every corner of your life.

Remind yourself daily that no winter lasts forever! Your time of inner joy and happiness will return to warm your burdened, grieving heart. Be encouraged as you watch the spring daffodils bursting forth in full splendor. God has not forgotten you! He has planted seeds of hope that are ready to burst forth in full bloom just for you!

**Because God makes no mistakes, we are showered with new hope every day.**

## Day 51

*"There is a friend who sticks closer than a brother."*
*Proverbs 18:24*

When harsh events come along unexpectedly in life and knock us down, it's hard to get back up again. We need help. We need encouragement. We need someone standing nearby whispering in our ear telling us we can do it. We need the comfort of a friend.

Studies tell us that people who have friends live longer and have fewer illnesses. Friends actually help our immune system to work. With this in mind, we should do all we can to cultivate friendships in our lives.

Don't be afraid to share your concerns and grief with a friend! A true friend will listen and not judge. A friend will hold your hand and dry your salty tears. A friend will encourage you to say whatever is on your heart and still love you for who you are.

Remember that this world is full of miracles, and sometimes those miracles come wrapped in the form of a friend. All it takes is one friend to help heal your broken heart. Keep looking about you. Your friend is there waiting to come by your side!

**Any sorrow in life is made easier when shared with a friend who offers a hug and a cup of hope.**

## Day 52

*"Trust in the Lord with all your heart and lean not on your own understanding." Prov. 3:5*

The road we travel is often cluttered with rocks and sharp twists and turns. Sometimes we stumble and fall and we feel too broken by grief to go on.

Right when we think we have no strength left God sends refreshment for our weary soul. A kind gentle word. A tender hug. A listening ear from a friend who truly cares.

When you think the road is too difficult to travel, take a break along the way and wait for help. God's love and compassion are never far away!

**An encouraging, hopeful word is like a cup of cold water in a hot, parched desert.**

## Day 53

*"I am the Lord, the God of every person on the earth. Nothing is impossible for me." Jeremiah 32:27*

Peace. You want peace in your life. You long to be at peace when the circumstances of life begin to unravel and pull from every direction. You want to know how to remain calm when you are being tossed about by the stormy seas of life.

The answer to attaining peace is really quite simple, yet people often spend a lifetime searching for it. To find peace, you simply refuse to see anything except hope even in the darkest hours of grief and pain. You will remain at peace when you place your hope in the absolute belief that tomorrow is a brand new day filled with countless new possibilities.

Place your hope in the knowledge that God is in control. As you watch the daily rising and setting of the sun, you can be certain that every tomorrow will unfold into a bright, new day of hope.

Peace and hope. You can't have one without the other!

**There is a calming peace in knowing that every tomorrow is an opportunity to begin again.**

## Day 54

*"Find rest, O my soul, in God alone; my hope comes from Him." Psalm 62:5*

There are times when it feels like the entire world is against you. Defeat becomes a word easily spoken and even more easily felt. One heartache after another leaves you feeling empty and completely alone.

When you are feeling totally drained, you need to hold on! Don't quit! Remind yourself that hope is still alive even during your darkest hour.

Hope places a melody in your heart when you feel like never singing again. Hope gives you new energy when you feel too weary to go on. Hope encourages you to invite tomorrow to come when it would be much easier to stay stuck in the pain and grief of yesterday.

Give your weary heart a much-needed rest! Lay your heavy burden down and watch the majesty of a morning sunrise. When you see the breaking of a new day, you will be reminded that with every new day comes a new reason to hope!

**Only hope can restore a broken heart.**

## Day 55

*"Blessed be the God of all comfort." I Cor. 1:3*

Sometimes it's really hard to see the sun shining through the dark clouds that are hovering overhead. Nothing in your life seems to be going right. You have strained relationships at home. Friends are scarce, and they seem to have disappeared right when you need their love the most. You feel the daily pain over the loss of a loved one, and the hole in your heart seems to be getting bigger by the day. It even seems like God has stopped listening and no longer cares.

Just when you least expect it, life has a way of taking a sudden change. A prayer is answered. A friend appears. New opportunities come into your life. The grief of loss is replaced with precious memories. Best of all, hope is restored. A song is placed back into your heart, and joy floods the soul. Once again you can feel the blessed safety and comfort of being wrapped in God's love and finally there is the new strength needed to go on!

**There is no such thing as a cloud taking permanent residence overhead.**

## Day 56

*"And we know that in all things God works for the good of those who love Him, who have been called according to His purpose." Romans 8:28*

There are times when life can become painfully overwhelming, almost like the bottom has dropped out. Problems pile up with no real end in sight. Days go by without any laughter. The nights seem extra dark and lonely. Nothing seems to make much sense any more.

Then, out of the most unexpected circumstance comes a hidden surprise of hope. You find a glistening rock among the dull, ordinary stones. You hear the joyful sounds of the starlings echoing across the lake. A bright and shining star appears from behind the clouds to light the path through the frightening darkness.

It helps to remember that nothing touches us that has not passed through the hands of our heavenly Father. Nothing. We may never know why pain has entered our life, but we can be sure that God is guiding us through.

All along the road to healing, reminders of God's constant love appear. What reassurance! What comfort! What hope!

**Life is noisy, but there is always a joyful melody of hope and peace hidden within the noise of confusion and grief.**

## Day 57

*"Light is shed upon the righteous and joy on the upright in heart." Psalm 97:11*

Life has a way of sending you the unexpected. Things are going along smoothly and suddenly you hit a major curve in the road. A serious illness. A broken relationship. A job loss. Or, the most heartbreaking of all—the loss of a loved one.

Days become dark, and it is difficult to feel the warmth of the sunshine in our lives. All of life takes on a cold, lonely chill

When the sun seems to be completely hidden, sit quietly and wait in hopeful expectation. Life also has a way of suddenly making things right. Just when you least expect it, new hope appears. A friend tells you of a job opening. Your health greatly improves following treatment. A broken friendship is restored. Peace gently enters the broken heart of grief and gives comfort to your weary soul. New hope was there all of the time waiting to be discovered!

**Hidden behind every cloud is a ray of sunshine waiting just for you!**

## Day 58

*In God I trust; I will not be afraid." Psalm 56:11*

There are times when circumstances are so painful that all we can do is pray. We somehow feel that prayer is most certainly second best. As long as we can try to fix things, continue to work and worry, and call in others for advice, we feel we're on track. When we are forced to fall totally on God we feel like such a failure!

Do you know that God wants us to rely totally on Him? He wants to take the ominous mountain that stands before us and break it down to size. He wants us to let go of our deep worries and anxious thoughts and let Him do what He does best. Allow God to be God.

Prayer shouldn't be the last item on our healing to-do list. Prayer is that all important first step. Prayer ushers peace into our hearts while we wait for God to take over and give us a much needed rest from carrying the heavy burden that was never meant to be carried alone.

**Prayer puts God where He belongs—first.**

## Day 59

*"Let me hear your lovingkindness in the morning; for I trust in You; teach me the way in which I should walk, for to You I lift up my soul." Psalm 143:8*

Sometimes it seems like our struggles and grief never end. We get through the pain of one sorrow only to be knocked flat by another. We struggle with poor health, disappointments, broken relationships, and the worst sorrow of all—the loss of the one we loved so much.

Nobody ever promised that life would be fair. In fact, God tells us that the sun shines on both the just and the unjust. Sometimes that's a really hard pill to swallow. We must remember, though, that God is the Master weaver in the tapestry of our lives. He has a plan for each of us, and that plan is meant to draw each of us closer to Him so that we can be His masterpiece of beauty.

It's so difficult to see the finished product when we have eyes dripping with tears. But, when His work in us is complete, we will positively know that we have been touched by the divine design of the Master's hand.

**When God is in control we have no need to fear. He knows the road ahead and will safely lead us to a place of comfort, replenishment, and joy.**

## Day 60

*"But those who hope in the Lord will renew their strength. They will soar on wings like eagles; they will run and not grow weary, they will walk and not be faint."*
*Isaiah 40:31*

When our world crashes in on us, it's difficult to see any beauty around us. Everything seems to be dark and hopeless. It feels like nothing in our life is right, and things keep going from bad to worse.

When life feels most empty, we need to cling to that hidden spark of hope that is planted deep within the heart. Hope listens for answers when God seems to be absent. Hope presses on even when life doesn't make sense. Hope pushes us high above the clouds to the sunlight of a brighter tomorrow!

**Hopes does not allow us the option of giving up!**

## Day 61

*"Uphold me according to Your word, that I may live; and do not let me be ashamed of my hope. Hold me up, and I shall be safe." Psalm 119: 116-117*

We go through times in our life when it's hard to look beyond the heavy burdens of today. Adversity touches us from every corner, and discouragement blinds our eyes to beauty. The happiness that once filled our heart has escaped us and only tears of grief drip from our eyes. The smile that adorned our face is now a frown of sorrow that cries out in pain.

What a blessing that God has given us the new joy and hope of a brighter tomorrow! What looks like barren, dry ground has the hidden potential to burst forth with fresh, new life.

Today's tears can be dried, and our eyes' sparkle can return with new determination as we watch the splendor of the rising sun. Tomorrow is a fresh day of fulfilled promises and renewed hope!

**God guides us into every tomorrow with promises of new hope and boundless joy.**

## Day 62

*"Know that the Lord is God. It is He who made us, and we are His; we are His people, the sheep of His pasture."*
*Psalm 100:3*

Are you facing a seemingly insurmountable task today? Does it feel like you have no strength left within you to meet the challenges of the day? Do you feel like giving up?

Right at the critical moment when you want to quit—don't! Look at the majesty of the sun, the moon, and the stars and be reminded that you've not been placed here to face the day alone. You have a Shepherd nearby gently nudging you, tenderly keeping watch over you, and softly whispering words of courage to you.

Hold on! Grab tight to the Shepherd's hand and allow Him to do what He does best—rescue you from the pain of the day. When you keep your eye on the Shepherd, there is no obstacle, no challenge, and no fear that is too great. The Shepherd will help you keep your focus on how you can do it, rather than why you can't. He will be your strength!

**When the road becomes rocky and clouded by grief, hold the Shepherd's hand tighter and continue to walk on!**

## Day 63

*"He has made everything beautiful in its time. He has set eternity in the hearts of men; yet they cannot fathom what God has done from beginning to end." Ecclesiastes 3:11*

All of us have experienced moments when our dreams have been snatched away and life changed in a mere instant. All of our energy is gone and our hope quickly vanishes.

Just as new life springs forth from the ashes, so does new hope burst forth from the brokenness. Hope can never totally be destroyed. Look all around you. Watch the robin looking for the first worm of springtime. Listen to the raindrops softly falling as they replenish the parched, dry land. Feel the sunshine warming winter's frozen, cold earth.

Hope is everywhere! Look to the heavens and dare to dream new dreams. Don't ever give up! With God, new possibilities are everywhere.

**Even a tiny flicker of light on a dark night can illuminate a path to a brighter tomorrow.**

## Day 64

*"Your light will break forth like the dawn, and your healing will quickly appear. Then you will find your joy in the Lord, and He will cause you to ride on the heights of the land." Isaiah 58:8,14*

Brokenness comes into the life of every person. A broken relationship. A broken promise. A broken heart. At some point, we must decide what we are going to do with all of the pain of brokenness.

We can easily become embittered and see situations where life has treated us unfairly. We can get caught in the trap of lonely, empty thinking, and begin to despise the world and all those who come into our lives.

We can also take this brokenness and look at it from an entirely different perspective. We can look at life through eyes that remain fixed on God. He has given us reminders of His love everywhere. The daily feeding of the tiniest sparrow. The faithful sprouting of the seed. The dependable rising of the sun ushering in a brand new day.

God's love takes our brokenness and gives us new hope, new strength, and a new vision. Take comfort in knowing that within each broken circumstance lies the very real possibility of a new and wonderful beginning.

**When you think you've exhausted all possibilities, remember this: you've only just begun!**

## Day 65

*"The Lord is good to all; He has compassion on all He has made." Psalm 145:9*

Are you dealing with some heart-wrenching pain right now? An illness that is not responding to treatment? Financial burdens that are multiplying daily? The sting of a broken relationship? The emptiness and grief of losing a loved one?

During moments of heartache, life can become so clouded by our tears that we no longer are able to see the rays of sunshine that appear each day. All of life looks like a cloud-covered season that will never have a sunny forecast of joy again.

It's vitally important to take an occasional mini break away from the pain of life so that your heart can be nurtured once again. Step back, take a long, exhilarating breath, and listen. Listen to the sounds of hope. Listen to the birds chirping a song of joy in the distance. Listen to the soft rain falling against the earth preparing the seeds to burst forth into the beauty of spring. Smell the gentle breeze ushering in the special aroma of nature. Listen to the peaceful sounds of nature and replenish your soul!

**Every day is an opportunity for a brand new beginning. What a wonderful gift!**

## Day 66

*"The things impossible with men are possible with God."*
*Luke 18:27*

There are times when the problems of life present themselves to us like a riddle. We think and think, and always end up at the same place. We have far more questions than answers. Life's circumstances are like strange, unanswerable mysteries.

Why do good people suffer while the uncaring, difficult people of this world often thrive? Why do bad things happen to good people? Why do innocent children suffer? Why do children die? The questions go on and on and we can't come up with meaningful, sound answers that make sense.

Somehow, we have the mistaken idea that God's blessings are equated with our goodness. That just isn't so! God never promises only happy, positive blessings to His children. What He does promise is strength for the day. He promises us that He is always in control. He promises to guide us as a Shepherd watches over His sheep. He promises us a new tomorrow. He promises us the gift of hope!

**Just because you cannot see the answer today doesn't mean that God has abandoned you.**

## Day 67

*"He is my rock and my salvation. He is my defender; I will not be defeated." Psalm 62:2*

Discouragement often resides in the heart of the weary soul. Emotional exhaustion settles over us like a dark cloud that hides the warmth and joy of the sunshine. Weariness of heart blinds our eyes to the blessings of life. We can no longer clearly see the mercy of God. All we focus on are the painful circumstances of life.

We need to battle discouragement so it doesn't overcome us. The best way to chase away the dark clouds of despair is not by our own strength. Rather, turn to God in faith, trusting God with every outcome no matter how bleak the situation may seem.

Complete trust in God builds faith and restores hope. Trust in God diminishes worry and creates an attitude of joy. Trust in God fans the flame of hope and pushes away gloom and despair. He's still in charge. He still tenderly cares. He still loves us!

**No matter what hour of the day or night our needs arise, God's love is there to carry us safely through. Depend on it. God's love never fails!**

## Day 68

*"The Lord is my light and my salvation. Whom shall I fear?" Psalm 27:1*

Fear is such a drain on our lives. Fear takes the joy out of everything and replaces happiness with only questions. Will this job really last? Will my health continue to be good? Will my best friend still be around ten years from now? Will one of my loved ones die? Fear propels us into a constant state of worry.

The reality of this life is that nobody knows what the next day or even the next hour will bring. Maybe there is a job promotion waiting around the corner. Perhaps you'll enjoy better health than ever before because you're eating healthier and exercising every day. Hopefully, your best friend will be with you through the thick and thin of life for years to come.

The flower blooms because of changes in soil, temperature, sunlight, and rain. Fear will never, ever produce the miracle of a flower. Trusting that all things will eventually work together to produce a bloom brings a measure of new hope every day.

Turn from your fear and remember that your life is like a flower. Eventually, the right circumstances will all come together to give you the most beautiful bloom ever!

**Hope and fear can never reside in the same heart.**

## Day 69

*"From the end of the earth I call to you, when my heart is faint. Lead me to the rock that is higher than I." Psalm 61:2*

Life can send a series of circumstances our way that leave us battle worn and shipwrecked. Often we're left feeling like we have no energy left to get up and move on.

God knows our every sorrow and feels our every pain. He hears our calls for help, and will answer in ways we never thought possible. Trust Him to send replenishment and hope for your weary, battered soul.

Tell God all that is on your heart, and then place your burdens at His feet. When you do, you will feel immediate relief from the pain. Nobody was meant to carry heavy burdens all alone!

Learn to lean on Him with perfect trust. As our Father, God knows the blessings that are waiting around the corner for us. He knows the joy that will return in the morning. He knows the relief from pain that we will experience if we have that enduring hope that simply continues to trust in a loving Father who genuinely cares.

**Faith has never promised to change my circumstances. Instead, faith changes me!**

## Day 70

*"He gives power to the tired and worn out, and strength to the weak." Isaiah 40:29*

You can't always control the circumstances of your life, but you can control how you respond to those circumstances. You can take your unfair pain and hurt and know that God is in your midst guiding you through the storm. It's not always easy to react positively, but sometimes it's necessary for survival.

When a field of trees is destroyed from a raging fire, momentarily it seems like all is lost. Because of that fire, though, there are valuable nutrients added to the soil giving much-needed replenishment. Seeds are scattered by the winds, and there will be a day when joy is spread into places far and wide. When the trees return, they will be strong and able to withstand the harsh elements.

Your problems and your pain just might be the seeds of many new beginnings. What looks like the end is often a fresh start. What defies all human explanation can really be the hand of your loving Father touching you in love, leading you to a place of peace and joy.

Replace despair with hope! Trust in the blessings of a new day! Trust God to carry out His plan for your life. Trust in the fact that His love never fails.

**By changing your thinking you can turn your scars into stars.**

## Day 71

*"Oh Lord, my God, I called to you for help and you healed me." Psalm 30:2*

Sometimes the circumstances in our lives seem far too big for us to handle. There are struggles in our relationships. We experience one financial crisis after another. Health problems grip us and we are left feeling depleted and worn out. The grief of losing a loved one settles in our heart, and we often want to surrender when the pain keeps running us into the ground.

Don't quit! Gather together enough energy to look upward. You will find the entire world stretching before you as you gaze at the expanse of the bright, blue sky. Watch the twinkling stars at the close of the day and feel new hope surging through you. Enjoy the thrill of a brand new sunrise every day and be filled with the assurance that God is still in control. Feel the gentle breeze softly touching your face, and hear the voice of strength and hope calling to you.

Every day comes to you wrapped as a brand new gift full of wonderful possibilities. Never give up! Always keep looking for special surprises that free you from the weight of worry and despair. New hope is everywhere!

**Life is tough but God's love is faithful. Never, ever give up!**

## Day 72

*"Blessed is the man who trusts in the Lord, whose confidence is in Him. He will be like a tree planted by the water that sends out its roots by the stream. It does not fear when heat comes; its leaves are always green. It has no worries in a year of drought and never fails to bear fruit." Jeremiah 17:7-8*

Have you been experiencing a succession of gray, bleak days? Does it feel like there will be no end to your streak of cloudy happenings?

Don't give up! Not far away there is a bend in the road with many new surprises waiting for you. Flowers are about to bloom. The sun is slowly breaking through the fog. The songbird is chirping a melody of hope just for your weary heart.

**Don't give up! God takes joy in surprising us with blessings when we least expect them and when we need them the most.**

## Day 73

*"Let us hold fast to the confession of our hope without wavering, for He who promised is faithful." Hebrews 10:23*

When we feel trapped in a tunnel of darkness and misery, we need something that will give us the feeling that circumstances will change for the better. We need hope! When we are so tired from dealing with the problems and difficulties of life that we feel like we have no energy left to go on, we need something that will give us new zeal and enthusiasm. We need hope!

When we become overwhelmed with fear and our imaginations run wild with worries that nothing in life is going to be safe or right anymore, we need reminders to show us that God is still in control. We need hope! When we aren't given answers to our questions, and we are forced to be still and wait, we need the courage to quietly sit back and rest. We need hope!

When all of life hurts and we have a pile up of grief and pain that makes us want to quit, we need encouragement, and we need hope!

Hope lifts us up and points us in a new direction. Hope calms our fears and gives us peace. Hope soothes our weary souls and gives us the reason to go on.

**Hope makes every day look like a bright, new beginning.**

## Day 74

*"The way of the Lord is a refuge for the righteous."*
*Proverbs 10:29*

Many times the problems and pain of this life overshadow our joy and we're left feeling like it's raining inside. The storm hits, and then we need to call on someone to help assess the damage of our life.

When it's raining inside, we feel sad, anxious, and empty. We feel wet from our tears, and we long for nothing more than the comfort of warmth and dryness again.

Is it raining inside your life today? Let someone know. There's someone standing nearby ready to share an umbrella. Someone is close who will help dry you off and help you get warm. Take a risk by asking someone to help you get out of the rain. There's an old proverb that says, "Rain does not fall on one roof alone."

You are not alone. Hope is near!

**God is in charge of all things, even the rain.**

## Day 75

*"Faith is the substance of things hoped for and the evidence of things not seen." Hebrews 11:1*

Sometimes we forget that life is fragile. We want to live life in the fast lane, always rushing from here to there, hardly taking time to breathe. When tragedy strikes, life suddenly comes to a screeching halt and we are reminded again just how fragile this life truly is!

We were meant to savor the sunshine moments of each day. It's important to take time to watch the billowy clouds slowly drifting by as you stretch out among the soft blades of grass. It's good for the soul to splash in a mud puddle and feel the freedom of laughing like a child again. It brings us peace to listen to the far away sounds of the babbling brook and be reminded of the beauty found in all of nature.

Learn to treasure these special moments of joy today so that when grief and pressures of life push you against a rock you will remember that life is still good. The sun does shine. Hope returns in the morning.

**Hope sees the sun shining through the darkest of clouds.**

## Day 76

*"My help comes from the Lord, the Maker of heaven and earth." Psalm 121:2*

So many circumstances make us feel alone. Broken relationships. Crumbling health. Job loss. And, worst of all, the death of someone we love. Loneliness and grief overtake us and we are left sitting in the ashes of darkness feeling very alone.

The human spirit has given us a special strength for times like this. We often refer to that strength as hope. Hope abides deep within the soul of every person, and even when hope momentarily escapes us, it's still there waiting to be discovered once again.

Hope is born on the wings of a butterfly. Hope is seen in the majestic soaring of an eagle. Hope is renewed when the first crocus blooms following the cold, barren days of winter.

When you're feeling all alone and abandoned by everyone, look for signs of hope greeting you with each new day. Your heart will be lifted as a song of new hope is discovered once again.

**The voice of God speaks to us through nature letting us know we are never alone.**

## Day 77

*"The Lord is good to all; He has compassion on all He has made." Psalm 145:9*

We know that in this life we each must pass through new and different seasons. When winter arrives and sends the chilling winds of despair and the bleak, dark clouds of loneliness it's difficult to imagine that spring will ever make its way into our heart again.

Hold onto your faith and believe with all of your heart that things will get better again because they surely will! Part of the blessing found in the seasons is that each season brings its own special seeds of new hope and joy.

If you're experiencing an especially painful winter right now, such as the death of a loved one, hold on. Rest in the knowledge that God is always near and His love is always pouring out upon us. Have you ever seen a winter that does not eventually unfold into a beautiful spring? Seeds of hope are planted beneath the cold, frozen earth. Sooner than you think, the warm sunshine will appear in the blue sky. The cold soil will be warmed, and beautiful flowers will suddenly appear.

Hold on! Your broken, empty heart will be replenished. Encouragement and comfort will come to you. Hope is surely alive!

**God's timing does not always perfectly work according to our plans, but His timing is always perfect.**

## Day 78

*"The Lord is my Shepherd, I shall not want." Psalm 23:1*

So many things in life make us afraid. We fear the unknown. What will happen now that I've lost my job? How will I survive now that the divorce is final? Will I ever smile again now that my child has died?

What we need during moments of questioning and fear is comfort. We need a strong arm placed around our trembling shoulders. We need words of comfort and wisdom to give us the assurance that things will eventually work out. We need someone to bandage our wounds and to love us unconditionally.

The good news is that God has not left us alone in our fears. He has given us the comfort, love, and protection of the "Good Shepherd." We need only to look at the stars lighting up the evening sky to be reminded that God is near. He is always watching over us. He is always leading the way. He never falls asleep on the job!

The next time you recite, "The Lord is my Shepherd, I shall not want," allow the words to penetrate your heart. Allow the words to bind your wounds. Allow the Good Shepherd to calm all of your fears.

**Because I know who holds the future, I am never afraid of tomorrow.**

## Day 79

*"If God is for us, who can be against us?" Romans 8:31*

There are times when the only question you ask is "why?". You wonder why another crushing blow has come into your life. The one person you loved so much walked away during a time of need. The job that meant everything ended and now you are facing financial ruin. Death came knocking at your door and suddenly took away your precious one. Shattered dream. Unending pain. People who don't understand. Why? Why do things like this happen?

During these questioning moments in life, it's good to ask "who?" Is anyone for me? Who is on my side? The answer lies within the reach of your prayers. When you feel lonely, forgotten, and neglected, take time to look about you. The Maker of the universe has left so many blessings within your reach. Call to Him. He is always ready to listen. Reach out to Him and He will touch you with His unexplainable peace.

The better question is not "why?" but rather "who?" If God is for me, who can cause me lasting harm? God is your Father. He is always near. He is your tender, loving Father who will never leave you in your time of need!

**God's love far outweighs any pain that dares to enter my life.**

## Day 80

*"He heals the brokenhearted and binds up their wounds. He counts the number of the stars; He gives names to all of them. Great is our Lord and abundant in strength; His understanding is infinite." Psalm 147:3-5*

Rain can really mess up plans for an outdoor picnic or a fun walk through the woods. Rain can dampen our spirit, as well as chill us to the bone by soaking our warm, dry clothes. Rain is often the most unwelcome, unwanted guest of the day!

We very seldom desire the rain, and yet we know that we need rain to keep our wells from running dry. Without rain, we wouldn't see flowers bloom, and we would never enjoy the sweet smell of freshly mowed grass. If it never rained, we would never get to enjoy the miracle of a rainbow painting God's promise of hope across the sky.

When rain comes into your life, try to remind yourself often that rain waters the sun scorched land and prepares it to grow plants that will bloom in the spring. Rain keeps our crops growing so that we can enjoy the blessing of daily food. Rain replenishes the earth and keeps it green and beautiful.

So, too, will rain help restore hope to your depleted soul. Rain will eventually touch your broken heart and promote blossoms of new beginnings to grow.

**Rain will bring new life in due season.**

## Day 81

*"Show the wonder of your great love, you who save by your right hand those who take refuge in you. Keep me as the apple of your eye; hide me in the shadows of your wing." Psalm 17:7-8*

There are times when the pressures of life become so heavy that it feels like the world is caving in on you. It seems like the clouds will never part long enough for you to see the beauty of the sun shining again. Joy seems to have vanished from your heart.

Losing a loved one steals so many dreams and brings about so much pain. Life feels empty and dark for such a long time. The worst part of all is feeling so misunderstood and alone.

Be assured that there is joy in the morning! With each new sunrise comes the promise of new hope. Every day brings a fresh, new day with countless possibilities of a miracle touching your life.

Listen to the sound of the gentle breezes rustling through the trees. Hear the happy melody of the songbird echo across the valley. Watch the dewdrops give a much-needed drink to the thirsty blades of grass. God's signature is everywhere! He has not forgotten you. You are never alone. Hope can be found everywhere!

**Hope is believing life will get better even when everything seems to be stacked against you.**

## Day 82

*"The Lord bless you and keep you; the Lord make His face shine upon you and be gracious to you; the Lord turn His face toward you and give you peace." Numbers 6:24-25*

When the daily path you're traveling keeps beating you down, it's hard to find a way to greet a new day with a smile. You feel too weary to even lift your eyes to see if the sun is shining. The bills are piled high. Friends seem scarce. Your heart is full of worry. It feels like God has moved away.

When the circumstances of your life have hit an all-time low, don't quit! Never, ever give up on life! Little reminders of hope are all around you. Look at the twinkling stars that illumine your pathway. Smell the crisp, fresh air following the spring shower. Listen to the whisper of the breeze rustling through the trees. Hear the voice of God telling you He is still near.

Remember that life isn't a destination. Rather, life is an incredible journey. As we experience the unexpected twists and turns, know that God is right there with you leading the way. Never stop looking for reminders of new hope each day!

**No matter what our response is to life's pain God never, ever gives up on us!**

## Day 83

*"If I go up to the heavens, you are there; if I make my bed in the depths, you are there. If I rise on the wings of the dawn, if I settle on the far side of the sea, even there your hand will guide me, your right hand will hold me fast."*
*Psalm 139:8-10*

I don't know what circumstances you're facing today. Maybe you were just handed some bad news about your health from the doctor. Maybe you are feeling the pain of loneliness and abandonment. Perhaps you just lost your job and you're carrying the weight of financial stress. Maybe your heart feels empty and your day seems black because death knocked at your door and took the one you loved. Maybe you want only one thing—to quit.

Look around you and experience the miracle of new hope! God wants you to watch the sun breaking forth on the distant horizon to welcome a new day. Kneel down and look closely at the flowers pushing through the dark, cold soil preparing to bring splendor and beauty to the unpainted landscape. Watch the birds leave their nest and begin to soar majestically as they explore new territory in the wide expanse of the clear, blue sky.

God wants you to feel His presence everywhere. He has left His signature for you to see so you can be encouraged and filled with the promise of new strength and new hope for today!

**During our darkest hours, God sends His love to give light and show the way.**

## Day 84

*"Yet those who wait for the Lord will gain new strength; they will mount up with wings like eagles. They will run and not get tired, they will walk and not become weary."*
*Isaiah 40:31*

When does the pain of loss end? Is there no relief? This is often the cry of the parent who has lost a child. The grief seems too big and too hard. There seems to be no end in sight for the pain and isolation.

You keep trying. You keep reminding yourself that you must take life one day at a time. Sometimes, you have to gather your strength one hour at a time. You work hard every day forcing yourself to move forward into this world knowing that it will never be the same again, but also understanding that you must choose to move forward into this new land beyond grief.

Hope is amazing as it teaches us that the very same sun that cast its warm rays before loss is still shining. Nature is still painting the world with beauty beyond words. Your Father is still giving you comfort and help in order to help fill the empty, painful void of loss. So, you slowly move forward knowing that one day the curtain of grief will be pulled back and you will be able to see life with new eyes and a heart filled with hope!

**There is no way out, but there is a way that goes forward.**

## Day 85

*"The Lord comforts His people and will have pity on those who suffer." Isaiah 49:13*

Do you feel like your shoulders are hurting from the weight of carrying extra burdens? Do you find yourself wearing a frown more often than a smile? Has the sun lost its ability to cast light onto your weary heart?

Worry is such a heavy burden to carry! There are times you feel as though you're going to buckle under the heavy load. When you worry, you're actually saying to God, "I can't trust you to be in charge. You are able to cause the rising and the setting of the sun, but I don't think you care enough about my problems to help me."

Sometimes God feels so far away that it's hard to believe that His mighty hand is truly in control of your life. It's easy during moments of defeat and discouragement to turn away from God and begin to crumble under the heavy weight of worry.

Look at the lilies of the field. Watch the birds gliding gracefully through the sky. Gaze across the expanse of the clear, blue heavens. His love is much greater than your pain. Give your worries to a loving Father who cares. His love never waivers. He will never let you down!

**When you pray, it is impossible to worry.**

## Day 86

*"Lord, even when I have trouble all around me, you will keep me alive." Psalm 138:7*

Sometimes it feels like the events in life are spinning out of control. Sickness. Loneliness. Broken relationships. Loss of finances. Death. In fear and with questioning we watch our plans being pushed aside as our life continues to stray off course at a rapid pace. Instead of being a joyous adventure, life has become a daily grief of facing the unwanted pain that arrives with each and every new day.

During stormy times, it's hard to remember that life is not careening out of control. It's difficult to remain at peace within when the events of life bring daily conflict and pain. It takes great amounts of courage to continue to trust when the clouds of life overshadow any joy that tries to touch the ache held deep within our soul.

When the hard, painful moments of life come, we know that no matter how tragic the circumstances, no matter how long and dark the days may seem, there will be a time when the sun will break through. Dawn will arrive. Joy will return. We see evidence of His faithfulness in the blooming of a flower. As the gentle rain replenishes the dry, thirsty earth, we are given new hope. What a burden is lifted when we know that He is always the one who is in charge!

**Even when you can't see Him, continue to trust. He's much closer than you think.**

## Day 87

*"It is God who arms me with strength and makes my way perfect." II Samuel 22:33*

Sometimes life grows so dark that the darkness seems almost impossible to describe. Void. Black. Nothing. Worst of all is that frightening feeling of being all alone. Painful circumstances can push us into the darkness at an incredibly fast pace. An illness invades our once healthy body. Nerves of steel disintegrate to worry, fear, and constant anxiety. The unthinkable happens—our child dies. And, we are left sitting alone in a cold, dark, room of lonely grief and despair.

Hope is an amazing thing, and next to impossible to destroy. Hope seems to know when that darkest hour has arrived, and hope appears in the most unassuming way. An unexpected tender smile. A song of confidence and encouragement. Listening ears when you thought nobody cared. Hope dares to give you that tiny nudge that pushes you into the light of a new day. Hope tells you to hold on when you feel like letting go. Hope stirs up new energy to keep on climbing when you want to drop out of the race.

Hope. It will arrive at the most unsuspecting moment, and it will always be on time. Hope shines brightest when your hour is darkest. Trust in it. Your hope is near!

**Hope sees blue skies even through the rain.**

## Day 88

*"The things impossible with men are possible with God."*
*Luke 18:27*

Are you facing what seems like an impossible mountain to climb? Bills that continue to spiral out of control. Unemployment with no real possibilities. Friends who have left your side during your time of sorrow. Some days leave you with an overwhelming feeling of aloneness. It seems much easier to give up than to face another one of life's difficult challenges.

Don't quit! Look at the mighty oak tree and remember that it once was small and seemingly insignificant. We marvel at a field of colorful flowers, yet obstacles such as harsh winds, freezing temperatures, and parched soil have all been part of the mountainous climb to the field of beauty.

Just when you need a spark of encouragement, it arrives! A cooling rain on a hot, sultry day. The winter crocus to remind us that spring is on its way. The moonlit sky to light a path in the darkness. God is near, and He is mightier than any difficulty you are facing. Look to the heavens and watch for the rainbow. It is your promise of hope!

**Impossible becomes "I'm possible" with just a small change.**

## Day 89

*"Be still and know that I am God." Psalm 46:10*

There are times when we grow so weak from the sorrow and pain of life that we think we can't go on. We die just a little bit more when others tell us to "buckle up and be strong." How can we be strong when we are so weak we cannot even open our eyes or lift our tired, weary heads?

How greatly we are tempted to become depressed and to feel lost in this big world of ours during our moments of heartache and loneliness. This is when we most need to remember the kindness and gentle caring of our Father. He gently and tenderly reminds us to simply trust Him and "be still." Being still during our weakest moments is necessary so that we can be revived. Rest. Be still! Lean completely into the arms of the Father who so intimately knows your pain and allow Him to dry your tears.

Be trusting and resting in His strength, you will gain new strength and hope. If today finds you feeling totally lost and depleted you are in need of complete rest in Him. That's all God really asks of us. Don't try to be strong. Just be still and allow His deep love, His tender caring, and His strength to transfuse you with hope and new strength once again!

**God reserves His best medicine for our times of deepest pain.**

## Day 90

*"How amazing are your thoughts concerning me." Psalm 139:17*

It's a feeling that everyone experiences but very few talk about. We feel alone. We feel like the world is way too big for us and we're lost in this huge space. There's nothing personal about life on this planet. Oh, what a lonely, forgotten feeling it is to be simply one who is lost among millions!

It's hard to imagine that we really do have someone who cares and is always looking out for us until we think about our relationships we have with our children. No matter how many miles away our child lives, no matter the age of the child, no matter the job our child has, we are always there watching and waiting and ready to help in the blink of an eye.

That's how it is with our heavenly Father. Do you know He never sleeps? He never leaves us alone. He is always there calling out to us to come to Him so that we can be embraced in the shelter of His arms. We have wondrous signs of God's love all about us as we look at the expanse of the heavens and see first-hand the care He has given to the tiniest of creatures.

Touch a flower. Feel the cool, refreshing breeze. Walk alongside the babbling brook. Listen to the birds chirping overhead. Hope is alive! God is good, and He truly cares! God is waiting in the very depths of my being to speak to me if only I will be still enough to hear His loving, tender voice!

**God paints the lily of the field, perfumes each lily bell. If He loves the little flowers, I know He loves me as well.**

## Day 91

*"Faith is being certain of what we do not see." Hebrews 11:1*

Grief is such a universal experience, yet when it happens to you personally, you feel so alone. Even when members of your family share the very same loss each person feels the pain at a different level and in a very personal way.

Our grief might be in common, but it is private as well. Your grief is your pain, and nobody experiences it in just the same way. It helps to remember that when you're walking down the pathway of grief, you are never alone even when it feels that way.

There will be a day when you find solace and hope. Trust that. Believe that! Place your hope in that!

Remember that your day of peace will arrive and it will be like having a heavy weight lifted off your heart and a new song placed there for you to enjoy. Hope will place a smile on your heart as you continue along in this journey called life.

Hope allows you to look at today and enjoy the beauty of this hour without worrying about the future. Hope gives you the strength for one day at a time, until slowly you realize that the future has arrived and you are living with new strength and a new sense of life that you didn't have before. Hope gives you the reason to go on!

**If you weather the storm, you will reach the port.**

## Day 92

*"My soul wait in silence for God only, for my hope is from Him. He only is my rock and my salvation, my stronghold; I shall not be shaken." Psalm 62:5-6*

Worry is the companion of loss. How will life go on? How will I ever begin to smile again? When will this shattered feeling leave? How much more can I take? And, the worst worry of all—what if this happens again?

All of these fears are normal for anyone who has gone through the pain of loss. Life will forever be more fragile. When suffering breaks into our world, we are made acutely aware of just how precious each moment "in the now" truly is.

The worry will begin to decrease as you allow yourself to trust in the beauty and miracle of life once again. There is no hurrying grief. The future will unfold one day, one hour, and one minute at a time. As it does, you will begin to open your heart slowly to new hope that builds new trust and new joy.

Be patient with yourself and begin with one small step at a time. Remind yourself often that you already have begun this walk of hope where worry will in time be left behind. You will make it! Hope is much larger than worry!

**I know that worry is useless and drains my energy. Today I will put down one worry, leave it, and walk away.**

## Day 93

*"Blessed by the Lord, who daily bears our burden." Psalm 68:19*

When loss comes into your life, dreams are snatched away and you are left wondering how to face the future. You feel like you've been thrown into a deep, dark hole with no way out. Loneliness becomes your only companion and you lose all interest in the daily routine of life. The very things that used to occupy your time and bring you pleasure no longer have any significance at all.

Grieving is hard work. There is no road map to follow so you don't know when the next bend or twist in the road in coming. You can't tell where there are steep hills or dangerous mountain ridges. You seem to be traveling alone okay, then suddenly you come up against a brick wall and it feels impossible to continue on. Grief is new, unexplored territory.

There is something amazing about this journey, though. It's hard to explain yet it happens all of the time. A rainbow appears out of nowhere and gives you hope. A butterfly lights on your windowsill and you find yourself smiling. A meal appears on your table from a neighbor and you suddenly feel less alone. The telephone rings and you have a much needed listening ear.

God will never allow you to travel this journey of grief alone. He sees to it that you have help all along the way. He gives you rest when you are weary, and hope when you feel lost. Just knowing that you have this inner strength will keep you going until one day you are no longer in that lonely hole, but you are sitting among the flowers and can see beauty in life once again.

**Hope is the friendly, unexpected voice pulling us back to a warmer world.**

## Day 94

*"For I hope in Thee, O Lord; Thou wilt answer, O Lord, my God." Psalm 38:15*

Sometimes all we want to know is when the lonely ache of loss is going to go away. We never knew that anything could hurt this bad. When will this painful throbbing in the heart go away? When will the world feel safe and happy again?

Loss changes everything about our "normal" in an instant. Suddenly our world feels upside down and out of control. Our thoughts race, but they only fall into a dark tunnel of fear and loneliness. Nothing seems to fit any more. The pain of loss is everywhere.

There's no easy way to explain how hope eases its way back into a broken heart, but it does. Hope is not pretending there isn't any sorrow. Rather, hope is calling on that inner strength that is part of each one of us to sustain us until we gradually find happiness again.

There is strength found in everyday things... smiles, kind words, the warm rays of sunshine, the listening ear of a friend. Even the far away sounds of the songbird whistling a thankful tune can begin to unleash that inner strength found in hope.

Be assured that hope is alive and it is gently tending to the needs of your heart. The day will arrive when you will know that joy has filled your soul once again!

**Yesterday's endings are the seeds for today's beginnings.**

## Day 95

*"He is our God, and we are the people of His pasture, and the sheep of His hand." Psalm 95:7*

People try to help us. They really do. "Get busy." "Get your mind off of this sadness." "Take a vacation." They want to help us when the grief is so fresh, as if we can really get our minds off of what has happened.

For the one grieving, there is no getting away for a long time. The pain is ours and we have to learn somehow how to face it, live within it, and finally move forward knowing that this loss will always be part of us.

We smile when others try to help. We know they mean well. But, inside our tears are cascading into the very depths of our soul. We know this is going to take time and lots of hard work. We know the emptiness won't be filled overnight. It probably never will. We appreciate what friends are trying to do, but there's no getting around it. The pain has settled in our hearts.

What do we do? We turn the conversation to something else knowing that not everyone understands the pain we're experiencing. It's not their fault. How can they know? They're trying to comfort, and for today that's good enough.

**I heard a bird sing and December was lifted from my heart.**

## Day 96

*"Walk by faith, not by sight." II Corinthians 5:7*

Sometimes things happen in our lives that are so hard to understand. A car accident that takes a life. A house fire destroys everything. A healthy, active person suddenly becomes ill with a terminal disease. The company downsizes and many jobs are lost, yours included.

There are no words to explain such painful circumstances. It takes lots of faith to work through the days of lost dreams, unrest, and brokenness. When the world you once knew suddenly becomes foreign territory, it's hard to stay focused and look to the future with hope.

God, in His wisdom and love, knew that we would need reminders of His presence with us during our moments of despair. We have only to look at the rainbow as it stretches across the wide expanse of the heavens to know that His promises are still true. When we watch the stars twinkling in the moonlit sky we can feel His presence in our darkest hour. When only bitter tears fall, we can look at the morning sun breaking through the clouds and know that soon our tears will be dried.

God is our Father, and even though we don't always understand the pain that comes into our lives we can trust Him to pull us close and give us shelter through the storm. God is a deeply personal Father and friend and He will bless us individually according to our needs.

Hope is alive within the heart of everyone and is awakened right at the exact moment when we need it most. That is a promise we can count on!

**Sometimes it takes a lot of rain before we see the rainbow. Don't ever give up! Your rainbow is there!**

## Day 97

*"I waited patiently for the Lord; and He inclined to me and heard my cry, and He put a new song in my mouth."*
*Psalm 40:1,3*

It happens so gradually that most often we don't realize it's taking place. We wake up one morning with the sun shining brightly and we smile and welcome the day. We go through twenty-four hours without crying. We join in on a conversation and there is laughter minus any guilt. And, we realize that we have finally reached our new destination.

The journey wasn't easy. In fact, we experienced every storm and hardship imaginable. We had many setbacks along the way. But, finally we have found that new place that we can call home. It is different from what we knew as our happiness before, but there is a joy here, too, and we know that we can peacefully settle in and call this new land our home.

Yes, without really knowing it, we have settled into our new place. There will be setbacks and reminders of our loss, but the pain will no longer take precedence over all that we think and do. Instead we will have gentle and fond remembrances, and we will shift most of our thoughts to loving gratitude for today. Most importantly, we will know that the dark side of our grief is no longer our landscape. Instead, we can live in the quiet, serene beauty of hope and peace.

**There is a melody in the air even when you aren't listening.**

## Day 98

*"The Lord is my rock, my fortress, and my deliverer."*
*Psalm 18:2*

The pain of loss is something that can't be explained by words alone. How do you explain a pain that runs so deep it makes the heart bleed? How do you tell others what it feels like to have a cloud always hovering above with reminders of the life that no longer exists? How can we possibly share the personal pain we feel to the extent that others will understand? It can't be done. Grief is too personal.

How do we move forward is the question we ask ourselves daily. How do we find our place in the new world that is now ours—the world that has been created by loss? How can we find a way to bring joy back into the heart that has been broken? Is it even possible to reclaim joy?

This world is full of pain and grief. That is a fact. But, it's also brimming over with joy and blessings. When we are in the miry pit of grief, we feel so alone and abandoned by all blessings. But, as we allow hope to ignite within us, it acts as a magnet drawing the blessings of life closer and closer to us until finally we reach that point where we can see joy again. No longer does grief rule our lives. Sure, grief is still there. The sting of loss will always remain, but no longer will it be the thing that fills our every thought and every action.

Hope is alive and it is bigger than any pain we are feeling right now. Believe it and cling to that thought. Hope will grow from a flicker to a flame and light the way out of the darkness into the light of a brand, new wonderful day!

**Although the world is full of suffering, it is also full of those overcoming it.**

## Day 99

*"The Lord is for me; I will not fear." Psalm 118:6*

When we are suffering intense grief, we find it difficult, if not impossible to remember what it felt like to be genuinely happy. We do not remember that feeling of energy and zest for living. We cannot recall how much fun it was to plan out the agenda for the day. We forget the small things like the background noise of happy chatter and laughter. We forget joy. We forget the wonderful feeling of waking up each new day with hope!

Grief and loss send us to a new place. We now reside in a foreign land where we are forced to learn a new language and adapt to new feelings and circumstances. We have been uprooted from what felt safe and secure and happy, and have been sent to a place that is unknown and so very frightening. This is our grief journey, and we don't know how we'll make it!

What helps us most is knowing we don't have to travel this road of grief alone. We have others beside us who have led the way, and they have found their new places in life and have begun to smile. You, too, will find a new joy, a new peace, and a new way to look at all of life again. You will find hope with the faithful unfolding of each new day.

**At first I was lost in the dark, then I looked upward and saw the sun peeking through the clouds and I knew with certainty that I was on the right path to call home!**

## Day 100

*"Why are you cast down, O my inner self? And why should you moan over me and be disquieted within me? Hope in God and wait expectantly for Him, for I shall yet praise Him, who is the help of my sad countenance, O my God."*
*Psalm 43:5*

When we are going through a loss, we often use the word "blue" to describe the state of our emotions. We are feeling sad, lonely, isolated, and depressed. We don't see the world as a place of peace and quietness, but rather our world is mixed up and out of sync.

Nothing feels right or in place. We feel displaced and upset. We are sad and blue. Oh, how we long or the time when we can see life as "sky blue" once again! With a heavy heart we wonder if that time will ever arrive.

If you're in a sad blue place right now, hold on. Remember that blue is an ever-changing color. Your day of hope and newness will arrive again. Today your world might look blue etched in the darkness of black and feel as though it is crashing apart. But, hope is alive and will return to bring you back to a place of blue calmness just as sure as the sun rises and sets each day.

Do you know that hope never dies—not completely? There is always a tiny flicker of hope sitting deep within your heart just waiting for the right moment to fan it into a flame. Maybe it's something as simple as a kind smile from a stranger that will turn your sad blue into sky blue. Keep looking upward and believe that your day of "new blue" will arrive. And, most assuredly it will!

**Who can resist the feeling of hope when staring at the expanse of the wondrous blue sky?**

## Day 101

*"Cease striving and know that I am God." Psalm 46:10*

Do you believe in Santa Claus? That's a rather odd question to ask, but do you believe? Most of us believe in the idea of a Santa. After all, Santa represents hope. Think about that. A jolly, round man who can deliver our wishes is really what the idea of Santa is about. What a shame that when we get older, we stop believing in miracles! We somehow toss aside the wonder of asking and receiving and become dull to the beauty of the world and the many possibilities all about us.

When we've lost everything, we need to cling to that amazing thing called hope. Too often we want to crawl into a deep hole and never come out. Why? Because we've convinced ourselves that things will never get better. We are certain that we will never feel love again following loss, so we stop hoping.

The next time Christmas rolls around, watch the spark and twinkle in the eyes of young children. They ask for the world, knowing that they'll be given a star. They ask, they believe, and they rest in the excitement of waiting for their gift to arrive. That's hope in its truest sense!

When you're feeling like there is no possibility for life to change for the better, become a little kid again. Ask your Father for whatever it is you need, and believe that He will grant you that wish. If He can make the sun, the moon and the stars, surely He can fill your empty, longing heart with hope!

**There is relief from this wound we call grief, and that relief is hope!**

## Day 102

*"To Thee, O Lord, I lift up my soul. O my God, in Thee I trust." Psalm 25:1*

Why do things happen as they do? Why are jobs lost leaving us without enough money to pay the rent? Why are relationships broken leaving us with more loneliness than we can bear? Why do people have to suffer through long, painful illnesses in agony day and night? Why do children have to die leaving us with a brokenness that can't be explained in human terms?

I won't pretend I can give you the answers to these mind-boggling questions. What you're faced with right now is way too big, too overwhelming, too personal for anyone to step in and say they have the answers. I can tell you this for a fact, though: you are not alone. God is alive, and He proves it over and over again by leaving His signature in all of life. Look to the mountains and see His majesty. Look to nature and feel the power of His creation. Look into the eyes of a loved one and feel His everlasting breath of life.

We have been given the promise of hope and the reassurance of knowing we are never alone. We are provided with just the right amount of love, faith, and hope to carry us through the darkest of times.

Turn to Him. Trust Him. Listen to Him as He whispers words of love and strength to use every day. You can make it out of this barren desert of grief! Hope is alive and will carry you through to the plush green valley of peace and comfort. Hold on, and never give up!

**All that I have seen teaches me to trust in the Creator for all that I have not seen.**

## Day 103

*"The Lord will guide you always; He will satisfy your needs in a sun-scorched land and will strengthen your frame. You will be like a well-watered garden, like a spring whose waters never fail." Isaiah 58:11*

There is so much dismal talk about the economy, the sad state of affairs of the family, and new illnesses being discovered weekly that it leaves a person feeling so discouraged and hopeless. When the blow of the death of a loved one hits, it seems like the pain of this life is too much to bear.

Remind yourself often that you have a Shepherd watching over you and He will never leave you alone. Your pain never goes unnoticed. In fact, do you know that every hair on your head is numbered?

Look at the mighty heavens and remember who made them. Watch the babbling brook and remember who is in control. Work hard to push fear to the side so that you can be comforted. Others have walked your difficult, lonely path and they are here to tell you that you will make it.

There will be a day when something or someone will awaken the hope inside of you and you will know that you are going to feel alive once again. There will be a day when you will see with news eyes and feel with a new heart. You will rediscover joy, and it will be doubly sweet because of all of the pain you've been through. Trust. Wait. Hope. Your day of peace and joy is coming!

**God's promises are like stars; the darker the night, the brighter they shine.**

## Day 104

*"Let us run the race that is before us and never give up."*
*Hebrews 12:1*

Every person alive has things happen in their life that makes them ask, "Why, God?" and all we can do is look to Him in faith. We don't understand. We get no answers that fit the pain we are going through. So we hold on. We hold on tight, hoping and praying that we'll make it through just one more lonely night.

Nobody has the answers—at least not the answers we want so desperately to hear. There is no easy way out of pain. It takes courage and stamina to withstand the daily drain. There are reminders, regrets, and the agony of losing someone precious to us. Yet, we hold on even when our world is spinning out of control.

We feel drained from so much pain. We're tired of people telling us it's going to get better when the reality is things have gotten so much worse. But, something inside keeps us holding on. That something is called hope. Hope meets our greatest needs and keeps us going when our own strength fails.

Hold on and never give up. Believe that your rainbow will appear because it surely will!

**Hope is believing when nothing at all makes sense.**

## Day 105

*"I find rest in God; only He gives me hope."* *Psalm 62:5*

Deep inside of us there is a little spark that glows all of the time. It's that thing that causes us to love when we don't want to. It causes us to forgive when we think we can't. It causes us to care about the world in which we live when everything seems too hopeless. We think our light has gone out leaving us helpless and hopeless, but that little light is always shining.

When we are grieving, we feel like there is no light at all. There are days when we can't even see the sun because of our tears. We become afraid and lonely and we try to hide ourselves in a corner.

What are you afraid of? You have your light guiding the way. Can you force yourself to take one step out of the dark today? Start small. Maybe your step is getting a shower. Or maybe your step today is going for a walk around the block. Try just one thing and build on that. You can do it!

Just one step at a time will get you out of the dark and back into the light of hope!

**Life becomes easier when we take it step by step, one day at a time.**

## Day 106

*"Be strong and take heart, all you who hope in the Lord."*
*Psalm 31:24*

If you've gotten through just one day while grieving, you've accomplished a lot. It's not easy to face a day when your heart feels utterly broken from the inside out. You shouldn't ever feel weak or ashamed to call on others to help you. That's why you have friends!

There's another thing you can do, too. Pray. Pray lots and lots, calling out to the One who is always there, always listening, and never sleeping. Your heavenly Father is like a parent to you. Remember how your mother stayed awake all night with you when you were sick? She never took her eyes off of you. That's how your Father in heaven is, too. He never sleeps and is always there watching and waiting for you to call for help.

In your grief, you might think you're weak, but you're not. You are strong and full of courage. You have the stuff that makes a hero. Don't ever forget that. When your grief grows dim and you're able to look at what all you've been through, you'll understand. And, you will then have the privilege to give someone else comfort in their time of grief.

Friends helping friends. Friends praying for friends. The grieving being comforted. That's what love and hope are all about!

**Remember that nothing in your daily life is too insignificant and inconsequential for God to help you by answering your prayer.**

## Day 107

*"The Lord of hosts is with us." Psalm 46:7*

When will I get relief? Will this empty feeling ever go away? Am I ever going to get over this loss? What we're really crying out is our wish that this never happened. We want to turn back the clock and go back to how things were before the loss.

But, the world as we once knew it doesn't exist. Our grief experience has changed that life. We now live in a new place, and it's up to us to work very hard to find a sense of belonging.

Little by little, hope begins filtering in through the cracks in our heart and we realize that even though our world is now totally different, we must find a way to go on. We begin to establish new traditions, find new ways to place peace in our soul, and we realize that we weren't alone at all.

Hope pushes us forward even when we feel like we can't go on. Hope helps us to see the beauty in small things such as a smile, a babbling brook, or a gentle snowfall. We understand more fully how to cherish the small moments in life, and we are so thankful for every ray of sunshine that touches our heart. Hope is alive and hope teaches us how to live again!

**Hope is waiting for what you know one day will come.**

## Day 108

*"He alone is my rock and my salvation; He is my fortress, I will never be shaken." Psalm 62:2*

Are you tired of being tired? Are you waiting for the next piece of bad news to hit? Do you feel like the storm is never going to pass? Has life hurt you so much that you're too afraid to let go and try to feel again? If you answered "yes," then you are in the middle of a full-blown grief attack.

Grief comes at us with a vengeance, and it immobilizes us for a while. We don't know what to think. Sometimes we don't even know how to think. We're all mixed up and we know that life is terribly off-balance and will never be the same again. We're left not knowing what to do.

When you are in the black hole of despair, it's so important to lift your eyes upward toward the heavens. After all, that's where you can find light. There is power and strength all around us and that's what we need when we are feeling battered and bruised from the fatigue of grief.

We may not know it until we're deep into the race, but we do have the inner strength to get through the dark days of grief. That strength is called hope. Hope gives us the strength to peek into the future with a new view. It helps us to hold on when all sense tells us to give up. It helps us to see that there is light at the end of the tunnel. It helps us to not give up!

**I don't see the big picture. I don't have a clue. But I know God does. I'm going to declare that, even if I don't feel it.**

## Day 109

*"Thou wilt keep him in perfect peace, whose mind is stayed on thee." Isaiah 26: 3*

Are you afraid right now? Does your heart feel heavy and broken? Do you feel like you've lost your very best friend and you have no one who truly understands you? Don't spend anxious moments worrying and being afraid to face each new day. If you stop and get very quiet, you will feel the very presence of God within you.

As you come to those dark places in your life, reach out for the hand of the Shepherd and He will take you under His wing and give you protection and help during the storm. God promises to take you to a cool, sheltered place where you can rest. And, no matter how steep the hill or the mountain, you never have to climb it alone.

Hope is believing in what you cannot see and continuing to trust when all else tells you to stop. You will gather strength from everyday things such as a bright smile, a warm hello, and special thoughts from friends and loved ones. Hang in there. God is near and hope is alive. You're going to make it!

**You can create an oasis of calm by thinking peaceful thoughts.**

## Day 110

*"Come to me, all you who are weary and burdened, and I will give you rest." Matt. 11:28*

When someone we love is snatched away from us by death we often wonder if there is ever going to be any relief from this pain. We wonder if there is any place that we can go to find relief from the loneliness. We ask ourselves if we will ever be able to smile again.

What we long for the most is for our world to return back to how it used to be. We miss the sounds, the smells, the laughter, the activities that now seem so far away. We wish that we had never taken life for granted, and we long to savor those moments we once had. We miss life as it used to be!

Deep within our heart we know that the world as we once knew it no longer exists. Our grief experience has changed our world, not just for today, but forever. Yet, we keep praying that something will happen to give us back that same joy and those same emotions. We wish, but we know it can never be.

Little by little we grow braver in facing our new life, and we realize that we now have a new relationship with the one who has died. We have a new relationship with the world, as well as with ourselves. We realize we are no longer in the past, but we have come face-to-face with the choice to keep moving in the only direction that is an option for us—forward. We slowly move forward into new territory and we do so with an inner strength called hope. And, deep within our soul we know we'll make it!

**As long as we keep faith alive, we keep hope alive.**

## Day 111

*"Find rest, O my soul, in God alone; my hope comes from Him. He alone is my rock and my salvation." Psalm 61:5*

Nobody knows exactly what you're going through when grief and loss hit your heart. They may say they know, but that's impossible. Yet, I know with full assurance that there are examples of others who have traveled this lonely path called grief. They have come through the tunnel and can see light again, and you can do it, too!

I don't have all of the answers; in fact, nobody does. Loss is far too difficult to understand, and the depth of pain you feel can't be explained by words alone. We "feel" pain, and that explanation of pain can't be found in the dictionary. But, there are real, visible signs of healing that we can see.

Did you notice the sun come up this morning? Did you watch the leaves gently swaying in the breeze? Did you look at your food and know that it was going to taste good? Did you choose your clothes with care when you dressed today? Did you look at the sky and compliment the blue? These are all signs that hope is penetrating your heart and you are going to make it!

With hope, you will bear this difficult time, and you will rise to a new tomorrow! No, you'll never be exactly the same, but you will be a "new you," and that "you" will include joy, purpose, and hope!

**The God who pays attention to the big things like the sun, moon, and stars, also pays attention to every small detail of my life. What matters to me, matters to Him, and that is my comfort.**

## Day 112

*"There is an appointed time for everything. And, there is a time for every event under the heaven. A time to weep, and a time to laugh; a time to mourn, and a time to dance." Eccles. 3:1-3*

Grief and loss can make even the sunniest of days feel like the middle of winter. You don't understand all of the emotional changes that are taking place, but you know that you feel terrible. Nothing seems right because everything is so new and different. Loss brings about so many changes.

One of the most helpful things you can do when going through that period of adjusting to a new and different normal is to give permission to feel the pain. Allow the tears to fall knowing that the pain you're feeling today won't always be this intense.

There is light at the end of the tunnel. There is a rainbow following the storm. Spring always arrives after winter. A caterpillar emerges from the cocoon as a beautiful butterfly. Hope will replace your sorrow, and when it does you will be able to smile once again.

**It takes a lot of courage to taste life when there is sorrow. Be reminded, though, that sweetness is soon to follow.**

## Day 113

*"But Thou, O Lord, art a shield about me, my glory, and the One who lifts my head." Psalm 3:3*

The sun is shining and there are sounds of joy all around, yet you don't feel any spring in your heart. Instead there is the lingering cold of winter and you don't know what to do about it. Any person going through grief and loss expresses those very words. Grief is a lonely word and it puts you on a journey to a lonely land for a while.

The good news is that this feeling of winter does not last forever. God, in His infinite wisdom, has provided hope for you when traveling this difficult path. Hope comes to you in ways too numerous to count, and comes in the most surprising ways to provide comfort and hope to your hurting heart.

The butterfly that you saw was bringing you a message that there is a new life waiting for you. Give it time to emerge. The rainbow brings you promises of blue skies and the truth that this storm will not last forever. The robin brings tidings of spring and the assurance that winter will end and flowers will soon bloom.

Today if you feel afraid and lonely, take a step back and look at nature. Nature doesn't worry, nor does it remain in a state of cold bleakness. Nature sprouts forth new life, new joy, and a promise of a glorious array of splendor for you to enjoy. Hope assures you that your spring is coming, and when it does, it will be wonderful!

**Hope helps me remember how to live.**

## Day 114

*"My God is changeless in His love for me." Psalm 59:10*

Robert Frost said it best when he penned, "The sun was warm but the wind was chill. You know how it is with an April day when the sun is out and the wind is still. You're one month on in the middle of May. But, if you so much as dare to speak, a cloud comes over the sunlit arch, a wind comes off a frozen peak, and you're two months back in the middle of March."

So it is with grieving. One moment you are feeling good, being warmed by the sunshine of life. You are active and happy and humming a sweet melody that's coming from your heart. Then, without warning, the storm clouds roll in and suddenly you find yourself in the middle of bad weather. You are seeking shelter from the storm, and you feel cold, afraid, and so alone.

These sudden, unpredictable steps back into grief will not always be so intense, and the spells of grief will grow farther and farther apart. You won't linger as long on your grief, and you'll begin to feel more in control of what is happening.

You will probably never be totally free of the bad weather and storm clouds of grief, but neither would we want to be, because those periods of longing keep us connected to the one we love.

As for those times when you leap into happy moments? You will remember the joy you felt watching the vibrant colors of the rainbow following the storm!

**I don't know how God does it, but ultimately if we trust Him with all of our being He can make things right.**

## Day 115

*"Taste and see that the Lord is good; blessed is the man who takes refuge in Him." Psalm 34:8*

Has life let you down? Are you feeling alone in your pain? Do the clouds seem to remain hovering above your head like a constant threat of another storm? If so, then you are walking the path called grief. Grief most often is a long, hard walk, but the good news is that for every step you take, you are one step closer to finding a place of peace and rest in the new normal where you must now live.

Nature has beautiful displays of hope and inspiration that have been placed on this earth for us to use for comfort, shelter, and inspiration. There are trees that have been weather beaten, yet they remain standing tall. There are flowers that have been stepped on, yet they bounce back. There are seeds that have been dropped and forgotten about, but they take root and bloom.

Remember that you, unlike the forgotten seed, have a Father watching over you who will never leave you alone. You have a special strength planted deep within your soul known as hope that will always be part of you. Take time today to reflect on nature and feel the peace that overrides your sadness. Take a moment every day to allow your heart, mind, and eyes to soak up some of nature's beauty and be encouraged. There is joy beyond this day of loss. There is peace to be found. There is a very special gift waiting for you. There is hope.

**A day with nature is a day of hope.**

## Day 116

*"Peace I leave you; My peace I give to you; not as the world gives, do I give to you. Let not your heart be troubled, nor let it be fearful." John 14:27*

When despondency creeps in and you feel like there is no way out of the dismal state that you're in, it's time to stop and look about you. Take in the sights and sounds of nature and be reminded who made the earth and all that is within it. Remind yourself that every creature, both great and small, has meaning and is genuinely loved and cared for by his creator. That means you, too!

Many times you fall into a state of feeling hopeless because your heart hurts so much that you can't ever imagine life without pain. Take time to reflect on past joys and remind yourself often of the rainbow. It is a promise of hope from your heavenly Father. Remind yourself of the hope that lives within you that is stronger than your fear.

I, like you, have gone through times of despair and darkness. To help me remember that I have a loving Father who watches over me, I began planting and caring for flowers. I also love to photograph those flowers. As I look at these beautiful scenes from nature I'm reminded that hope is very much alive. When you place visual reminders of hope all around you, you will feel your heart being replenished and filled with new hope.

**A picture is worth a thousand words, so choose your pictures wisely.**

## Day 117

*"Be of good courage, and he shall strengthen your heart, all ye that hope in the Lord." Psalm 31:24*

Facing change under the best of circumstances is difficult and a bit frightening, to say the least. What will it be like? How can I be prepared? When will this awful feeling leave? How long will it take me to get to a place of feeling normal again?

Change brings about many new things for us, and the loss of a child is perhaps the worst change anyone will ever go through. You no longer can find the ground beneath you, much t less travel the road of grief that you have now been placed upon.

Mercifully, the sharp edges of pain that accompany grief will not always be there. With each passing day, you are making progress in finding your way through all of the new grief, even if it doesn't feel like it. Time stops being your enemy and actually begins to help give you what you need to help navigate through this dark, winding path called grief.

If you are in the newness of grief right now, life is not at all routine for you. Everything is different from the rising of the sun to the close of the day. Millions have walked this path you are now on, and they have also struggled. They searched. They fell down. They suffered battle fatigue. They asked hard questions. They cried millions of tears, but they made it, and you will make it, too!

Hope is much stronger than the grief you are experiencing today. Hope will eventually help you to begin to feel alive again. Hope will emerge strong. Hope will give light to your path. Hope will brighten your journey. Hope will give you purpose again. Hope will carry you through.

**Hope is stronger than any grief, and when my aching soul surrenders to hope, I will begin to see light once again.**

## Day 118

*"He who dwells in the shelter of the Most High will rest in the shadow of the Almighty." Psalm 91:1*

It's so difficult to be thankful when your heart is hurting. It's difficult to be thankful when you are in the presence of happy, busy people while you are feeling so sad and alone. Life can be brutally painful when you are expected to say thank you but you cannot even begin to mouth the words.

How can you give thanks in the midst of job loss, illness, broken relationships, and death? How is it possible to thank God, your Father, when you have been pummeled by the storms of life? How does a heavy heart find the strength to look heavenward and say thank you during moments of doubt?

You can only say thank you when you understand who your Father is. You can only feel peace when you are aware of the blessing of hope. You can only whisper words of praise when you understand that the pain will not last forever.

You have a Heavenly Father watching over you and He has promised to be faithful and never leave your side. He has given you the blessings of the sunrise and the sunset, the starry skies, and the changing seasons. He also knows when you need your heart to be held, and right at that moment He sends help to carry your through.

Who is your help today? The kind voice of a friend. A strong shoulder to lean on. A person to hold you close and dry your tears. The warm sunshine against your face. The rainbow painting the heavens with splendor.

Yes, even at the deepest point of your pain, God assures you that He is near, and you can face the day with hope!

**A day without hope is a day without sunshine.**

## Day 119

*"My soul, wait in silence for God only, for my hope is from Him." Psalm 62:5*

When the clouds are hanging heavy above us like huge billows of tears ready to fall, we often become afraid that we will never see the light of the bright sunshine again. Loss takes so much away from us that we fear the sun is dying, too.

During the winter of our lives, we live in anticipation of those moments when we will be welcomed into a safe, warm haven and feel secure. We long for our tired bodies to get some rest from the heavy burdens of grief we've been carrying, and we yearn for the feelings of loneliness to go away. We want to taste the sweetness of life again, but we fear that the day of joy will never return.

The predictability of the changing seasons becomes part of our hope that we will taste laughter and abundance in our lives again. Our season of comfort and peace will arrive, and we will be able to feel the warmth of sunshine comforting our soul. Friends will engage in lively conversation with us, and we will know that we are not alone. There will be a day when the clouds part and the bright, blue sky appears with the sun's light giving new hope to our soul.

Look to the heavens. Gaze at the evening stars twinkling brightly in the sky. Take in a breath of fresh air, and be filled with new hope!

**When we listen carefully to the sounds of nature, we can hear the ongoing message of hope and love being spoken.**

## Day 120

*"Blessed are those who mourn, for they shall be comforted." Matt. 5:5*

Grieving has its seasons, and autumn seems to be a particularly difficult season for those who have gone through loss. Maybe it's the visual of seeing the flowers stop blooming and the leaves falling off of the trees. Perhaps it's feeling the warm summer sunshine fading and suddenly feeling the lingering chill in the air. For most who have experienced loss, autumn is a time of reflection and bracing for the days of winter that lie ahead.

What if you viewed autumn a bit differently this year? What if you reminded yourself of how beautiful spring will be when it arrives again? What if you took the time to plant flower bulbs in the fall so that you can look for your spring following the dark days of winter? What if you promised yourself to keep focused on the beauty of spring and summer rather than facing autumn with fear and dread?

Many years ago following the loss of a baby boy, I went through a terrible autumn of grief. Winter was even worse, and I was not certain that springtime in my life would ever return again. I'm not sure what moved me to plant daffodil bulbs that fall, but I did. As I planted them, they were watered with my tears. The more I dug into the chilled, barren earth, the more my tears fell. Yet I continued to dig and plant. Dig and plant. Dig and plant.

Autumn passed, the ground lay frozen and covered in snow for months in the mountains of Pennsylvania.

My sorrow remained heavy. Little did I know how much spring would awaken in my soul that year! Little did I know how much my grief would be lifted when I saw the first signs of those daffodils breaking through the ground that was finally beginning to thaw. Little did I know how much my grief would be lifted as I saw those first springtime blooms of daffodils! Hope returned, and it will return for you, too!

**Grief endures for a season, but spring always returns!**

## Day 121

*"The Lord is near to the brokenhearted and saves those who are crushed in spirit." Psalm 34:18*

Sometimes the days are long and dreary. In fact, most days feel that way to anyone who has suffered a major loss, especially the loss of a child. Time is measured by tears, and there are days when nothing seems to offer any kind of relief from the pain of loss.

If you're suffering today, why not take a few minutes to listen—really listen—to the sounds around you. Maybe you're hearing exactly what your Heavenly Father wants you to hear—silence. There is so much peace found in silence when we are meditating on heaven and all of the beauty that awaits us.

Remind yourself often that this earthly home is only temporary. You have a beautiful place prepared for you that is free from all heartache and tears. There will be no more pain and suffering. And, best of all, you will be reunited forever in this wonderful place with those you love and miss so much. What a thought! What comfort and peace! What hope!

**When the days are empty and my soul aches, I know I can find hope and comfort by trusting in God who is the keeper of my soul.**

## Day 122

*"I will trust in God's unfailing love forever and ever."*
*Psalm 52:8*

There are times when it seems like your life will never feel right again. So much loss and pain have become part of you that you've somehow forgotten how to notice the blessings that touch you each and every day. All you can think of day and night is how to get rid of this ongoing pain.

What you need most during moments of your loneliness and loss is a large injection of hope! You need to know there is a reason to get up in the morning. You need to know there will be a song on your heart again. You need to know that you won't always have this huge emptiness right in the center of your heart.

Can you say goodbye to a loved one and still know they will always be present with you? Can you look at life through different, more hopeful eyes? Can you crawl out of the hole of despair and look upward to the heavens with peace and learn to trust once again?

Yes, it is not only possible, but each day that you breathe, you're taking one step closer to finding new hope. When you can not only see the sun shining, but also feel its warmth, you know you are walking in hope. When you hear the birds sing happily at the break of dawn, you know you are finding new hope. When you walk among nature and feel God's mighty presence once again, you know you are experiencing new hope. When you can pray and give thanks, you know you have found hope!

**Death was a painful mystery, but now I see hope in the beauty that surrounds me.**

## Day 123

*"You will go out in joy and be led forth in peace; the mountains will burst into song before you, all the trees of the field will clap their hands." Isaiah 55:12*

Every day brings its share of sunshine as well as its share of troubles and pain. Sometimes the pain you experience is beyond what you ever imagined possible. It is during those times that you need to remember all those who have walked before and traveled similar journeys and have made it. When tragedy hits, you wonder how will you ever bring joy back into your life again? That's a question everyone asks and the answer is often more clear than what you think.

Joy in its purest form comes from the simple and natural things of life. Sunbeams streaming across an open meadow. Raindrops pitter-pattering on the rooftop. A beautiful rainbow following a springtime shower. Birds chirping their early morning songs of thanksgiving. A butterfly flitting across the petals of summertime flowers. The gentle breeze sweeping across the ocean waves. Joy cannot be bought with money. Joy is not found in a jar on a shelf. Joy is a presence—a state of being that can only be found when you have come to a place of peace.

If you are struggling today, look around you. Do you see the joy? Look at all of the little blessings of life that are found in nature and allow your heart to slowly, steadily be refilled once again with that peaceful, quiet sustaining hope and joy!

**"Hope is the little voice you hear whisper 'maybe' when it seems the entire world is shouting 'no.'"**
**—Unknown**

## Day 124

*"Rejoice in hope, be patient in tribulation, be constant in prayer." Romans 12:12*

There are so many losses that come into our lives, but nothing can compare to the loss of a child. This loss is never supposed to happen. It crosses the boundary of falling within the norm. There is nothing right or good or purposeful when a child dies. This tormenting pain suddenly becomes so real when child loss occurs. We feel so broken.

How do we pick up the pieces of life and continue to live following the loss of a child? This has been the age-old lament of parents from the beginning of time. As we can reason, we don't ever put back our lives as they were before such a loss. There is impossible to do.

Our hope is not in this world, but our hope is in heaven. Our hope is in God. Our hope is believing that we have a Heavenly Father who cares. Without this hope, our life feels empty and meaningless.

Every day, as we breathe in the sights and sounds of all creation around us, we are breathing in whispers of hope. Slowly and surely life will return to our broken spirit, and we will gain new meaning from this crushing wave of grief brought on by the death of one we loved so much.

One day, one hour, one breath at a time. That's how it's done. We breathe in the essence of God, and that fills us with new life and new hope!

**Hope is revealed to us one moment at a time. Stop and rest in each new moment.**

## Day 125

*"Love never fails." I Corinthians 13:8*

Where do you go when life comes crashing down like a heavy weight on your heart? Most often people try to hide from the pain or try everything in their power to make the pain go away as quickly as possible. The truth is that it's not always possible to make your pain vanish. This is especially true when going through a loss.

Sometimes the best you can do is to make it through one day, one hour, or one minute at a time. At first the pain is so hard to carry that you fall from exhaustion.

Slowly you begin to understand that the hope that was snuffed out so suddenly is still residing deep within your heart. It might only be a tiny flicker, but it's still there.

Look around you right at this moment. Can you find one blessing? Focus on that blessing and keep your heart and mind fixed on that. Allow that blessing to bathe your heart in hope.

Every day that you do this—just focus on one blessing—you will feel that flicker of hope swelling up into a flame until finally you realize that you haven't been alone through this storm. Hope has made a permanent residence in your heart and never left you even for one second!

**You can make it through anything when you live one day at a time.**

## Day 126

*"When I am afraid, I will trust in you." Psalm 56:3*

Sometimes it feels like life is falling apart right before our very eyes. We pray but don't get answers. We try seeking wisdom, help, and support of others, but to no avail. We work hard only to find we're in one big mess, and we just don't understand. Life has become one big pile of pain and anxiety.

During these moments of not understanding why all of the bad stuff is happening to us we stop and ask ourselves the really hard questions. Is this my fault? Why do evil people seem to flourish while so many good people suffer day and night in pain? Why did my mate walk out on me? Why is my child addicted to drugs? Why did the car accident have to happen? Why?

On and on we go without ever really finding answers. The truth is that sometimes there are no answers. The hard truth is that bad things really do happen to good people. Life is unfair. And, most often there is no explanation that makes sense out of what has happened in life.

This is when we need to lean on perfect trust. We need trust that God is working His will in our lives every day, every hour, and every minute of the day. Is this kind of trust easy? Not at all! In fact, it's downright hard to trust until we let go of everything and say, "Okay, this isn't about me anymore. This is about God working in my life. This is about total surrender."

It helps to walk among nature and view the mighty works of God. Look closely at a raindrop and find its beauty. Stare at the evening sky and notice all of the twinkling stars that have been perfectly set in their place. Watch a sunrise and feel your heart race as you experience the miracle of a brand new day.

Strength and hope come from learning how to fully trust that God is in control and that He knows what he's doing. Try practicing perfect trust for thirty days and see what happens. Guaranteed you will be filled with new hope and brighter days!

**Where flowers bloom, so does hope.**

## Day 127

*"The Lord is my strength and my shield; My heart trusts in Him, and I am helped." Psalm 28:7*

Do you sometimes feel like every step forward you take you get knocked back two? Or for every dollar saved, you lose five more? Do you feel like you are one of those people who has had the misfortune of having a streak of bad things happen in your life over and over again no matter how hard you try?

Rest assured, you're not alone. At some point, every one of us has gone through a time in life when it feels like the entire world is working against us. We experience one heartbreak after another without any opportunity to heal. What we need during times like this is some kind of assurance that things will get better. We need something or someone to help us through the dark pathway into a place of some peace and light. We need our heavy burden to be lifted!

When we are anxious we are often sick at heart. We know that worry keeps us from feeling good, it's a total waste of time and energy, and it makes us feel miserable. Yet, human nature is to worry and be anxious about the cares of life.

When you are burdened and feel weighed down by worry, take a walk among nature. Look up to the heavens and breathe in the fresh air. Look at the expanse of the sky and marvel at the miracle of it all. Remind yourself over and over how many times you've felt hopeless only to have hope arrive in the center of your heart exactly when you needed it the most.

Worry erases the promises of God from our minds. When we worry we focus on us. When we place our hope and trust in God, we focus on life and its abundance. Life is beautiful, even in the midst of our turmoil and problems. When we center our eyes on our blessings, the worries and cares of this world shrink by comparison, and our hope in life and the wonders of living expand.

**The most exciting, rewarding walk you can ever take is a walk with God!**

## Day 128

*"Those who wait on the Lord shall renew their strength; they shall mount up with wings like eagles."* *Isaiah 40:31*

Sometimes our tears fall like raindrops. We feel weak and overcome by the trials we face each day. We don't know where we will get the strength to face another day. The storms of life hit us hard and leave us feeling alone and shipwrecked.

We look around and we are all alone. Our tears continue to fall and the weight of the storm weighs heavy on our heart. We long to be wrapped in love and hope once again.

Have you experienced a loss this week? Have the walls of your life caved in and all of the problems of this world seem to have come crashing in at once? Let someone know! Call out to the Lord in your pain and He will send help. He promises that our cries will not go unheard.

You are not alone. You are never alone in your time of need. And, even better, God is never late in answering our calls for help.

Remember the beauty of the sunrise as a brand new day awakens. This is God's promise to you that new hope has arrived!

**Just when it seems the darkest morning appears.**

## Day 129

*"In the day of my trouble I will call to you, for you will answer me." Psalm 86:7*

Many times we cannot understand why life has turned out so different than how we had planned. No matter how hard we try, our finances don't add up. We work and work to build good, solid relationships only to be misunderstood. Our health gives us problem after problem even though we exercised, eat right, and get proper sleep.

Bad things really do happen to good people, and we become all too aware of this when unforeseen tragedy strikes. We're left wondering why there's so much sorrow in this world.

Twists and turns in the road of life can present us with challenges we never thought we would have to face. Things we used to count on are no longer certain. Life is all mixed up! Our hearts fill with doubts and fears, and we have no idea who to lean on for comfort and help.

During moments like this, only God Himself can put our minds and hearts at rest. He has given us the promise of hope found in the beauty of a rainbow. We experience the majesty of a new day with the dawning of every bright and glorious sunrise. We see the faithfulness of His love found in the stars that light up the evening sky.

The events in our life might not make any sense to us, but our Maker knows every detail and He will be with us every step of the way. The more we let go and let God, the easier it is to see hope in the midst of pain, courage in the face of fear, and peace in place of anxiety. Watch and see how God holds true to His promises. The sun always comes out following the rain!

**Every smile plants a new seed of hope that will take root and grow.**

## Day 130

*"He will cover you with His pinions, and under His wings you may seek refuge." Psalm 91:4*

Grief does such strange things to our moods. One minute we can be busy and happy and thinking only about positive things. Then, at the passing of a second, our mood can change and we are out of sorts with the entire world. We can't stand being around anyone, and we are certain that nobody in the entire universe cares about us. Grief seems to play with our minds and our emotions, and we feel out of control, alone, and afraid.

Grief is like the invisible visitor that is always hiding in the background ready to pounce on us when we least expect it. Maybe it's a certain song that plays on the radio that triggers grief. Perhaps it's that little boy smell that we miss so much. Maybe it's the smell that comes following a soft, gentle rain that reminds us of playful times splashing in the mud puddles with our little one. Grief is tricky because we can never predict when it will pay us a visit.

There is no sure-fire way to make grief go away, but it helps to do all that we can to give us some extra strength when the unwanted visitor appears. We need to constantly fill our minds with hopeful thoughts. Before we go to bed each night and when we wake up each morning it helps to remember that each new day is a miracle. In fact, every day is a special gift to us that is waiting for us to enjoy.

We are never alone, even though there are times when loneliness overcomes us. All we have to do is look at the sky and be reminded that there is a star shining just for us. When we feel the warm rays of sunshine against our face we know that God is mighty and much more powerful than our unwelcome guest called grief. We are never alone; hope surrounds us always! God's love is tender enough to hold us when we are weary, and strong enough to carry us when we feel we cannot go on. Lean on Him, listen to Him, and call to Him often. He will see us through!

**When we have hope, we can make it through anything!**

## Day 131

*"Let Him have all your worries and cares, for He is always thinking about you and watching everything that concerns you." I Peter 5:7*

Worry is the companion of loss. How will life go on? How will I ever begin to smile again? When will this shattered feeling leave? How much more can I take? And, the worst worry of all—what if this happens again?

All of these fears are normal for anyone who has gone through the pain of loss. Life will forever be more fragile. When suffering breaks into our world, we are made acutely aware of just how precious each moment of today truly is.

The worry will decrease as we begin to allow ourselves to trust in the beauty and miracle of life once again. There is no hurrying in grief, and so this winning over worry is a step-by-step process. The future will unfold one day, one hour, and one minute at a time. And, as it does, we will begin to open our hearts slowly to new hope that builds new trust and new joy.

Be patient with yourself and begin with one small step at a time. Remind yourself often that you already have begun this walk of hope where worry will in time be left behind. You will make it! Hope is much larger than worry!

**I know that worry is useless and drains my energy. I will try, today, to put down one worry, leave it, and walk away.**

## Day 132

*"Because He has inclined His ear to me, therefore I shall call upon Him as long as I live." Psalm 116:2*

Where do you go when you need comfort? Who do you turn to in your sorrow? Far too many times we try to handle it on our own and sorrow has a way of swallowing us up, so-to-speak, until we feel like we have fallen into a pit of dark, lonely grief.

We have so many choices, and we need different kinds of comfort and reassurance at different times and moments in our lives.

Sometimes we need the quiet and comfort of nature. We need to see the sunrise and the sunset, and we need to hear the sounds of birds singing, crickets chirping, and frogs singing their night time songs of peace and joy.

Sometimes we need other people. We need hugs, and lots of them. We need comforting, uplifting words. We need to see the smile on the face of a friend. We need to feel compassion!

Other times we need to hear the voice of God, and only God. We need to clear our minds of all clutter and concentrate on Him and be reminded that He is still in control of our world that seems so out of control.

Where are you in your sorrow today? Don't sit in the deep pit of loneliness. Reach out. Make a choice to get some help. Walk among nature. Call a friend. Better yet, make plans to meet a friend and share a meal together. Talk. Cry. And, yes, allow yourself to smile and laugh—even in your sorrow. Comfort is all around us. Reach out and grab some comfort and hope today!

**Each new day sings a message of hope.**

## Day 133

*"For the Lord God is a sun and shield; The Lord gives grace and glory." Psalm 84:11*

Grief seems to hit us like a tidal wave at times when we least expect it. We can be plodding along in life okay when all of a sudden we get smacked hard with the reality of our loss and we're left feeling like we're drowning in a sea of sorrow with no life jacket in sight.

Being aware of how grief works is a critical part of the grief journey. Knowing that we can get these grief attacks unexpectedly can actually help us to prepare for them.

When your tidal wave of grief hits, take some long, deep breaths, and prepare to wait it out. Don't fight it or try to swim against the tide. You will only exhaust yourself both physically and emotionally. Feel the pain with the knowledge that following this storm, the seas will once again return to calm, and you will have better days ahead.

The pain will begin to subside as you begin to acknowledge the fact that grief attacks are only momentary in nature. The raw part of grief work has already been done, and you will be able to manage your grief by thinking calm thoughts, journaling your emotions, taking a walk among nature, and calling on a friend for some encouragement.

Did you get hit by a tidal wave today? Take courage in knowing that you're going to make it. Others have walked this path before you and they've made it and you will, too. Your hope is bigger than your fear. Your courage is stronger than your pain. And, your hope is always alive and at work!

**I will face my pain with courage, and I will make it!**

## Day 134

*"A merry heart doeth good like a medicine." Proverbs 17:22*

Any kind of loss is hard. Loss of job. Loss of your home. Loss of a beloved pet. Loss of a friendship. The most difficult of all to bear is the loss of a loved one, especially the loss of a child. Children are never supposed to die before their parents.

How can you ever find hope when every ounce of hope seems to be gone? Somewhere on this journey of grief you will begin to remember happy times. At first it's painful and often seems a bit disrespectful. Eventually, though, these memories bubble up and fill your heart with so much joy.

The happy memories become a healing salve to the raw pain that you once felt. One of the greatest gifts you can give to yourself is to be able to remember the times of laughter and fun shared with your loved one.

Give yourself permission to remember the happy times. When you do remember those times of laughter, fresh hope will flood your soul with healing peace and joy!

**Help a person laugh and you've helped heal a broken heart.**

## Day 135

*"Behold God is my helper; the Lord is the sustainer of my soul." Psalm 54:4*

In a perfect world, life doesn't hurt. There is no pain, and we don't have to shed tears because all is perfect and well. Reality tells us, though, that we don't live in a perfect world. Instead, we experience lots of pain, sorrow, and tragedies that come into our lives quite unexpectedly.

Sorrow is a new language that must be learned by those who experience loss. Sorrow gives us new eyes by which we view all of life. At first we feel like foreigners struggling to find our way without a map. In time, we struggle less until finally we find a new place to call home. It is here that we learn the new language and we have a keener, sharper eyesight in which we can see all of life's beauty.

If you are struggling today in the land of sorrow, hold on and continue putting one foot forward until you find your place of level ground. Trust that as you travel this lonely path, you will find others along the way who will reach out and help you. They will speak your language and you will no longer feel alone.

You will be filled with new hope each day until finally your small flicker of hope will turn into a sunbeam that will light the way for you from the dark path of sorrow into the healing light of a new-found peace and inner joy.

**Behind every cloud is a special rainbow moment when life begins to make sense again.**

## Day 136

*"Now may the God of hope fill you with all joy and peace in believing, that you may abound in hope by the power of the Holy Spirit." Romans 15:13*

When you are walking the pathway of loss, it often feels like you're walking all alone. Everyone around you seems to be happy and carefree and surrounded by friends and laughter. The pain of loss turns your world upside down for a while and takes away your clarity of vision. You see things through tear stained eyes and you feel things through a heart that has been broken. Nothing feels or looks right, and loneliness temporarily sets you apart from everyone.

Hope is a seed that has been planted in the heart of each and every individual. Hope lies hidden during times when life is moving along at a strong, happy pace. But, when you begin to falter and feel like life has lost its meaning, hope comes to the surface and helps you to go on.

Hope arrives at just the right moment and in just the right way. God has planned it that way. Along comes a comforting smile that seems to let you know that joy will return. You feel the warmth of the sunshine against your cold, lonely heart, and it reminds you that friendship will once again give you warmth and comfort. The evening stars that light up the sky remind you that you are never walking the path of sorrow and grief alone. There is always a light to help guide you along the way.

Hope is the link to your heavenly Father. Hope reminds you that you are never alone. Hope reassures you that there is joy in the future. Hope gives you a reason to go on!

**Better times are ahead, so hold on!**

## Day 137

*"Be glad for all God is planning for you. Be patient and prayerful always." Romans 12:12*

When you reflect and look back upon your life, it's always good to take the time to remember the many ways that God has been by your side and has given you an anchor to hold onto when you've felt like you were lost and floating out to sea. God's love is never changing, and He remains faithful in His promises to you.

There are times when God's faithfulness is questioned, and that's okay. That's part of your grief over the losses you've experienced. Everyone questions during moments of pain and anguish. That's often how you will get your answers.

Take the time to look at the stars and see the darkness of the evening wrapped in the twinkling light. Wake up and look to the heavens to see the faithfulness of a new day being ushered in. Take a long, deep breath and allow your guardian angels to watch over you. Feel the peace that only God can give as you allow Him to touch your heart with new hope.

Isn't it a good feeling to put away some of the old stuff of life and begin new? Hold onto the hope that God is faithful, and He has a special blessing chosen for you in the days ahead. Allow your mind to rest in those thoughts. Hope will soon begin to fill the empty cracks of your soul, and you will soon be singing a song of joy again!

**Even when we don't understand, have confidence that God's love stands behind it.**

## Day 138

*"Do not fear, I will help you." Isaiah 41:13*

Grief is so difficult to explain. How do you tell what a broken heart feels like? How can you explain the feeling of emptiness that echoes like a hollow hole? How can you explain the constant gnawing that overrides every thought you have day and night reminding you of your loss? Grief is something that's really not able to be understood completely unless you've been through it.

Life following loss feels as though you have been placed in a foreign land and you can't speak the language. You try hard, but nobody understands. Your words consist of sorrow and pain. You feel as though you're not to make it in this new land of pain and grief, yet you know that there's no way out. Not just yet.

Hope is something that crosses over all borders and travels into every land. Hope can find even the tiniest crack and begin to take root and grow. And, when hope anchors to an empty heart, it begins to fill in the holes, and you will start to feel as though you're no longer a stranger in a foreign land. Hope gives you a reason to go on when all logic says that you can't.

God has given an abundance of hope that surrounds you every day to provide healing when you feel so alone and lost. The sun, the moon, the stars all point in the direction of God. The ocean and the miracles that lie below the sea remind us that God is always in control. You are never alone, and you have not been forgotten. And, the best part of all is that hope arrives at just the moment when it is needed most!

**Hope refreshes and replenishes the weary soul.**

## Day 139

*"Give thanks in all things, for this is God's will for you." I Thess. 5:18*

Do you ever wonder why the verse about giving thanks in all things is in the bible? I'm sure a lot of people have struggled with that verse over the years.

Most people can be thankful when the tide is flowing in our direction, when the sun is shining on our face, and when all good things are coming our way. But, when our lives are shattered, battered, and tattered, it's another story. The words "thank you" don't even come to mind. Yet, we are told that it's good and right to give thanks even during the worst of times.

When grief enters the chambers of our heart, we cry tears of pain and loneliness and our hearts ache so bad that we can't even think. The only utterances that come from us are groans of pain. The emptiness that we feel can't be described. How is it possible to give thanks?

I am convinced that God understands our hearts when they are full of grief, and He allows us to feel the pain, walk the journey, and come back to Him. This is in order that we might once again say thank you for the countless blessings of life and for all of the many miracles that are found in each day.

If you are struggling in your walk today and cannot say the words "thank you," don't allow the additional burden of guilt weigh you down. God knows you, He knows your heart, and He loves you. He will instill within you enough hope to carry you to a place of thankfulness. For today, rest in His arms and allow His love to warm your broken heart and feel the comfort of His peace.

**Hope is like a country road; there never was a road, but when many people walk on it, the road comes into view.**

## Day 140

*"I will send down showers in season; There will be showers of blessing." Ezekiel 34:26*

Grief is so much like the weather. Some days the sun shines and we feel so warm and good all over. Then, without any warning, a storm begins brewing and before we know it, we're running to find shelter.

The life touched by grief never really knows how to dress for the weather. Will it be raining today, or will there be only sunny skies? Will laughter touch my heart, or will my tears flow fast enough to fill a river?

There is one thing we do know for certain. The sudden flashes back into intense grief will not always be that way. There will be a day when our grief no longer is the focus of our entire attention. We will be "okay" if a brief shower comes because we know that soon the skies will part and the sun will shine once again.

What triggers the rain in our lives? It could be something as insignificant as seeing a baby kitten rolling around in the grass. Or a butterfly fluttering to and fro. Maybe it's a song that comes on the radio that reminds us of the emptiness in our lives. And, we weep tears of sorrow.

We'll probably never be totally free of these grief flashes, but there will be a day when hope overrides our deep sense of loss and our heart will wear a smile—even in the rain!

**God's love is big enough to carry us through any storm.**

## Day 141

*"Many blessings are given to those who trust the Lord."*
*Psalm 40:4*

When we are walking the pathway of loss, it often feels like we're walking all alone. Everyone around us seems to be happy and carefree and surrounded by friends and laughter. The pain of loss turns our world upside down for a while and takes away our clarity of vision. We see things through tear-stained eyes and we feel things through a heart that has been broken. Nothing feels or looks right and loneliness temporarily sets us apart from everyone.

Hope is a seed that has been planted in the heart of each and every individual. Hope lies hidden during those times when life is moving along at a strong, happy pace, but when we begin to falter and feel like life has lost its meaning, hope comes to the surface and helps us to go on.

Hope arrives at just the right moment and in just the right way. God has planned it that way. A comforting smile that seems to let us know that joy will return is sent our way. The warmth of the sunshine against our cold, lonely heart reminds us that friendship will once again give us warmth and comfort. The evening stars that light up the sky remind us that we are never walking the path of sorrow and grief alone. There is always a light to help guide us along the way. Hope is our link to our heavenly Father. Hope reminds us that we are never alone. Hope reassures us that there is joy in the future. Hope gives us a reason to go on.

**When God allows extraordinary trials, He gives extraordinary comfort.**

## Day 142

*"....and hope does not disappoint, because the love of God has been poured out within our hearts through the Holy Spirit who was given to us." Romans 5:5*

Sometimes it's so hard to remember life as it was before our loss. We try to "get back that feeling," but we can't. When the bottom dropped out from below us, we were crushed, and the healing seems to be an ongoing work. We forget what life was really like before our loss.

So, we begin to mark the calendar with all of the firsts. The first time since it happened...the first birthday, the first movie, the first time in church, the first vacation, the first holiday. And, every event seems to be shadowed by the darkness of our loss.

We wonder how we are ever going to go on. Will it get any better? Will the heaviness ever lift? Will laughter ever be part of life again?

Our loss changes the entire constellation of our lives. That fact will never go away. That is etched into our hearts forever. But, the edges will soften, and events and people that enrich and bring love into our lives will bless us so that our loss will not always take a front seat, but will in time become part of the tapestry of our lives that will add its own bit of special beauty that we will wear with special affection forever.

If your heart feels like it's breaking in two today, remember with patience and hope that your life will not always feel this fragmented and broken. Hope will embrace your heart and allow love to bless you as joy slowly returns.

**When life caves in, you need comfort. God's gift to you is just that—holy comfort.**

## Day 143

*"Preserve me, O God, for I take refuge in Thee." Psalm 16:1*

Once the reality of loss has settled in on our heart, the difficult job of working towards some type of healing begins. We often don't have a clue where or how to begin to heal a broken heart. All we know is that the pain is real and it's unlike anything ever felt before!

God was so wise when he created this earth. He knew we would be in need of distractions from the hurt in this life. He knew that we would need places to go and things to see that would calm us and give us reassurance. He knew that He must create a place of beauty for all to see and enjoy as they begin the hard process of healing.

Where is your place of healing? Is it sitting under the clouds and watching them roll by? Is it climbing atop the highest mountain and looking in awe at the view? Is it taking a nature walk through a garden of butterflies and flowers? Is it sitting on the sandy shore and watching the rhythm of the waves rolling back and forth?

Once we find our place, we have to be willing to let it speak to us. We have to allow our place to touch the innermost part of our hearts and give us the comfort we need in knowing we are not alone. We need to allow our place to fill us with new hope. When we find that special place, it will whisper to us in a mysterious sort of way and tell us that all is going to be well!

**Prayer is an end to isolation. It is living our daily life with someone; with Him who alone can deliver us from all pain.**

## Day 144

*"Light rises in the darkness for the upright; the Lord is gracious, merciful, and righteous."* Psalm 112:4

When grief is new and so raw, it takes up all of our time and energy. We forget what day it is, and worse yet, we don't even care. We stop going out, we miss appointments, and we withdraw from life as we once knew it. Grief affects every part of our being!

At first, we expect this kind of response to our grief. We need to do so much adapting to a new world, a new place to call home, and a new way to find joy. We can't rush through this process!

But, there comes a time in our lives when we will be faced with the most difficult choice of all. Do we stay in our deep grief, or do we make a conscious effort to take one step at a time and try to move forward into a place of hope?

Most of us make the choice to move on because we know that's what is best. If we stay in that deep black hole of grief for too long, we'll miss another spring. And, we don't want to miss the blue skies, the budding of the flowers, seeing the first robin plucking his worm from the earth that is beginning to unfold with so much life and beauty!

Even though grief will always be a part of our lives, there comes a time when we can move it from a place of everyday top priority, to a place of subdued recognition that we carry deep within our soul. Spring comes once a year, and it's full of hope. Give yourself permission to enjoy the beauty of this season of hope and new beginnings!

**When I am in sorrow, my soul longs for a touch of fresh air, blue skies, and sunshine! Spring is a gift, and I will enjoy all the beauty of it!**

## Day 145

*"The Lord is my rock, my fortress, and my deliverer."*
*Psalm 18:2:a*

The pain of loss is something that cannot be explained by words alone. How do you explain a pain that runs so deep that it makes your heart bleed? How does you tell others what it feels like to have a cloud always hovering above with reminders of the life that no longer exists as you once knew it? How can you possibly share the personal pain you feel to the extent that others understand? It cannot be done. Grief is too personal.

How then can you move forward? How do you find your place in your new world—the world that has been created by your loss? How can you find a way to bring joy back into your heart that hurts so much each day? Is it even possible to reclaim joy?

This world is full of pain and grief. That is a fact. But, it is also brimming over with joy and blessings. When you are in the pits of grief, you feel alone and abandoned by all blessings. But, as you allow hope to ignite within you, it acts as a magnet drawing the blessings of life closer and closer to you until finally you reach that point where you can see joy again. No longer does grief rule your life. It is there. You will always feel that sting of loss, but no longer will it govern your every thought and action. That's hard to believe right now, but it's true.

Hope is alive, and it is bigger than any pain you will ever feel. Cling to hope and it will ignite a fire within your heart so that you can find your way out of the darkness into light!

**Prayer is exhaling the spirit of man and inhaling the spirit of God.**

## Day 146

*"But Thou, O Lord, art a shield about me, my glory, and the One who lifts my head." Psalm 3:3*

The sun is shining, there are sounds of joy all around, yet I do not feel spring in my heart. Instead there is the lingering cold of winter and I don't know what to do about it. Any person going through grief and loss has expressed those very words. Grief is a lonely word and it puts you on a journey to a lonely land—for a while.

The good news is that this feeling of winter does not last forever! God, in His infinite wisdom, has provided hope for us when traveling this difficult path. Hope comes to us in ways too numerous to count, and comes in the most surprising ways to provide comfort and hope to our hurting hearts.

The butterfly that you saw was bringing you a message that there is a new life waiting for you. Give it time to emerge. The rainbow brings promises of blue skies and the truth that this storm will not last forever. The robin brings tidings of spring giving the assurance that winter will end and flowers will soon bloom!

Today if you feel afraid and lonely, take a step back and look at nature—God's gift to you. Nature doesn't worry, nor does it remain in a state of cold bleakness. Nature sprouts forth new life, new joy, and a promise of a glorious array of splendor for you to enjoy! Hope assures you of that! Your spring is coming, and when it does, it will be wonderful!

**Hope helps me remember how to live.**

## Day 147

*"I will lie down and sleep in peace, for you alone, O Lord make me dwell in safety." Psalm 4:8*

Winter months leave us longing for color and refreshment in our lives. When springtime finally arrives, we are often in awe of nature and all of the daily miracles that unfold before our eyes with the changing of brown to green, cold to warm, sticks to leaves, and bitter wind to warm sunshine.

Perhaps more than anything, the changing of seasons gives us hope. Hope that our day of darkness will not last forever. Hope that tomorrow is one more step forward in the journey towards healing. Hope that every day is a miracle. Hope that my miracle is waiting to unfold right before my very eyes!

If you are feeling lost in a sea of grief today, please remind yourself that winter does not last forever. Spring does arrive, and when it does, it will bring with it a refreshing new time of nurturing and hope!

**God's fingerprints are everywhere. Nothing has been left untouched by His love.**

## Day 148

*"I have good plans for you, not plans to hurt you."*
*Jeremiah 29:11*

Grief is common among all people, yet it is something that makes us feel so terribly alone in our pain. Even when members of a family share the same loss, the type of grieving we do can be so uniquely different. We each experience the pain of our loss in different ways that make grief so hard to understand.

Is there a common thread in grief that we can each see and feel? Yes! That one thing we long for, that one thing we each understand is that we need hope when feeling such despair. We
need to find a way to move forward in life and not stay stuck in the lonely prison of grief.

How do we do this? How do we find this hope that we so desperately need? The only true and lasting hope can be found by trusting. When we know with full assurance that our Shepherd is watching over us, we can rest in Him. When our faith stretches to the point of understanding that if He calmed the stormy seas He can also calm my storm-battered heart, then I can find hope and strength in Him.

Walk among nature and experience the mighty presence of God. Read His word and allow Him to comfort your hurting heart. Look to the heavens and be filled with awe as you know He is always with you. Cling to the promise of the rainbow—our visible promise of hope! Grief is real, but hope is eternally alive.

**Without hurry or fear I will dwell in the house of my grief and wait for the promise of my hope to return.**

## Day 149

*"My hope is in Thee." Psalm 39:7*

There are times when life hurts and religion doesn't seem to give comfort. In fact, religion can make us feel worse when we are seeking answers and we get only silence. It's a hard fact to understand and accept that bad things really do happen to good people, and there is no solid explanation that gives us any comfort.

Many times, life's painful circumstances do not make any sense at all. The undeserving person gets the promotion at work. The person with a heart of sincere caring gets struck with an illness that causes a lifetime of pain and suffering. A person's life's savings are lost because of one poor decision. An accident takes the life of a loved one. Or, the most unthinkable pain of all—a child dies a senseless death leaving behind only brokenness and a lonely, aching heart.

How can a person go on when life hurts so badly and leaves us in a pile of ruin with no logical answers to life's problems and pain? Even though we do not receive the comfort and answers we are looking for today, there is relief found in that inner strength we call hope. We have only to look at the breaking of dawn to understand that life offers new possibilities each and every day. As we watch the expanse of the blue sky, our hearts fill with the fresh sense of new hope. When a star brightly shines in the dark sky we know that there is no night so dark that we cannot see hope.

God has not left us alone in our pain. Rather, He has tenderly covered us in His love so that we cannot lose sight of a brighter tomorrow. He has spread His arms around us and allows us to feel His strength carry us through the pain. He gives us rest from our burdens and places a song on our heart by giving us the rainbow painted sky with promises of new hope.

**Forgiving the unfairness of life releases us from the shackles of pain.**

## Day 150

*"Behold, God is my helper; the Lord is the sustainer of my soul." Psalm 54:4*

Most of us don't like change. We get to a place in life where we feel comfortable, and we are fine with staying there. Then, out of the blue, there comes something that knocks us flat and leaves us wondering if we'll ever get to a place in life where all feels okay again. Loss brings about so many changes in our lives!

Are you struggling with finances today? Broken relationships? Loss of health? Lost dreams? Loss of a loved one? The unthinkable—the loss of a child? If so, please know that you're not alone in this pain. Countless others have walked the lonely path of grief and pain and have been faced with many changes, and they've made it. The good news is that you, too, will make it to a new place of peace and joy!

While dealing with all of the changes that come about due to a loss, surround yourself with others who can support you. Look to those who have gone through similar circumstances for some much-needed guidance and encouragement. Remember that by sharing your pain, you have cut that pain in half. You'll be surprised at how many people will encourage you when you open up your heart and let them into your life.

Slowly but surely, changes will take place, and you will find yourself once again able to enjoy the small blessings in life. Day by day, the sun will begin to shine once again, and you will find yourself able to face the day with renewed hope and strength!

**If you can't see the answer, it doesn't mean it's not there. You don't have to see the bird to hear its beautiful melody.**

## Day 151

*"The Lord has been my stronghold, and my God the rock of my refuge." Psalm 94:22*

Sometimes life feels empty and we can't seem to shake loose our fears, sadness, and anxiety. We try so hard to get back into the groove of a meaningful, purpose-driven life, but the pain of loss overrides all of our attempts of finding joy.

During our moments of emptiness, it's helpful to take out a piece of paper and begin making a list of our blessings. Begin with the basics of food, shelter, and clothing. Then dig deeper. Look far into your life and start the process of noticing the blessings we don't often think about. Be thankful for freedom. Be thankful for access to your bible. Be thankful for prayer. Be thankful for the sun, moon, stars, and every rainbow that paints a message of hope across the sky.

Being thankful when going through trials and pain in this life is not always easy. But when we count our blessings, naming them one-by-one, heart changes begin to occur. Discouragement exits our heart and joy enters. Tears dry and smiles form.

God has not left us alone to be swallowed up in a sea of pain. Even in our darkest hours, He is near us supplying us with all of our needs and filling our hearts with new hope!

**A thankful heart cannot lose trust in God.**

## Day 152

*"Have I not commanded you? Be strong and courageous! Do not tremble or be dismayed, for the Lord your God is with you wherever you go." Joshua 1:9*

Grief often leaves us feeling depleted, hopeless, and in many ways disoriented and confused with life. It's hard to cope with the daily strains of living, but it's an emotional and physical drain to cope with everyday life when dealing with the daily pain and heartache of loss.

Try to remind yourself often that you are only asked to do this for one day. You can do it! You can look at the sunrise and enjoy it for one day. You can accept others as they are for just one day. You can manage your pain for only one day. You can get dressed and get out among people for just one day. You can smile at someone just for today. You can believe that your tomorrow will get better just for one day. You can feel less alone just for one day.

Hope is a seed waiting to germinate and grow, and it will change your heart completely. Allow hope to come alive—just for today. Allow hope to thrive and guide you—just for one day. Allow hope to be yours—just for today!

**We don't have to look to the future; we are only asked to live today with hope. And, when we do, we have created a future of enduring hope!**

## Day 153

*"But as for me, I trust in Thee, O Lord." Psalm 31:14*

As hard as this concept is, remember that life is not always fair. Bad things really do happen to good people. And, sometimes we get a bigger portion of difficulties and pain than we ever imagined we would be asked to bear.

But, also keep this in mind. Life is full of everyday heroes who have somehow managed to unlock the door to their hearts and find that inner spark of hope. Eventually they do go on, and they do so with dignity, grace, and peace.

Loss is a lonely, painful road to travel when you're trying to do it alone. The good news is that we have not been left alone—not even for a second! We have a Father who knows every detail of our life, and He cares. He knows our thoughts, our pains, our sorrows, and more importantly He calls out to us in so many different ways each and every day to help ease our pain.

Look at the sunbeams streaming from the heavens and be encouraged! Gaze at the twinkling stars at night and be filled with awe at the details of the universe. Watch a butterfly and be filled with hope as you trace the steps of its formation. God's imprint is all around us, and His hands are tenderly holding our hearts and giving us the assurance that we will get through this pain.

Trust in His promises, hold tight to His hand, and be assured that He will never let go!

**Hope is seeing the rainbow after the storm before the sun comes out.**

## Day 154

*"I wait quietly before God for my hope is in Him." Psalm 62:5*

Special holidays are times when we are supposed to be filled with joy and thanksgiving, yet it is so difficult to even say those words during times of painful loss. There is an emptiness that won't go away, that can't seem to be filled, and that continually gnaws at the heartstrings letting us know that something is wrong.

Remind yourself often that grief is a very private matter, and it affects all of our relationships with family, friends, and our world. Inwardly we know that there will be a day and a time when we can freely and easily say thank you, but maybe that day is not right now. The important thing is to know that there will be a day when you will feel joy and thankfulness again.

A good alternative to thankfulness is trusting...trusting that one day you will feel thankful. Trusting that you will smile again. Trusting that you will laugh with others again. Trusting that you will love again.

There is a seed of inner strength we call hope that is embedded deep within the center of your heart, and in due time that seed will sprout. And, you will know because what is now dark will come alive. What is now sorrow will be joy. What is now pain will be peace. Trust and hope, and thankfulness will follow!

**I will trust when I cannot see, knowing that there is a bright light at the end of the tunnel.**

## Day 155

*"In you, Lord my God, I put my trust." Psalm 25:1*

What am I going to do today? That is the most difficult question that a person who is suffering loss faces every day. Am I going to get up and get out of bed, or am I going to pull the covers up over my head and not face the day?

Grief is hard work. It is painful. It is lonely. And, nobody can do the hardest part of grief work for you—feel the pain. Yet, we have help along the way. Every one of us has an extra source of help called hope that is laying dormant inside the depths of the heart. And, when we call on this hope, we can be certain we will be given the strength we need to face the day—hour by hour at first, but we will be given the strength to get through each day!

Are you having trouble facing today? Call on your source of hope and wait for an answer. Sometimes it comes in the form of a butterfly lighting upon your windowsill. Maybe you will see hope in a fluffy white cloud that is in the sky. Perhaps you'll see hope spelled out in a rainbow that follows a storm. Or maybe your hope will come in the still whisper of the gentle breeze blowing in your ear that reminds you that you are never, ever alone.

Take courage in today, and look for your special hope! It's there, and it will not fail you. Don't worry about tomorrow as that's another day. Just look for your hope for today, and be assured that you will get through!

**Today I will deal only with today, and I know that I can do it hour by hour, minute by minute, hope by hope!**

## Day 156

*"Blessed are they who mourn, for they shall be comforted." Matthew 5:4*

What a conflicting thought that in our deepest hour of pain from loss we are so keenly reminded of life! There is nothing that makes us more acutely aware of how much we should savor each moment of life than when we experience the death of a loved one—especially the death of a child. We never expect a child to die before his parents!

Though we deeply mourn our loss every day, we learn to cherish every moment of life. We learn of the brevity of our time on this earth. We understand more completely the child-like wonderment of stopping to examine every leaf, every insect, and every stone that comes into our path. We see more clearly the beauty in all of creation, and we more fully understand the miracle of each new sunrise.

Our loss will always leave a spot deep within our heart that feels empty. There is nothing that will ever replace that ache. But, as new hope emerges into our heart, we will experience a clearer understanding of how to live today—this day—to the fullest. We will live in the hope that the beauty of this life is a mere glimpse of the beauty and peace of the life to come. Through death we have been given the priceless gift of new hope!

**Hope is like a sunbeam. It brightens the innermost places of the heart.**

## Day 157

*"As the deer pants for streams of water, so my soul pants for Thee, O God." Psalm 42:1*

Loss changes so many things in a person's life. There are times of loneliness and feeling helpless. There are moments of not understanding why this had to happen. There is often a feeling of regret and overwhelming sadness. And, almost always there is a feeling of wishing that the loss had never happened.

How do we find our way to joy once again when so much of life and happiness were taken away in the blink of an eye? How can we find balance when our world suddenly feels like it has been turned upside down?

The way to hope and joy is a slow, steady path of many turns and changes. The answer lies within. Grief changes us, and along with the changes come new perspectives and new insights on life.

Listen to the softly falling raindrops. Take time to smell the scent of the lilies of the valley in bloom. Look upward and linger as you watch the rising sun. Gaze for an hour at the starry sky. Linger over a slice of warm apple pie. When our hearts have been broken, the things we once took for granted become the very things that will restore our faith and spark hope within our hearts once again.

**There is more beauty in one butterfly than can be written in volumes of books. And, therein lies the beginning of my newfound hope!**

## Day 158

*"Blessed are those who mourn for they shall be comforted." Matthew 5:4*

How will I do it? How will I get through the next day when I can't see the light at the end of the tunnel? Who really understands? Does anyone want to sit down beside me and help me through this mess in my life? I feel so alone, so broken, and so helpless!

Every person who has experienced loss has felt those same feelings of helplessness and abandonment. Life feels shattered and it seems to us that we will never be put back together again. Our burdens seem far too big for us, and so many times we give up searching for hope.

Hold on! Take a moment to stop and breathe slowly. Close your eyes and reflect on the moment. Listen to your own heart beating and know that as long as you have life inside of you, you have hope!

We each have had deep moments of pain and darkness, and during those times it is hard, if not impossible, to imagine ever seeing the light of day again. But, God designed us in His image, and He has not left us alone. Our Creator has sent us the sun, the moon, and the stars to shed light even during our darkest hours.

Take a walk outside for a moment every day just to listen to the sounds of nature. Do you hear the gentle breeze blowing through the trees? Can you hear the songbird singing a song of thanks and praise in the distance? Look to the heavens and follow the clouds. Stare at them until you can see beyond the misty blue to find the breaking of a new dawn. These are gifts of hope for us! These are our daily reminders that each day brings new hope and new strength! We have not been left alone in our pain! Rather, our heavenly Father has wrapped us in His arms of love and promised to never let go!

**Every sunrise is a personal reminder of new hope!**

## Day 159

*"Your love, O Lord, reaches to the heavens, your faithfulness to the skies." Psalm 36:5*

Grieving has its seasons, and autumn seems to be a particularly difficult season for those who have gone through loss. Maybe it's the visual of seeing the flowers stop blooming and the leaves falling off of the trees. Perhaps it's feeling the warm summer sunshine fading and suddenly feeling the lingering chill in the air. For most of us who have experienced loss, autumn is a time of reflection and bracing ourselves for the days of winter that lie ahead.

Are you facing autumn with dread and fear? What if you viewed autumn a bit differently this year? Why not buy a bag of flower bulbs and plant them now? And, then wait patiently and knowingly for the beauty of spring to return after the dark days of winter. What if you promise yourself to stay focused on the beauty of spring and summer rather than facing autumn with fear and dread?

**The best thing about the future is that it comes one day at a time.**

## Day 160

*"Trust in Him at all times, you people; pour out your heart before Him; God is a refuge to us." Psalm 62:8*

Hurry, hurry, hurry! Rushing here and there and really getting nowhere seems to be the way we live life when all is normal and well. But, when grief strikes the depths of our heart, we suddenly find that a song of a different beat is sung: "time stands still."

Quiet times become much harder to handle. Our loneliness seems to shout out to us in the silence and reminds us that nothing is right, and life has been turned upside-down. We grasp for some normalcy of the hustle and bustle of life again, but it doesn't happen. Not yet. Not when grief is raw and new. Busy lives are most generally happy lives, but there does come a season when it is good to be still. Sometimes we have to wait out the storm and regroup. We need time and space and even some silence to find that place called our new normal.

In the battlefront of our tears and grief, we often find comfort in retreating from the hurriedness of life for a while and just being still. Sitting among the solitude of nature is often grief's most helpful comfort. In the still of the night is the time we can most clearly hear the whisper of our closest Friend, our Father, our Comforter. Don't fear the quiet; rather embrace it for a season. Take time to listen for the quiet yet powerful voice of hope whispering in your ear daily. Hope will eventually take root in the very depths of your heart and grow into a spontaneous, healthy new joy!

**I will sit quietly for a season in my house of grief until my newfound hope appears.**

## Day 161

*"The Lord lifts the burdens of those bent beneath their loads." Psalm 146:8*

Any kind of loss is hard. Loss of job. Loss of home. Loss of a beloved pet. Loss of a friendship. Most difficult of all to bear is the loss of a loved one—especially the loss of a child. Children are never expected to die before their parents!

How does one find hope when all hope seems to be gone? Somewhere on this journey of grief, we begin to remember happy times. At first it's painful and often seems a bit disrespectful, but eventually those memories bubble up and fill our hearts with joy! Precious memories bring healing to the soul.

The happy memories help take away the edge of the raw pain that we once felt. One of the greatest gifts we can give to ourselves is to be able to remember the times of laughter and fun shared with our loved one! Yes, we will always shed tears and we will always wish for our loved one to be with us, but by remembering the joyful times together our hearts feel less empty.

Give yourself permission to remember the happy times! When you do remember those times of laughter, fresh hope will flood your soul with healing peace and joy.

**Precious memories are like sunshine to my soul.**

## Day 162

*"Guide me in your truth and teach me, for you are God my Savior, and my hope is in you all day long." Psalm 25:25*

It's a new day, so why don't I feel so new? Why am I still carrying around yesterday's fears, pain, sorrow, and problems?

This is a question that most of us ask every day. We all know that changing a page or a date on a calendar does not make all things new, but it does give us new hope that we can begin our next day with a new mental attitude of resolve to gain inner peace, joy, and happiness in spite of our outward circumstances.

Try something different today. Every time you have a negative, sad thought replace that thought with a statement of thankfulness. "I am thankful for my daily food. I'm thankful for the sunshine. I'm thankful for warmth during those cold, frigid days of winter. I'm thankful for the changing seasons. I'm thankful for the air I breathe, the evening stars that twinkle, and the many small blessings that touch my life each day."

With practice, you can soon find more and more things to be thankful for, and you will even be able to find some hidden blessings in the pain you are experiencing.

Hope is much stronger than fear. Hope is alive and never dies. Hope is a resource that every person alive has been given. Tap into your reserve of hope to help you—one day, one hour, one minute at a time!

**My hope helps me stay strong even when life makes no sense at all.**

## Day 163

*"Do not fear, for I am with you; do not anxiously look about you, for I am your God. I will strengthen you; surely I will help you. Surely I will uphold you with My righteous right hand." Isaiah 41:10*

There are times in our lives when our faith seems to fly right out the window. Life can hand us some brutal circumstances and we're left feeling like we're drifting out to sea without a life jacket or a captain to steer the boat. It's a terrible feeling of being lost and shipwrecked.

If you're facing some of the harshness of the day such as job loss, financial insecurities, broken relationships, or the loss of a loved one, that's the time when you most need your faith and hope. But, how does that happen when all looks dark?

During your desert times of faith there are two things that will help you. One is to saturate yourself in the Psalms. There are cries of hopelessness followed by the assurance that God is alive and real. And, that's just what you need whenever the unrelenting seas of grief and pain are battering you.

The second is to walk among nature. Just seeing the many wonders of nature will calm your soul. Nature is God's display of His wondrous love and care and power. Nature speaks volumes to us about hope. The seasons come and go, and we know that there is always a spring that follows the depths of winter.

Hope is alive, and hope is the key to restoring our faith. Faith and hope are the keys to survival! When obstacles and trials seem like prison walls, we can break free by clinging onto our hope in the power of our Maker.

**When there seems no chance of being set free from my grief, hope bathes my soul with new strength and I am set free.**

## Day 164

*"Behold, God is my helper; the Lord is the sustainer of my soul." Psalm 54:4*

When we're going through pains, trials, and loss, it seems like there is no end in sight. The bills continue to pile up. The work seems to fall more and more behind. The clutter builds until soon we can't even find a chair to sit in. And more than anything, that overwhelming feeling of loneliness seems to be worse than ever!

Does it ever end? Does the sadness ever go away when we've lost someone? Do we ever find a place in our hearts for joy again? Can we ever feel whole when we've been torn apart by disaster and pain? Grief pushes us onto a new road that we've never traveled before and the path seems all uphill, rocky, and impossible to climb!

Hold on! Stop right where you are and take a few minutes to reflect, to catch your breath, and to understand that today is one day, and you can make it through! You can take things hour by hour, until you can say with positive affirmation, "I've made it!" That's all we're ever expected to do. We need only to make it through today.

Expect the sunrise to come with brilliance and strength and new hope. Today is almost gone, yesterday is over, and tomorrow is a brand new beginning with opportunities for new hope and new miracles.

Don't confuse mourning your loss with forgetting how to live. It's a difficult climb to reach that point of getting there, but when you do you will know it. The flowers will gain back their brilliant colors. The sky will once again look bright blue. The warmth of the sunshine will touch your soul. And, you will no longer feel alone.

**Every cloud holds within it the potential to give showers of blessing.**

## Day 165

*"The Lord is for me; I will not fear; What can man do to me?" Psalm 118:6*

Most often, when we think of the coming of spring, we think of positive, beautiful changes. Spring is a time when life seems to awaken from its long winter's nap, and quite miraculously nature begins painting the world in an array of beautiful colors from the backdrop of the bright blue sky to the ever-stretching landscape of blooming trees and flowers. Animals are coming out of hibernation, and new life is seen everywhere during the spring awakening.

For the one who has suffered a loss, spring may be a difficult, painful reminder of life that was taken away, and springtime grief casts showers of tears on each new day. Rather than a season of joy, this is a season of mourning for the grieving heart. It is a time when hope is needed so badly!

As the grieving heart seeks comfort, it is important to remember that springtime isn't always marked by a date on the calendar. More importantly, springtime is a season of the heart. If your heart is heavily burdened with sorrow today, take comfort in knowing that your personal season of spring will arrive. God is never too late in sending the sunshine! He always knows when you need to see the rainbow painted in the sky as a reminder of his awesome, faithful promises.

Take heart, weary one. Your season of spring will arrive at just the right time. Hope will adorn you, and your heart will be bathed in peace and joy once again.

**Spring is a season of the heart—a gift from God that arrives exactly on time.**

## Day 166

*"Lord, I am in great trouble, so I call out to you. Lord, hear my voice; listen to my prayer for help."*
*Psalm 130:1-2*

When we are suffering intense grief, we find it difficult, if not impossible, to remember what it felt like to be happy. We do not remember that feeling of energy and zest for living. We cannot recall how much fun it was to plan out the agenda for the day. We forget the small things like the background noise of happy chatter and laughter. We forget joy.

Grief and loss send us to a new place that seems like a foreign land where we are forced to learn a new language and adapt to new feelings and circumstances. We have been uprooted from what felt safe and secure and happy, and have been sent to a place that is unknown and so very frightening. This is our grief journey, and we don't have a clue how we can make it.

What has helped most of us who have been called on this journey is knowing that we never have to travel alone. We have others beside us who have led the way, and they have found their new places in life and have begun to smile again. You, too, will find a new joy, and a new peace, and a new way to look at all of life again. You will find hope with the unfolding of each new day!

**At first I was lost in the dark, then I looked upward and saw the sun peeking through the clouds and I knew with certainty that I was on the right path to home.**

## Day 167

*"Pray without ceasing." I Thessalonians 5:17*

Are you feeling overwhelmed by loss today? Does it feel as though life has abandoned you and you're all alone in your grief? Have you come to the point of almost wanting to give up?

Hold on! There is hope beyond the grief, and that hope never fails to arrive at just the right moment in your life!

Take a walk alone today and look at the sky, slowly breathe in the air, and feel the breeze brush gently across your face. Hear the whispers of God in all of nature and allow His presence

to touch your heart. Feel His nearness and be assured that you have not been left alone in your pain.

Prayer is an amazing avenue of healing because it allows you to talk to the Physician and the One who truly understands. You can say what's on your heart and mind without fear of being misrepresented or misunderstood. There is no fear being placed on you when you speak to God in prayer. He listens. He understands. He sends comfort. He is your tender Father who cares.

What is on your heavy heart today? Sadness? Emptiness? Loneliness? Feeling forgotten and misused? Feeling abandoned? Then walk among the fields. Touch the lilies. Catch a butterfly.

Allow the raindrops to fall gently across your face, and know that you are never alone! Hope is alive and will continue to grow stronger with each passing day when you open your heart to prayer.

**Even on the bleakest day the sun still shines.**

## Day 168

*"My soul clings to Thee; thy right hand upholds me."*
*Psalm 63:8*

Today is another day in the 365 days that make up a year. I find myself being swallowed in a sea of grief and pain today, yet I have an inner knowing that somehow, someway it is still going to be good. I know because I have seen another sunrise. I know because I have experienced the joy of hearing the birds in the distance chirping their songs of praise and thankfulness. I know because I've seen others fall into a similar sea and come out onto dry land strong and filled with new hope.

My greatest moment of knowing comes when I look at creation. Not all of us have the opportunity to walk along the sea, or to pick wildflowers from a field, but each one of us has the sky. Can you even begin to fathom the expanse? Study the moods of the sky by following the clouds and their many changes from dark to white and fluffy billows of cotton floating through the air.

When I look at the heavens I am filled with hope! I know that I have a Creator who takes great pain in every detail, including the very details of my life. I can feel His presence in my life, and I am comforted. I can see His workmanship and know that He is very involved in my life. I can see His mighty power in all of His creation and I feel embraced in His strength.

What are you going through today? Pain? Doubts? Loss? Fear? Look to the heavens and allow the Maker of it all to hold you in His strong arms and to keep you safe! Hope is near. Strength is yours. Peace is your gift today!

**The day the Lord created flowers was the same day He knew we would understand hope.**

## Day 169

*"The Spirit of God is upon me, because the Lord has anointed me to bring good news to the afflicted." Psalm 61:1*

Facing those first holidays after a loss are horrible. Our mind is scattered with all kinds of thoughts about escaping the day. If only I could just get out of my skin for a day and become someone else, things would be better." We know that's not possible, but we sure would like to do it—just for one day. If we could just forget about the terrible loss just for today things wouldn't be so hard. But, we can't forget.

What are we to do? How do we make it through? This seems so hard to hear, but we must bear with the suffering and work our way through it. Face our fear and pain, and just allow the tears to fall. When we do, we are actually working towards the day when we will be better, stronger, and more able to cope.

Keep reminding yourself that you can make it through today. And, when you do, you can make it through tomorrow. And, you'll keep on going until there comes a time when you feel good again.

Hope is an insidious friend who never leaves us alone for one minute. Hope is always at work, keeping the heart sealed off to too much pain, but allowing us to feel enough that we will know there will be a day when we feel better. Hope is alive, and it dwells within. Get through today...one day at a time. And, remember often that there will be a day when hope grows much larger than your pain! You can do it. You can make it through today.

**The sky is endless; so is your hope.**

## Day 170

*"Depend on the Lord; trust Him, and He will take care of you." Psalm 37:5*

When sitting in the ashes of loss, we lose all hope for a while. How do we pick up the pieces and move on? Where will we get the energy? Who will stand by our side and help us? How will life ever seem worth living again? Where's the hope?

Our mind seems to go crazy with anxious thoughts during times of despair. We cannot seem to come close to even imagining what life would be like without this pain. During moments of utter despair, it's good to take time to walk among the beauty of nature. Allow the big, blue sky to speak to us. Look at the stars and watch how they light up the night giving us just the right amount of light to guide our way to safety. Take the time to watch the morning sunrise. Watch how perfectly timed it is. The sun never forgets to show its face!

Never, ever give up hope! Every day is our chance to begin anew. Every day gives us a fresh start. Every day is wrapped in love and has the potential to unleash miracles. Every day gives us a reason to live!

**Hope gives a peace that goes beyond all human understanding.**

## Day 171

*"The heavens tell the glory of God." Psalm 19:1*

Sadly, we often complicate grief with our own thinking. We forget that we are humans and loss is part of this life. That's a painful fact to hear, but it's the truth. Why do we act like death is such a stranger when we know that this life is not meant to go on forever?

If we're honest, we understand that death will come to all. Our problem is we miss the one who has died terribly. It's painful to the point of heartbreak.

We've been given such blessings within the beauty and masterpiece of nature. When we are feeling overcome by sadness and the despondency of our grief, it helps to stop thinking and go take a walk among nature. Spend some time walking among the flowers and trees. Gaze at the morning sunrise and allow it to speak to you. Sit in your favorite outdoor chair and watch the butterflies fluttering about in search of the finest nectar. Study the designs found in the leaves that adorn the trees. Take an evening walk and watch the sun slowly fading away against the horizon.

Allow the miracles of nature to speak to your heart as never before. Nature's creation didn't happen by chance, but rather by design and purpose. Can we believe that God has a design and purpose for human life, too? Why do we think that God has left us unattended in our grief? If God takes great patience with the birds and flowers and trees found in nature, how much more love will he show to us? Spending time with nature is like medicine to our grief.

**In the stillness of the night you will rediscover that God is still God.**

## Day 172

*"We walk by faith, not by sight." II Corinthians 5:7*

The journey through grief is so different for each person. Nobody feels a loss in quite the same way no matter what the relationship was to the one who is gone. The time spent together and the memories created were so personal. You know from past experiences that well-meaning friends are going to try to tell you how you should grieve and how long you should grieve. This is one time when it's okay to be a bit selfish. You can be polite, but firm. You don't have to answer to anyone but yourself when it comes to grieving your loss.

If you feel like visiting the cemetery every day for one year straight and that helps you, then do it. If you feel like continuing to set the table for your loved one, don't let anybody tell you that you're crazy. You know what you're doing to help get your through this valley of despair.

If you feel like sleeping with your loved one's shirt every night, don't let anybody talk you out of it. This is your personal grief walk. Do you know what? You're going to be okay when you grieve in your own way! By making your own grief decisions, you're carving out your personal journey to hope and healing.

**Sometimes it takes a lot of rain before we see the rainbow. Don't give up! Your rainbow is there!**

## Day 173

*'Tis better to have loved and lost than never to have loved at all." —Alfred Tennyson*

Death is the greatest robber of all. When a child dies our hearts are broken forever. When we lose a spouse suddenly without warning, we lose our faith in life. If this can happen, what else can be taken away? We get angry. We feel broken. We question why? We go around and around with our thoughts, but one thing stands out. Oh, how blessed we were to have this precious loved one as part of our lives if only for a short while! We had the most precious gift taken away, but...we also were given that gift to love and cherish, and we will forever be thankful.

**My pain overcomes me, but in my greatest hours of grief I remain thankful for the precious gift of the one I held so near and could love.**

## Day 174

*"The Lord will accomplish what concerns me; Thy lovingkindness, O Lord, is everlasting." Psalm 137:8*

Will today be the day that the clouds of despair begin to lift? Every time we are greeted by a new sunrise, we are given the gift of new hope. We never know exactly when that special smile or kind word will be sent our way, but we can be certain that it will arrive at just the right moment to help ease the pain of our broken heart.

When grief becomes part of our lives, we are suddenly living in a world that seems lonely and barren. There is nothing at all that looks, smells, feels, tastes, or sounds familiar. We find ourselves wandering in circles, not knowing where we are going. All we know is that we want to go back to that place in life where things felt safe, happy, and secure. Yet, we know that we can't.

God, in His infinite wisdom, gave us a universal language that we can all understand. It is the language of love, and everyone can speak it. When we are grieving, though, we often don't hear any spoken words of love, because our hearts are too heavy to listen. That's why God gave us very real symbols of His love.

Listen to the peaceful sound of the babbling brook and feel the gentle touch of God's love. Smell the fresh air following a soft rain and understand that you will be renewed after the falling of your tears. Watch the clouds part to display the rainbow following a storm and remember the promises of God. Watch the lips of a stranger passing by form a smile and feel the warmth of someone who cares.

Every time your heart is touched by God's love, a bit more hope grows within your heart until one day you will find you are no longer a stranger in a foreign land. Instead, you are a beautiful flower blooming among a field of many wonderful friends. Hope instills new life in you.

**Prayer is when you talk to God; meditation is when you listen to God.**

## Day 175

*"I have written your name on my hand." Isaiah 49:16*

Today is a brand new day, yet when our hearts are hurting nothing seems to feel right. The thrill of unwrapping the gifts of a new day isn't there, and our hearts seem to fill with only loneliness and pain. We are left wondering when we will get our enthusiasm back for life. When will our joy return? When will we be filled with a song in our heart?

Grief is a hard word to say, and it is even more difficult to understand. When grief knocks on the door of our heart we know it is there because we can feel the raw pain that so suddenly overtook us. However, grief leaves us very slowly and we often don't realize that our unwelcome guest is inching its way out of the door of our heart until is has been replaced by the wonderful blessing of hope.

Every time we look at a butterfly or the colors of a rainbow, we take one step closer to hope. Each time we feel the warmth of the sunshine upon our face, we grow closer to recognizing the miracle of a brand new day. For every flower that we see bloom, we push aside one sad thought and allow space for a bright, new thought of hope to visit our heart.

Grief is a difficult journey, but we have not been left alone. God has placed his signature of hope in the morning sky, in the twinkling of the evening stars, and in every soft whisper of the wind. He has given us the assurance of His love by showing us all of His creation. He is our Shepherd, and we are His sheep. His tender care will carry us through every dark valley into the green pastures where we will find rest and replenishment.

**Joy comes in the morning when hope is planted in the heart.**

## Day 176

*"But the plans of the Lord stand firm forever, the purposes of his heart through all generations." Psalm 33:11*

People try to help by saying this was God's will. The loss hurts so bad, that it's impossible to think that this kind of pain was in a special plan for your life. You push aside that thought, and try to figure out what went wrong in your life to cause this loss.

Were you a bad person? Did you do something that caused this much pain to the one you loved so much and now you're being punished for it? Were you born under an unlucky star and this is your lot in life to have horrible things happen to you? Why were you singled out among millions of others?

These thoughts swirl through your head for days, weeks, and months following a loss until one day you realize the futility in that thinking. When you walk among nature it teaches you about the goodness of God and the love of your Creator. You know, though, that storms pass through and cause pain. Both the good and the bad are hurt. That's the part that is so hard to accept. But, only when you begin to see life as more fair than unfair and understand that the sun shines on both the just and the unjust can you understand that others will go through terrible losses, too.

In time, your pain will begin to ease and you will see life in a new way. You will understand more of the blessings that came your way than the pain. This is the beginning of your healing.

**Always begin anew with the day just as nature does. It is the most sensible thing to do.**

## Day 177

*"Preserve me, O God, for I take refuge in Thee." Psalm 16:1*

Once the reality of loss has settled in on your heart, the difficult job of working towards some type of healing begins. You don't have a clue where or how to begin to heal a broken heart. All you know is that the pain is real and it's unlike anything you've ever felt before!

God was so wise when He created this earth. He knew you would be in need of beauty to soothe you from the hurt in this life. He knew that you would need places to go and things to see that would calm you and give you reassurance. He knew that He must create a place of beauty for all to see and enjoy as the hard process of healing begins.

Where is your place of healing? Is it sitting in a meadow under the expansive blue sky and watching the clouds roll by? Is it climbing atop the highest mountain and looking in awe at the view? Is it taking a nature walk through a garden of butterflies and flowers? Is it sitting on the sandy shore and watching the ebb and flow of the waves?

Once you find your place, allow it to speak to you. Allow your place to touch the innermost part of your heart and give you the comfort you need in knowing you are not alone. Allow your special place to fill you with new hope. When you find that special place, it will whisper to you in a mysterious sort of way and tell you that all is going to be well!

**When hope guides all your thoughts, even problems and pain become lined with sunshine.**

## Day 178

*"Do not fear, for I am with you." Isaiah 41:10*

When grief comes into our lives, we often act in ways that we never did before, and it scares us. We suddenly feel out of control and so alone. We feel like crying one minute and screaming the next. Nothing really feels right, and our stomachs have an achy feeling that is hard to explain. Empty is probably the best way to describe the feeling when we are struggling with grief.

What do we do when grief overtakes us and we no longer know who we are or where we're supposed to be? During times of questioning and feeling alone, it's good to remind ourselves often that we will get through this. Our grief won't always be raw like an open wound. Little by little, the sunshine of hope will cast sunbeams on us, and our hearts will begin to heal. No, we'll never be the same as before, but we will feel joy and peace again.

When the fear of facing a new day creeps in, remember that with every new day comes the possibility of new miracles. Every sunrise, every rainbow, every singing bird is a reminder of the miracle found in the awakening of a new day.

Grief relief comes in the most unexpected ways and at the most unexpected times, and one thing is for sure. It always arrives on time!

**Anything worth worrying about is worth praying about.**

## Day 179

*"For you have been my hope, my confidence since my youth." Psalm 71:5*

When tragedy strikes, you feel wounded. You can't get up for a while because the air has suddenly been knocked right out of you. You wander around in a daze with no real place to go. All you know is this pain is relentless and you want it to go away.

You seek out help from your doctor. He gives you a pill and tells you to sleep. You try taking walks, but the loneliness is too much so you come inside and lie down. You try going to church, but the pastor doesn't seem to understand at all what you're going through.

You try everything that you can possibly think of, and then one day a neighbor walks up to your door carrying a freshly baked apple pie. In the awfulness of the day, you are touched by the comfort of love and friendship, and it's something you never forget.

Your senses are made keenly more aware during times of grief. The smallest act of love speaks to your broken heart more than a thousand eloquent words without passion and meaning.

**A true friend will weep with those who weep and temper every word with new hope.**

## Day 180

*"Be strong and courageous. Do not be terrified; do not be discouraged, for the Lord your God will be with you wherever you go." Joshua 1:9*

When caught up in the tangled messiness of grief, there are some hard words that you have to hear. You hear the sounds of people all around you laughing, busy with their daily chores of life, and carrying on as though nothing at all had happened. You withdraw to a corner and wonder how could this be. How can others around you be experiencing normal life? How could others be genuinely happy when you are struggling so hard just to breathe? Your loss hurt so bad that you expected the world around you to shut down for a while just to sit with you, to help you, and to mourn with you.

Instead, the world rushes on as though everything was okay. It's hard to see this. Perhaps this is one of the hardest parts of grieving. You know others care, but they just aren't showing it, and that hurts. You have to step back and remember how life works. When you were in your happy place, you felt real sympathy for others around you who were hurting, but life didn't stop for you. And, it's not going to stop for your friends either. This is tough, but it helps to remember that in our humanness life really does go on. It has to. That doesn't mean that others don't care. They care, and they are waiting for you to let them know how they can help you find some hope once again.

**May I be reminded that others are walking this difficult uphill path, too. How often I forget and think I am the only one.**

## Day 181

*"Your word, O Lord, is eternal; it stands firm in the heavens." Psalm 119:89*

As much as you try to deny it, grief has sharpened our awareness of the beauty of life. Oh, how much you wish you didn't have to have such a bitter teacher as death, but that loss did something internally to you. Stop doing what you're doing right now and take a look inside of you. Can you see the changes? Can you notice the way you never look at a flower the same? Do you notice how often you step outside onto the porch, taking a deep sigh and stare at the mighty blue sky?

Listen right now. What do you hear? There are sounds that you never picked up on before. You can even hear the distant thumping of your own heart beating to the rhythm of life. It's true that every one of your senses are much keener now. You see and hear things that you never paid attention to before.

The hard truth is that when you lose someone you love dearly, your eyes are opened up to a whole new world. You see through the meaningless banter, and you focus more on the spiritual. You look at the sky and imagine what heaven will be like. You take time out of your busy schedule to say "I love you" more. You know what it is like to feel utterly and completely lost and without hope, so you are there for others around you who need the words of comforting hope that you can give.

Sometimes you go through these fires of hell to come out stronger, see more of God's beauty, and to be more willing to help others who are in need. Grief and loss are terribly hard, but they also instill a spirit of love deep within your heart that you never knew existed. Grief paves the way for a new, deeper, more enduring hope.

**God doesn't make mistakes. He loves you far too much to allow that.**

## Day 182

*"I will lift up my eyes to the hills; where does my help come from? My help comes from the Lord, the maker of heaven and earth." Psalm 121:1-2*

People come to us with all kinds of special sayings and quotes when we are desolate and without hope. They mean well, but what they don't understand is that most of the time we really don't want to hear anything. We need to feel. Lost hope strips us of our ability to feel love, compassion, gentleness, and kindness. When we lose hope, we lose our ability to see life clearly. We look at everything and everyone through tear stained eyes.

As hard as it is to do, it helps when we take out a pen and a piece of paper and begin writing down our blessings. When we've just gone through a loss, thinking of blessings isn't easy to do. We resist because our heart is too wounded. It's too exhausting to think beyond our pain.

Force yourself to write down just one blessing today. Then tomorrow write down one more. And, the next day do the same. You'll surprise yourself at the end of the month with a beautiful hope journal that will help draw life back into better perspective for you. It's a simple exercise, really, with big benefits for the heart.

**A thankful heart is a heart filled with hope.**

## Day 183

*"He will wipe every tear from their eyes. There will be no more death or mourning or crying or pain." Revelation 24:4*

Have you ever wondered what our loved ones would say to us now that they are gone? What kind of message would they give to us? Would we be told to slow down our pace of living and stop rushing so much? Would we be told to forgive more? Would the message be one of cheer?

Maybe our loved one would say to dry those tears because all is well in heaven. Maybe the message would be to remember that there is no loneliness or pain in heaven. The message would probably say to remember that the road is rocky and difficult here on earth, but heaven is waiting and so is the one we love so much.

Our message would be one of hope and beauty. Our message would be to stop worrying and grasp hold of the beauty all around and seize the moment. Our message would be a loud, clear, wonderful message of hope!

**Breathe life into the everyday by looking for the extraordinary in the ordinary.**

## Day 184

*"Do not let your hearts be troubled. Trust in God; trust also in me." John 14:1*

Months after a loss you begin to feel so much better. There are days when you find yourself whistling a happy tune and there is a skip in your step. You breathe in the fresh air and can say that all is well.

And, then it happens. Grief returns out of nowhere. Your heart drops to the floor as you remember the one you love, with tears flowing like a river. It's as though the entire veil has been lifted and you are feeling raw, stinging pain again. Your heart hurts worse than it did before.

Don't be afraid of these moments when you temporarily slip back into the valley of grief. This is quite normal. These moments will come when you least expect it, but they won't last long. Take some deep, cleansing breaths. Focus on how far you've come since your loss. Sit down and rest for a while. That's okay. You've been through a lot, and a temporary setback every now and then is to be expected.

In a few days you will see that you are gaining strength back and you can clear your thoughts once again. You're not immobilized as you once were. Hope is holding you together and will continue to do so. Your hope is much larger than your grief!

**Slow down and listen to the music that is found deep within your soul.**

## Day 185

*"All who humble themselves before the Lord shall be given every blessing and shall have wonderful peace."*
*Psalm 37:11*

As a kid you loved going to the amusement park and trying out all of the rides. Without doubt, one of your favorites was the roller coaster. It gave you a ride that was wild! You climbed up the steep hills, rounded the turns at breakneck speed and then came soaring down the track. Oh, what fun!

When we lose a loved one, we are put on a roller coaster. This one, our emotional roller coaster, however, isn't by choice. Our emotions seem to take off every day and we never know quite where this ride is going to take us. Anger. Tears. Guilt. Shame. Blame. Brokenness. The ride is wild but definitely not the kind of roller coaster ride we enjoyed as a kid.

We wonder when this terrible emotional ride is going to end. The truth is it's different for each person experiencing loss. As hard as this is, we must remember that this is our ride, and we need to ride it until the end. As the months move on, we'll notice the ride slows down and becomes much more predictable. We can live life in a more balanced, joyful way now. Our grief is beginning to be tamed more and more each day until, finally, our hope becomes a beautiful light that shines from us, lighting the way of each new and precious day!

**It is with God we travel, and while He is at the end of our journey, He is also at every stopping place along the way.**

## Day 186

*"In quietness and trust shall be your strength." Isaiah 30:15*

Remember when you played with buttercups as a kid? You'd pick one and place it under someone's chin and if there was a yellow shadow, that meant sunbeams were shining. The petals on a buttercup are soft and tender, yet they have such a glow that they are a powerful reminder of the hope found in all of life.

When we are experiencing the pain of loss, we need reminders such as the buttercup. We need to see something visible that shows us that hope is alive, even when we are feeling so down and out. Nature has a way of ushering in gifts of hope in ways that we could never begin to think of ourselves.

Are you feeling really blue today? Do you feel lost in a sea of tears and confusion? Take a walk someplace where there are trees and flowers and signs of nature. Pick up a leaf or a branch off of a tree and study it. Look at the intricate design and know that there is nothing in nature that was made by mistake.

God took great care with His marvelous creation, and that includes you, too. God knows everything about you. He knows every tear you've cried, and every heartache that you've felt. You're not alone. He is near, and just as the buttercup is able to shed sunbeams of hope and joy, there will be a day coming when you can, too.

**God has promised strength for each day, rest from our labor, and light for our path. Rest knowing that His promises are sure!**

## Day 187

*"And we know that in all things God works for the good of those who love him, who have been called according to His purpose." Romans 8:28*

There are times when everything looks so dark. The dark is so bleak that it feels as though there is no hope left. During these moments we get anxious and we feel like we should be doing something to get rid of this horrible feeling. But there is no energy left. And, all we can do is wait.

Waiting isn't something that comes very easily to most people. We fidget and fuss and we want to take control and fix what is wrong. When loss has become part of our life, there's no real way to fix this kind of brokenness. We are forced to sit and wait.

During our times of waiting something happens to us. When our hearts empty of all hope, we learn to lean on God. It's like the newborn child who cannot do for himself. He must wait to be fed. He must wait to have his diaper changed. He must wait to be held and rocked. That's just how we are when we are emptied of all hope. We've come to that place of total emptiness and we must wait.

In our waiting, God speaks to us in so many different ways. We feel the gentle whisper of the wind brushing against our cheek and we know that is our mighty God nearby. We watch for the morning sunrise, and it comes exactly on time, and we know that God has planned it that way. We wait for the evening sunset and just at the designated time with complete accuracy the sun sinks down into the horizon.

As we wait, our empty heart is slowly filling with new hope. We breathe in the certainty of God and breathe out the relief that hope has been restored.

**When all seems to be lost, remember who you have as a Father.**

## Day 188

*"In you, O Lord, have I taken refuge." Psalm 31:1*

Can you remember watching storms when you were a kid? The clouds would roll in, the rain would come pelting down, the winds would blow, and you sat in awe of the power of the storm. It seemed like the landscape would be changed forever.

But, the storm passed really quickly and moved on to another place. When you walked the same path the next day, you noticed that you could hardly tell a storm had passed through. But, if you could talk to the grass, it would say that part of the storm remained with it. The same is true of the flowers. During the storm they were knocked down, but the next day when the storm passed and the sun was shining, there they were standing tall and beautiful.

If nature could talk, do you know what it would say? Part of the storm is what has produced the beauty you see in me. The same is true for us. When we've weathered a storm and regain our strength, we can look at ourselves and know that we've endured the hard parts of life and we have increased the beauty within. We have a greater love and appreciation for all of life. We are much more forgiving. We have patience that we didn't have before. And, our heart is full of a newfound gift of hope.

**Just when we think we're too exhausted to stand up God sends more of His grace and hope.**

## Day 189

*"Hope deferred makes the heart sick, but a longing fulfilled is a tree of life." Psalm 25:25*

One of the hardest things you will have to deal with after losing a loved one is anticipating all of those times when the one you love isn't with you. Birthdays. Holidays. Vacations. Church. Meals. Ball games. Family gatherings. Parties.

It's human nature to think about these things and to begin to fill up with worry wondering how you are going to handle each of these situations. What will Christmas be like? What will every birthday be like? How will it feel to go on a vacation without the one you're missing?

This is very hard to hear, but sometimes the hard times are needed. You cannot know what the future is going to be like, so all of the worrying is robbing you of the precious and beautiful joy of today. There is no possible way you can look into the future and see what troubles are going to come your way. This is true for everyone. So, why not practice living in the hour?

Just for today, enjoy the blessings that surround you. Is the sun shining? Get outside and enjoy it. Is the rain falling? Put on a raincoat and boots and splash in mud puddles. Is it summertime? Pack a picnic lunch and invite some friends to join you. Make some memories today that will hold you up during the stormy seasons of life. You can't change what has happened, but you can change the way you live today. Why not choose to enjoy today's blessings and set aside the joy robber of worry?

**There is a calm, hopefulness to a life lived in gratitude and joy.**

## Day 190

*"Wait for the Lord; Be strong, and let your heart take courage; Yes, wait for the Lord."* *Psalm 27:14*

When loss takes place in our lives, we feel like the weight of the world is on our shoulders as well as on our hearts. It feels like if we move one step the wrong way, our world is going to completely come tumbling down. Life hurts so much when we lose someone we love!

Trust in the fact that there will be pockets of time when you can find some relief and peace from all of the pain and heaviness of heart. Be sure to look to the heavens each day, and remember Who created the great expanse. Listen to the song of the birds, and remember that there will be a day when a song will return to your heart. Look at the evening stars twinkling in the sky, and remember that there is light to lead you down the path of the unknown.

Hope. Continue to hope and believe. You are far stronger than you think. When you remind yourself that your Shepherd is always near, that will give peace and strength when you grow weary along the way.

Comfort and new strength come to us in the most surprising of ways. A friend from the past calls out of the blue and gives your heart a lift. An envelope arrives in the mail with no return address. Inside is a crisp fifty dollar bill letting you know someone cares about you. When you are crying a butterfly lands on your arm and won't go away. Coincidence? Not hardly! That's your hope and it has arrived to carry you through!

**Never give up–ever! Reach out your hand and there will be help to pull you across the chasm of despair. That help is called hope, and hope will never abandon you.**

## Day 191

*"I will keep the Lord before me always. Because He is close to my side, I will not be hurt." Psalm 16:8*

Healing from grief comes to us so slowly that many times we don't see it happening. We begin noticing small things like fields of flowers blooming or the cows grazing in a pasture. We drive by a stream and pay attention to the quiet beauty of the water trickling over the rocks. Sometimes we even make it an entire day without putting ourselves to bed in tears.

These changes taking place in our grief journey are such welcome changes. We've struggled daily to find something to smile about since our loss and step by step, day by day we are beginning to see the sun shining upon us once again.

We can see the miracle of a butterfly emerging from its cocoon. We pause and make the time to appreciate each and every evening sunset. We have found the childlike joy of splashing through mud puddles. Watching a bird fly through the sky is thrilling. We say a prayer of special thanks for every meal that sits before us. We can see with new eyes—thankful eyes—and that is part of our new joy!

Yes, without really knowing it, we have settled into our new place. There will be setbacks and reminders of our loss, but the pain will no longer take precedence over all that we think and do.

Instead, we will have gentle and fond remembrances, and we will shift most of our thoughts to loving gratitude for today. And, most importantly, we will know that the dark side of our grief is no longer the landscape of our daily life. Instead, we can live in the quiet, serene beauty of hope and peace grasping hold of the small miracles given to us each and every day.

**I will walk through this pain of grief one day at a time until I reach my new home of peace and hope.**

## Day 192

*"Anxious hearts are very heavy, but a word of encouragement does wonders!" Proverbs 12:25*

Grief is common among all people, yet it is something that makes us feel so terribly alone in our pain. Even when members of a family share the same loss, the type of grieving we do can be so uniquely different. We each experience the pain of our loss in different ways that make grief so hard to understand.

Is there a common thread in grief that we can each see and feel? Yes! That one thing we long for, that one thing we each understand is that we need hope when feeling such despair. We need to find a way to move forward in life and not stay stuck in the lonely prison of grief. We struggle to desperately find a new place of joy and belonging.

How do we find our peace and joy? What can we do to find our hope when it feels as though all of life is hopeless? Most often we cry out to God for help. When our faith stretches to the point of understanding that if He calmed the stormy seas He can also calm my storm-battered heart, then we can find hope and strength in Him.

Walk among nature and experience and you will feel the very presence of hope surrounding you. Read His word and allow Him to comfort your hurting heart. Look to the heavens and be filled with awe as you know He is always with you. Cling to the promise of the rainbow—our visible promise of hope! Grief is real and it hurts so badly that we think we can't take it another minute. But, we have something greater than our grief and that is hope.

Hope is bigger than any grief we have to bear. That doesn't seem possible right now, but when we tap into our reserve of hope, strength will pour through our veins and give us the energy and the desire to continue on!

**Without hurry or fear I will dwell in the house of my grief and wait for the promise of my hope to return!**

## Day 193

*"For the Lord God is a sun and shield; the Lord gives grace and glory. Psalm 84:11*

When loss occurs, there is one thing that is needed to sustain us during our time of pain. Hope. Hope calms the storms at night. Hope turns fear into courage. Hope turns the darkness into light.

Hope is the one thing that provides comfort when peace seems so far away. Hope gives a reason to keep on going when all logic says to give up.

Because we are made in the image of God, we have seeds of hope planted within our soul. When we anchor to our heavenly Father, we will find shelter from the storm, and we will feel the security needed to pull us safely ashore.

When we place our hope in God, the tears of grief will be dried and the sun will gradually return to paint a beautiful rainbow across the innermost part of our heart.

God has not promised a life without tears, but He has promised to carry us through every pain that we have to endure. That promise is one we can stand on and claim as our very own!

**Pray, then let God take care of all of the details.**

## Day 194

*"And now, Lord, for what do I wait? My hope is in Thee."*
*Psalm 39:7*

Grief is as unpredictable as the weather in March. One day the sun can be shining brightly in our lives and the next day we are seeking shelter from the blowing winds and cold chill of the snow beating against our face. When we experience a loss, we are placed aboard an emotional roller coaster that takes us through dips and valleys, peaks and fast turns, then speeds down the slope and spits us out onto the ground leaving us breathless.

There's one thing we can count on, though. The speed of the roller coaster finally tames, just as the unpredictability of the weather in March. Spring finally arrives giving us an opportunity to catch our breath and to see our grief from another perspective.

While it's true that our grief will never end completely, it's just as true that our grief will become less raw. There will be a time when we will be able to withstand the storm clouds and look beyond them to a place where the sun shines and flowers grow.

**Trusting God through my hour of despair is the only way to show God I know He is still in control.**

## Day 195

*"Let me hear Thy loving kindness in the morning; for I trust in Thee." Psalm 143:8*

Are you struggling with pain and sorrow today? Does life have you feeling like there is no light at the end of the tunnel? Is your heart feeling broken and hopeless? Then, think on this:

Just for today—
I can face my fears with courage.
I can set aside my worries.
I can think healthy thoughts.
I can read something hopeful.
I can say thank you for one blessing.
I can look to the heavens with awe.
Just for today—
I can remind myself that I am never alone.
I can forgive others and myself.
I can imagine a time when I will feel happy.
I can step out of the darkness and appreciate the sun.
I can count the stars and know that I am counted among them.
Just for today—I can choose to live with hope.

**It only takes a spark of hope to ignite a fire within the heart.**

## Day 196

*"I wait for the Lord to help me, and I trust His word."*
*Psalm 130:5*

There are times when life hurts and prayer doesn't seem to give comfort. In fact, prayer can make us feel worse when we are seeking answers and we get only silence. It's a hard fact to understand and accept that bad things really do happen to good people and there is no solid answer as to why.

Many times, life's painful circumstances do not make any sense at all. There are so many circumstances in life that are unfair. When we think of the big picture of starvation, wars, hospital beds overflowing, natural disasters that take thousands of lives at a time, it's overwhelming. We can find ourselves very discouraged sitting in the ashes of our pain.

How can a person go on when life hurts so badly and leaves us in a pile of ruin with no logical answers to life's problems and pain? Even though we do not receive the comfort and answers we are looking for today, there is relief found in that inner strength we call hope. It's hard to explain this inner strength, but we know it's there. We can feel it nudging us to go on when all logic tells us to curl up in a ball and quit.

Not all answers will be known today to life's painful questions. In fact, a lot of times we're left without answers. That's when the magic of hope kicks in coupled with the reassurance of trust. All we have to do is look at the ebb and flow of the tide to know that we have a mighty God much larger than any pain we are called on to endure. Trust completely and the flame of hope will be rekindled.

**God speaks in the silence of the heart. Listening is the beginning of prayer.**

## Day 197

*"In all these things we are more than conquerors through Him who loved us." Romans 8:37*

Grief carries its own set of burdens, and among all of them, we don't need to deal with the burden of worrying about when it is okay to shed tears. It's okay to cry—anywhere, at any time, and any amount. Allow the tears to flow, and think of them as healing rain from heaven, for our tears bring cleansing and comfort. We were designed to cry when we are in pain! So many times we put on our fake happy mask in order to protect others, when in fact, we are only hurting ourselves and others by not allowing our tears to fall. Tears are a God-given gift of provision for our release of pain.

Little by little, as we work through some of the most difficult days of pain, our tears will begin to lessen, and the tears that have fallen will now be the life support for the new joy that will begin to sprout from the innermost being of our hearts.

If you are struggling with grief and pain from loss today, remember that your sadness and tears will not last forever. Deep within your being is a seed of hope that is being watered daily by your tears. God holds each one of our tears close to Him and will provide comfort.

**Even in my sorrow, hope holds me in its embrace**

## Day 198

*"The heavens are telling of the glory of God; and their expanse is declaring the work of His hands." Psalm 19:1*

Whenever grief enters our lives, it is often described as feeling like a hole has been placed right in the center of our hearts and nothing in the world can ever fill that void. That's grief at its worst, and for a long time it hurts like nothing we've ever felt before. Loss touches every area of our living, and we feel drained, and devoid of all hope. Well meaning people urge us to move on in life before we've even had time to process what has happened. As hard as this sounds, until we meet our grief head-on we'll never be set free from its terrible grip.

God, in His infinite love and wisdom, knew that we would need to know with absolute assurance that hope is still alive within our grieving hearts, so He gave us daily reminders to serve as hope boosters. All we have to do is look to the heavens, and we can see the mighty works of God. We see the sun, the stars, the moon, the clouds, and the vast expanse of the sky. All of those are reminders of what a mighty God we have as our Father.

God did not design a world of chaos and despair, but rather a world of beauty and miracles. When we look at the intricate makings of a flower, our hearts fill with hope because we know that if God cares that much for a flower, He truly cares for each one of us! We are never alone. Hope lives within our hearts forever!

**Every new day is a gift of hope sent from God.**

## Day 199

*"When I am afraid, I will put my trust in Thee." Psalm 56:3*

Days of grief are faced with dread and fear because that gnawing feeling of emptiness and loss dictates every waking minute. The nights are long and lonely, and sleep comes in fitful spurts. The grief of loss is so overwhelming until our eyes begin to open from this dark, lonely place of sorrow and pain.

Thankfully, hope is much stronger than despair. Hope is far more alive and empowering than discouragement! Step by step, moment by moment, hope begins to fill the immense void left by our loss.

At first we don't notice the changes being made by new hope. The pain feels far too big. Then, one day we begin to pay attention to things like the background noise of birds singing their good morning song. We take joy in walking the dog around the block. We walk into a restaurant and, for the first time in months, the aroma of food smells good. We notice people smiling all around us, and it feels good to be alive.

As hope grows, our pain of loss takes on new meaning until one day we are filled a new purpose in life. Joy has returned and so has our hope!

**Grief lives for a season, but hope lives forever.**

## Day 200

*"Now may the God of hope fill you with all joy and peace."*
*Romans 15:13*

There are times in our lives when we feel utterly hopeless. Problem after problem comes our way, and we wonder when and how this cycle of pain is going to end. One thing after another...bills, sickness, broken relationships, more bills, job loss, and then the unthinkable happens. A loved one is snatched away by death. Our world suddenly doesn't feel like it is worth living in anymore.

Life without hope is not a life at all. And, for a period of time following loss, hope seems to be absent in our lives. Then, something strange begins to happen when we least expect it. We get a phone call from a friend. We see a caring smile. We feel an arm around our shoulder. A tissue is handed to us to dry our tears. Someone places a meal on our table and sits with us while we eat.

Hope arrives in many different ways, and when it does we begin to see life differently once more. There is meaning again because we have been shown love. We know that we can make it, because we are able to draw on the strength of others in our time of weakness. We begin to feel less alone, because we know that there are others who care.

Hang on! Your day of hope will arrive, and when it does, the sun will begin to shine for you, too!

**Hope is everywhere and it will eventually find us if we just wait a little while longer.**

## Day 201

*"I can lie down and go to sleep, and I will wake up again, because the Lord gives me strength." Psalm 3:5*

When grief enters your life everything looks and feels so different. You feel lost, lonely, and frightened beyond words. How are you going to do this? Where are your friends? Where do you belong in this world that is far too big for you now?

Grief shatters from the inside out, and when it does you long for the familiar. There's safety and comfort in routine. Take heart. Everything feels different to you right now, but you haven't lost everything. Step back and take a long, deep breath. Take two or three breaths, if you need. Pause, and look around you.

You see familiar faces. Those are your friends who want to help. Look upward and you will see the big, blue sky still there displaying majesty just for you. Look on the streets by your home. You'll see cars driving to and fro, going about their daily business. There is comfort in seeing the familiar. Take time every day to soak up as much routine life as you can. While living in the brokenness of your grief, the familiar will speak volumes of healing to you.

**God sends us the sunrise so that we might know His personal welcoming of each new day.**

## Day 202

*"Yet those who wait for the Lord will gain new strength; they will mount up with wings like eagles." Isaiah 40:31*

All winter, in many parts of this land, the earth has been barren and cold. Nothing has been growing, and the ground has seemed lifeless. However, during this time, the roots have been gaining nourishment in preparation for the season of spring! Spring is a time when the earth comes alive again and blooms with magnificent beauty!

Allow this thought to break through the chains of distrust that often comes with loss. Remember that the season of sorrow will in time give way to a new season of hope and joy. Remind yourself often as you look out your kitchen window for signs of spring. Just as surely as spring will thaw the frozen ground and sprout forth new life, hope will push forth in your heart causing new life and many new beginnings to bloom. Wait. Be patient. Trust. It's a fact that spring always follows winter. It can't be any other way.

**Just as I trust the changing of the seasons, I will trust that my winter will turn into spring, my sorrow will turn into joy.**

## Day 203

*"Since the Lord is directing our steps, why try to understand everything that happens along the way?"*
*Proverbs 20:24*

If there is one real truth taught by death it is to do what you can do today. Don't keep pushing those things you want to do to the background of your mind because they'll never get done. All of us have experienced the death of someone we love, and we have conversations with ourselves asking why we didn't make that visit that would have given so much encouragement. Why didn't we make those cookies and deliver them? Why didn't we use the phone for five minutes to brighten up someone's day?

It might be too late to do these things for the one already gone, but there are others around us who need our love. Look for people around you and let them know that you're thinking of them. Say I love you. Extend forgiveness. Hold someone's hand and tell them how special they are.

Do you know that one of the greatest remedies for grief is to extend love to another? When we open up our heart that way, we receive precious blessings back that help to give our aching heart comfort. Grief is an amazing teacher when we allow it to be.

**There are no mistakes, no coincidences. All events are blessings given to us to learn from.**

## Day 204

*"When doubts filled my mind, your comfort gave me renewed hope and cheer." Psalm 94:19*

Every person grieving a death wants to know how long this grief lasts. Society wants to set limitations on the way we grieve and also tries to place limits on the amount of time it's customary to grieve. It has been said that it takes seven years to adjust to the loss of someone close to us. Seven years! Why do you feel the need to apologize if you're crying only months after your loss?

We need to learn how to treat ourselves with kindness and patience. The world can often overlook those in grief and put impossible demands on us. You know what is best for your heart. Only you know the best way for you to grieve. And, you are the sole person in charge of your grief. It's hard to stand strong against those trying to direct your path of grief, but you can gather the strength to do it. Do you know how much courage you're already showing when you stand up each day that you're living within your loss?

Remind yourself every day that you are strong, you are courageous, and you are doing this thing called grief the best way that you can—one day, one step, one breath at a time.

**Friendship with yourself is all-important, because without it you cannot be friends with anyone else.**

## Day 205

*"For lo, the winter is past, the rain is over and gone; the flowers appear on earth; the time of singing of birds is come." Solomon 2:1-2*

When you experience a loss, the pain gets rough. There is an aching clear to the soul that you just can't shake. Grief drains your energy, and no matter how hard you try to eat right and drink enough fluids you just can't get enough energy to make it through the day without a nap.

Then, the cycle begins. If you nap, you can't sleep at night. Before you know it, you're stuck in this pattern and you don't have a clue what to do.

Most times, the old remedies are the best ones. They are tried and true and reliable. You're probably not going to like it, but put on those tennis shoes, get outside, and start walking. You might be saying you don't have enough strength to walk to the bathroom, let alone walk around the block, but you can give it a try. Guaranteed you will surprise yourself.

Walking has so many health benefits that you can't overlook it. When you walk your body releases chemicals that help elevate your mood. It's worth a try. A side benefit of walking is getting to experience some of the joys and wonders of nature. The birds will sing to you as you walk. The gentle breeze will cool you down when you feel too warm. And, the big, blue sky is a beautiful work of art. The best part is it's all free!

A little bit of walking every day—even ten minutes—will help you to gain some much-needed relief from the heaviness of grief, and it will begin cultivating the seeds of new hope!

**With the Lord as my companion and guide I never have to walk alone.**

## Day 206

*"An anxious heart weighs a man down, but a kind word cheers him up." Proverbs 12:25*

Do you worry? Of course you do! Very few people have mastered the practice of releasing all worry. When loss becomes part of your life, worry seems to increase. You worry about countless things that never entered your mind before. Your biggest worry is likely the anticipation of what could go wrong in your life next.

Slow down and take some long, deep breaths. Exhale slowly. Do this a few times so you can clear your head. Now look all around you. If you can, find a nearby window and look outside. Do you see the sky? Do you see tall, stately trees that have been withstanding storms for years? Do you see the sun shining across the horizon?

All of these powerful gifts to us have one thing in common. They never worry. They know that they will be taken care of by the laws set forth in nature when they were created.

Do you know that you've been promised you would be taken care of, too? Just as your heavenly Father watches over the trees and fields and flowers, He is watching over you. You haven't been forgotten in your pain.

Try this each day. Write down one worry on a piece of paper and give that worry to God. Continue doing this every day until you can finally say that you have cast off the heavy burden of worry. Do you know what else will happen? The heaviness of grief will begin to lift because new hope and trust are making their home within your heart.

**Hope is placing all trust in God's promises—no matter what!**

## Day 207

*"You have made known to me the path of life; you will fill me with joy in your presence, with eternal pleasures at your right hand." Psalm 16:11*

When loss takes place, grief enters our lives and takes residence. Grief is a tricky kind of beast. If we allow it to have full reign, grief will swallow us up and grip us tightly, not wanting to let go. We feel trapped, and that is a terrible feeling.

So, what are we supposed to do while in this state of sorrow? We know grief will most assuredly be part of our life, but we certainly don't want it to overtake us forever.

Ever so slowly, we begin taking tiny steps. We simply get through one day. Make a list if that helps. Today you will walk to the mailbox get the mail. Tomorrow you will wash one load of laundry. The next day you will spend fifteen minutes reading something positive.

What we are doing is slowly, steadily teaching ourselves how to live again. We can't experience a loss and then jump back into life right away. It takes time. Slow and steady. That's how you can do it. One day, one hour, one breath, one step at a time.

After a few weeks you will notice something happening. Without thinking, you are doing some of the routine things that once were part of your life. You're taking steps without thinking and your steps are a bit lighter. Hope has jumped on board and is now your daily companion.

You're doing it. You're learning how to walk back into life again.

**Look for the beautiful and you will read the handwriting of God in places you never thought possible.**

## Day 208

*"If I go up to the heavens, you are there; if I make my bed in the depths, you are there. If I rise on the wings of dawn, if I settle on the far side of the sea, even there your hand will guide me, your right hand will hold me fast." Psalm 139: 8-10*

Sometimes we feel like hiding from the world. We don't feel like facing people and the things they say. They mean to help, but sometimes it comes out all wrong, and we're not ready to face another day of that. We could just hide behind a door or under a pile of blankets like when we were kids.

There's one thing wrong with hiding, though. We can't get away with it for long. As long as we're alive we will have people in our lives. We have jobs and other responsibilities. We have to go to the supermarket, the doctor, and the dentist. We know that we can't hide forever, but we don't know what to do. If we could just go into hiding for a while maybe we would emerge a new person.

Grief plays tricks on us like that. Rather than hide from people, the truth is we need our friends now more than ever before. Our friends might not always say just the right thing, but having them walk beside us is a comfort. We can't do this alone. We weren't meant to do this alone.

Reach out, grab a friend's hand, and start walking this journey of loss together. It's a lot easier than trying to do this all alone.

**God never intended for us to carry our burdens alone.**

## Day 209

*"My flesh and my heart may fail, but God is the strength of my heart and my portion forever." Psalm 73:26*

How much we want to talk about the one who has died! We have a need to say their name over and over again. In our grief, saying the name of our loved one is necessary. It helps so much to give validation to the life that was so precious to us.

Others might get uncomfortable at first hearing us mention the name, but they will soon learn that this is a big part of our grief walk. Talking freely of the one who died gives us the opportunity to have a connection of sorts. They don't feel so distant when we mention their name.

Oh, how much we miss the one who died! Our hearts hurt so much from the inside out. We miss seeing their face. We miss hearing their voice. We miss the way they smiled. We miss everything. Just saying their name is comforting.

We have a new relationship with the one who has died, and we know that. We understand that life will not ever be the same. That's one more reason why we have such a need to say their name and to hear their name being spoken by others.

They were important to us! They lived! We walked and talked together. We ate meals together. We want to somehow preserve a bit of that relationship, and one way we can do it is simply saying their name. There is profound hope in healing in saying a name!

**Stop and listen. The voice of God can be heard all around.**

## Day 210

*"I will send down showers in season; there will be showers of blessing." Ezekiel 34:26*

Yes, we understand that our loved one has died. We understand what that means. We also know that a part of us died, too.

Death brings about so many unwanted changes. Our present day is so different from what we expected it to be. When we lose someone close to us, the daily interaction is gone. We miss that. We miss seeing the one we love. We miss the laughter that we enjoyed together. We miss those serious moments when we talked about the deeper issues of life. We miss the daily routine. We miss everything.

We also understand that so much of our future was wiped out in the blink of an eye. All of the hopes and dreams we had of spending time together. We are missing out on the vacations, weddings, grandchildren, and so many other beautiful occasions.

Our future seems dismal. There are times when we simply don't know how to navigate on this earth any more. We are lost and so lonely. One of the hardest phrases we'll ever hear is to "let go." "Let go, and let God." We cry out in our pain that we don't want to let go, yet we know we must.

We must let go of the painful part of death in order to allow room for new hope and joy. We now have a new and different relationship with our loved one who has gone on. But, we can only enjoy the treasure of precious memories when we let go of the pain.

**When you suppress grief too much it will swell up and double. We must learn to let go.**

## Day 211

*"Happy is he whose hope is in the Lord his God." Psalm 146:5*

Do you have a special place of healing? Most of us do. We might not call it that, but it's the place we go to when we are wounded and need to feel comfort. It's that place visit when we want to reconnect with nature and with God. It's that place we escape to in our minds that gives us peace.

My special place has always been the ocean. I grew up along the Atlantic coast and I can remember walking along the sandy shore in every season. I went there when my sister died. I went there when my parents divorced. I went there when my life was a mess during my first year of college.

The ocean is still my place to visit when I need rest. There's something so healing for me when I watch the ebb and flow of the waves. I love the sound, the smell, and the beauty of the big, wide, wonderful sea. That's the place I visit when I need to find balance and hope in life again.

What's your place? Where do you go when you're feeling broken and so empty? Find that place and claim it as yours. Maybe it's only a tiny space in a closet in your bedroom, but if it works, then deem that as your sacred healing place.

**A garden of joy blooms from seeds of hope.**

## Day 212

*"Because He has inclined His ear to me, therefore I shall call upon Him as long as I live." Psalm 116:2*

Where do you go when you need comfort? Who do you turn to in your sorrow? Far too many times we try to handle it on our own, and sorrow has a way of swallowing us up until we feel like we have fallen into a pit of dark, lonely grief. Loneliness is not the place to be when we're in need of encouragement!

Sometimes we need the quiet comfort of nature. We need to see the sunrise and the sunset, and we need to hear the sounds of birds singing, crickets chirping, and frogs croaking their night time songs of peace and joy. There is great solace found in the consistency and beauty of nature.

Sometimes we need other people. We need hugs, and lots of them. We need comforting, uplifting words. We need to see the smile on the face of a friend. We need to feel compassion! There's nothing quite like listening ears, shared tears, and genuine words of encouragement!

Other times we need to hear the voice of God, and only God. We need to clear our minds of all clutter and concentrate on Him and be reminded that He is still in control of our world that seems so out of control. We need to feel the presence of our Lord. We need to be infused with his strength when we are too weak to make it on our own.

Where are you in your sorrow today? Don't sit in the deep pit of loneliness. Reach out. Make a choice to get some help. Walk among nature. Call a friend. Better yet, make plans to meet a friend and share a meal together. Talk. Cry. And, yes, allow yourself to smile and laugh—even in your sorrow.

**Kind words give rest to a weary heart.**

## Day 213

*"He will keep in perfect peace all those who trust in Him, whose thoughts turn often to the Lord."* Isaiah 26:3

If you're like me, you don't like change. We get to a place in life where we feel comfortable, and we are fine with staying there. Then, out of the blue, something happens in our life that knocks us flat and leaves us wondering if we'll ever get back up again. Loss brings about so many changes in our lives that we lose the face of familiarity. Everything looks so strangely different.

Are you struggling with the loss of a loved one today? That's a change that came into your life that you never wanted, never expected, and would never welcome. Yet you find yourself in the middle of this chaotic place of change.

When dealing with all of the changes that come about due to a loss, surround yourself with others who can support you. Look to those who have gone through similar circumstances for some much-needed guidance and encouragement. Who better to help you than those who have traveled a similar road? Never be afraid to ask for help! You'll be surprised how many people will come to your side and give you help and encouragement.

Slowly but surely, the changes that take place in your heart will lead you to a calmer, more restful place of grief. Day by day, the sun will begin to shine once again, and you will find yourself able to face the day with renewed hope and strength.

**Hope places new life into every soul who expectantly waits for it!**

## Day 214

*"From the fullness of grace we have all received one blessing after another." John 1:16*

When the clouds are hanging heavily above us like huge billows of tears ready to fall, we often become so afraid that life is never going to feel good again.

During the winter of our lives, we live in anticipation of those moments when we will be welcomed into a safe, warm haven and feel secure. We long for our tired bodies to get some rest from the heavy burdens of grief we've been carrying, and we yearn for the feelings of loneliness to go away. We want to taste the sweetness of life again, but we fear that the day of joy will never return.

The predictability of the changing seasons becomes part of our hope that we will taste laughter and abundance in our lives. Our season of comfort and peace will arrive, and we will be able to feel the warmth of sunshine comforting our soul. Friends will engage in lively conversation with us, and we will know that we are not alone. There will be a day when the clouds part and the bright, blue sky appears with the sun's light giving new hope to our soul.

It's hard to let go of fear and put some trust in life again. Keep reminding yourself that if the seasons can change with complete predictability, so can we. Your grief will not last forever.

**I don't know how long I have on this earth so I'm choosing to live with sunshine in my soul.**

## Day 215

*"Our help is in the name of the Lord, who made heaven and earth." Psalm 124:8*

Sometimes things happen that are hard to understand. In fact, sometimes the painful happenings are impossible to understand and we're left with only questions.

We often hear that God will see us through, and that each star represents a special miracle waiting for someone to take, but that has little meaning to us when we are walking the lonely path of grief and loss. The last thing we want to hear is that everything is going to be okay!

But, the truth is that God is all around us, and He is trying to show us that He really does have a world full of miracles waiting to be recognized. It's difficult to see through tear-stained eyes, but when we do, we can see that His love and care are all around us. Just when we least expect some sun to come shining through the darkness, it appears! God's timing is always right!

Hidden within the heart of every person is enough faith and hope to pull us through. When we begin to look for the miracles found in each new day, we begin to see them and we can feel the mighty hand of God drawing us close, giving us the comfort and shelter we need.

Did someone give you a smile today? Did you hear the rushing wind telling of God's mighty power? Did you see the white, fluffy clouds floating through the bright, blue sky? Did someone say, "I love you" today? Did you feel a moment of calm and peace?

Miracles are all about us, and you have the faith to see them! When you look for miracles you will find them, and then your faith will grow strong enough to carry you through!

**Nothing can stop a miracle from happening to you!**

## Day 216

*"An anxious heart weighs a man down, but a kind word cheers him up." Proverbs 12:25*

There are times in our lives when we are overcome by the cares and pain of this world and we need some special attention. Our souls need to be nurtured. We long to be drawn out of a place of darkness into a place of light. We need hope!

There are many different ways to get a glimpse of hope and to feel it momentarily, but the most significant way of all is to draw close to God. When we draw near to Him, He has promised to draw even closer to us and to continue to take care of us and fill us with His love.

Lay your heavy weight of grief down for a moment and walk beside God through nature. Look at the clouds and the mighty sea and feel His power and peace. View the birds soaring through the air and feel the freedom found by giving your cares to Him. Look at the flowers blooming, and feel His very presence! Guaranteed if you spend just five minutes a day nurturing your soul by taking nature walks, breathing in the fresh air, and filling your mind with hopeful thoughts you'll see a big shift in your life. Grief was never meant to be your constant companion.

**Hope puts a song in your heart even when you forget how to sing.**

## Day 217

*"I will lie down and sleep in peace, for you alone, O Lord, make me dwell in safety." Psalm 4:8*

There really isn't much of anything that gives us comfort when we're entering into the house of new grief. When we lose a loved one we feel as though part of our heart is now missing.

We struggle to understand what this thing called death is, but we can't really know because we've never been there. Day and night our minds wonder what it's like. Is our loved one resting okay? Is the one we love able to enjoy peace and laughter?

It helps to think of death as being a place of eternal rest. Take a long, deep sigh and let out the air slowly. That feels so good. We're able to relax and our bodies and minds seem to have an overall feeling of peace.

What if? What if death was similar to that? What if the one we love is experiencing total bliss? What if we can experience this with the one we love when we die? That's not such a bad thought. In fact, that's a thought to hold onto when we feel overcome with grief. Hold that thought in your mind—forever in the presence of those you love. That thought will bring much comfort in the days ahead.

**Peace is found in the acceptance of things we cannot change.**

## Day 218

*"Sustain me, according to your promise, O God and I will live; do not let my hopes be dashed." Psalm 119:116*

Keep busy. That's what people tell us to do after a loss. Keep busy and your mind will stay off of things. There's one problem with that kind of advice. It doesn't work.

No matter how hard we try, we can't hide from the fact that someone we love died. Keeping busy only works momentarily. At the end of the day, we still have the empty house to enter. We still have the bed that no longer holds the one we love. The place setting at the table remains empty.

Sure, it's great to stay busy. But, if we think that staying busy will erase our grief then we're making a big mistake. Grief finds us eventually, and when it does it demands to be heard.

When we wear our grief, we actually stop fighting it. It's so exhausting to keep pushing grief away because it's faster and stronger than we are. When we let grief have its way, we will learn how to live within our grief. Eventually we will work our way through the really hard stuff and find a place where we can be comfortable in life again.

**I can feel the heartbeat of hope pulsing through my veins when I stop fighting my pain.**

## Day 219

*"This is the day the Lord has made; let us rejoice and be glad in it." Psalm 118:24*

It's so hard to try to trick ourselves into being happy when everything inside of us is screaming in pain. Losing a loved one is like a hundred toothaches plus a hundred headaches, plus more. The pain can't be described.

Right now it's nearly impossible to imagine being happy again. It hurts too much to think even one day into the future. But, if we occasionally allow our minds to drift away from the pain, we can catch a momentary glimpse of life down the road when grief isn't so all-consuming and so raw.

For today, we need someone to sit beside us and acknowledge our pain. We don't need lofty words. We simply need someone to see us in our grief and to lay a hand on our shoulder to let us know that they are trying to understand.

In time, the grieving will move from the center of our heart to a less prominent place. But, for now we don't owe anyone any apology for our pain. Grief is real, and it hurts.

**Only by living in my grief will I be able to walk away from it.**

## Day 220

*"Look to the Lord and His strength; see His face always." I Chronicles 16:11*

If you're like me, it's difficult to say thank you during times when you're in pain. In fact, it's almost impossible to do, especially when going through the dark, lonely days of loss.

Remind yourself often that grief is a very personal matter, and it affects all of our relationships with family, friends, and our world. Inwardly we know that there will be a day and a time when we can freely and easily say thank you, but maybe that day is not right now. The important thing is to know that there will be a day when you will feel joy and thankfulness again.

A good alternative to thankfulness is trusting. Trusting that one day you will feel thankful. Trusting that you will smile again. Trusting that you will laugh with others again. Trusting that you will love again.

There is a seed of inner strength we call hope that is planted deep in the center of your heart, and in due time that seed will sprout. And, you will know because what is now dark will come alive. What is now sorrow will be joy. What is now pain will be peace. Trust and hope and thankfulness will follow.

**I will trust that there is light at the end of the tunnel even when I cannot see.**

## Day 221

*"Blessed is the one who trusts in the Lord." Psalm 40:4*

How will I get through the next day when I don't even have the strength for today? Who really understands? Is there anyone who cares enough to stop and help? Does anyone want to sit down beside me and help me through this mess in my life? I feel so alone and so broken.

Every person who has experienced loss has felt those same feelings of helplessness and abandonment. Life feels shattered and it seems to us that it will never be put back together again. Our burdens seem far too big for us, and so many times we give up searching for hope.

Hold on! Take a moment to stop and breathe slowly. Close your eyes and reflect on the moment. Listen to your own heart beating, and know that as long as you have life inside of you, you have hope.

**Without hope our hearts would break.**

## Day 222

*Peace I leave with you; my peace I give you. I do not give to you as the world gives. Do not let your hearts be troubled and do not be afraid. John 14:27*

It's so helpful for families to grieve the loss of a loved one together. Each person has had a different relationship with the one who has died, and that is helpful in the process of experiencing grief. Some will have funny stories to share. Others will have work stories to share. Still others will share about their intellectual relationship. Every person can bring a different face of grief to the table.

The difficult part of this sharing is to be non-judgmental and to overlook a lot. Allowing for differences in grieving is a must. You might not like hearing a loud, unreserved telling of a story because that's not your style, but it's important to realize that everyone has their own way of telling a story and of working through grief.

There is no right or wrong way to grieve, and there is nothing that will speed up the process. Patience, unconditional love, and a huge serving of forgiveness all help when learning how to grieve a loss as a family.

**Life is God's novel and we must allow Him to complete the work in His time and in His own way.**

## Day 223

*The Lord is close to the brokenhearted and saves those who are crushed in spirit. Psalm 34:18*

Has life been a series of ups and downs lately? Have you been tossed to and fro in the sea of grief and feel like there is no way out of the churning waters? If so, then you are in need of some rest and replenishment. You are in need of some encouragement and a reminder of the sincere promise that there is joy beyond grief. You are in need of hope.

Hope is not pretending that there's never any sorrow. Hope is knowing that our sorrows will not be this deep tomorrow. Hope is knowing that we have an inner strength to call on to help hold us together until our sorrow finds its proper place in our hearts, where there is also room for love, joy, and peace to abide. Hope knows that there will be a day when we will feel alive once again.

It's not easy to trust in something you can't see, but the alternative of not trusting causes more grief. You trust in the wind, and you can't see it. Can you also trust that hope is alive even though you can't see it?

Step by step, one breath at a time, we are moving away from our grief. Guess what's waiting for you? Hope. Lots and lots of hope!

**I believe in the sun even if it isn't shining. I believe in love even when I am alone. I believe in God even when He seems to be silent.**

## Day 224

*"I sought the Lord and He answered me and delivered me from all of my fears." Psalm 34:4*

Dealing with grief is scary. We sometimes think and act out of control. One minute we're crying, the next minute we're angry. Our emotions make no sense at all. Our thoughts don't even seem like they belong to us.

We utter sounds that we've never heard before. We cry from deep within the wells of the soul. Grief is a journey that we never wanted, and one that we fight every step of the way. We've entered unknown territory without a map or a guide, and we feel so lost and alone.

We want to know when this terrible agony is going to end, and nobody seems to have an answer that makes sense. Somehow, we seem to emerge from this dark pit of despair a little bit at a time. Every day that we wake up, we know we must put one foot in front of the other and when we do we've made some progress. This journey of grief and loss is slow, but that's the only way we can travel this haphazard road of unknown twists and turns.

Remember the old saying that it's always darkest before dawn. Hope seems to know when to arrive, and it's always on time!

**God cares about every detail of my life every minute of every day without fail.**

## Day 225

*"How precious to me are your thoughts, God! How vast the sum of them. Were I to count them, they would outnumber the grains of sand. When I awake, I am still with you." Psalm 139:17-18*

In our lonely hours of grief we sit and wonder if anyone is thinking of us. Sometimes it's hard to believe that anyone is around. The phone remains silent for days. Oh, at first the phone rang constantly, but now that the newness of the loss has worn off for others, they've gone on about their business of daily life.

Friends have stopped delivering meals, and most days we don't have the energy to cook. Fast food becomes the substitute for healthy eating. Comfort eating has put extra pounds on us, so not only are the pangs of loneliness part of us now, but also there is the grief of looking into the mirror and seeing how much our physical self has changed.

It would be so good to be remembered by others in our pain! There are many who truly do remember. We're sure of it. It would be better to say, "it would be so good for others to *show* that they remember." People become afraid to mention our loss after a few months because they think that we've settled into our new life and we're okay.

How good to know that God is always there. He never falls asleep on the job, and we can call to Him in prayer any time we're feeling lonely and forgotten. God is our twenty-four hour a day keeper, and that is such a help on those long, lonely nights when it feels as though nobody remembers.

Prayer works. Prayer helps. Prayer gives a direct line between us and God. All we have to do is call!

**God can hear even the most quiet whispering of a prayer because He cares so much.**

## Day 226

*"The Lord's promises are pure, like silver refined in a furnace, purified seven times over." Psalm 12:6*

Everything seems to fall apart at the seams when we go through a loss. Words become meaningless when people try to tell us that it's not so bad, and we'll be feeling better soon. What does better mean? When is soon? Can anyone tell us that?

We seem to dig deeper into our hole of despair. We want to withdraw from everything and everyone for a while. We feel utterly and completely hopeless and nobody around us seems to understand.

This is when we need a friend so much. Just a listening ear helps more than anyone can imagine. We don't need lectures or promises about how great things are going to be. We just need ears to listen.

God designed friends to listen. We feel abandoned, but have we really tried calling a friend and asking that friend to sit by our side? Nine times out of ten, the person we call will be more than glad to come stay by our side. If that doesn't work, our best friend of all is always available. We can talk to God any time we want, and He will always listen and always provide the comfort that we need.

**Prayer frees us from our fears and gives us strength and courage to face our hurts and pains.**

## Day 227

*"For the Lord God is a sun and shield; the Lord gives grace and glory." Psalm 84:11*

Oh, the fears that we have following a loss! Death causes a separation and makes us fear that we will lose all connection to the one we love. We need constant reminders that this separation won't happen unless we allow it to happen.

Our relationship with our loved one has changed, but it hasn't ended. The one we love will always be part of our life, and part of our hope. We can no longer see, touch, or hear our loved one, but we can experience the joy that was shared by constantly tapping into our memory bank.

What if we tried this for a while? Every day recall one memory that we have with our loved one. Make it a happy one. Visualize the occasion when you watched the movie, ate a delicious meal together, or walked to the park to feed the birds. Close your eyes and remember the colors you saw. Feel the feelings you felt. Soon you will feel your tense shoulders begin to relax. You will notice a smile forming on your lips. Your mind will begin to feel less stress. You will know that your relationship hasn't ended, it has only changed.

Grief can't rob us of the happy memories that made our relationship so special. Only we have control over what we remember. Make those memories ones that will hug your heart and bring relief to your grieving.

**Never miss an opportunity to recall those memories that are beautiful.**

## Day 228

*"Blessed is the man who makes the Lord his trust." Psalm 40:4*

Why is it that some people are more prone to grow from a grief experience than others? It actually has to do with the ability to grieve. When we try to stuff our grief into a closet, or hide from our grief, we don't allow ourselves the pain of experiencing the grief. While feeling pain is not pleasant, this is what actually pushes us into a place of better understanding, a closer walk with God, and having an open communication about our grief.

Have you tried to create some kind of meaningful purpose to the death of your loved one? That takes lots of time and hard work to do, but if you can, the end result is you will experience life in a new, more hopeful way. You will have a stronger, more connectedness to nature and the beauty all around you. And, you will be far more tolerant in dealing with daily life experiences.

Put some kind of validity and meaning to your loss if you can. Has your heart changed? Do you now see life from a different vantage point? Are you more aware of the pain others have in their lives? Do you feel an urgency to want to help others? If so, your pain and your grief have pushed you into a place where you are growing from your loss.

**When you face your grief head-on and experience its pain, you will eventually come through the dark tunnel to a place of peace and hope.**

## Day 229

*"Turn to me and be gracious to me, for I am lonely and afflicted." Psalm 25:16*

What can help a grieving heart? That's the question everyone asks over and over again. There are some simple but practical things that help. Sure, we've thought of these things because others have suggested them to us, but we've tossed these ideas aside.

What if you actually tried something today? What if you sat down and wrote out some of your thoughts? What if you became open and honest with the thoughts you've been unable to share yet with others, and wrote these thoughts in a journal? Do you know that journaling thoughts brings about some very positive results?

You don't need a fancy journal. A dollar notebook will do. Begin by writing just one grief thought into your journal. Maybe it's something that you feel is too big or too personal to tell someone else. After you write it down, read it once then put away the journal until tomorrow.

Keep this practice going for the next thirty days and you will begin to notice a small shift in your thinking. No longer are you avoiding your grief. You are writing down thoughts and questions and seeking answers. You are becoming more aware of your feelings turning from an overwhelming sadness to that of coping and wanting to learn from your grief. Slowly, one day at a time, your thoughts will change from hopeless to hopeful. That's one very good reason to get our your pen and begin to journal those thoughts!

**Hope ignites our hearts to love.**

## Day 230

*"But the Lord is my defender; my God is the rock of my protection." Psalm 94:22*

When we're in grief, everything means something to us. We see signs everywhere. That feather that landed in front of me is a sign. The red cardinal sitting in the tree brings hope. The glove that was missing and now appeared is a sign. The summer flower that blooms in the winter has great meaning to us.

Are we just dreaming up these things or did they happen for a reason? We can begin to drive ourselves crazy with doubt. Why not take the happening and accept it as having special meaning? Do you believe that we are spiritual beings? Maybe you don't understand how the spirit world works. None of us will know for sure until we enter that realm. But, we can take great comfort in seeing these signs and trusting that they have significant meaning from our loved one.

There's always room for doubt, but there is also room for trusting and hope. Why not err on the side of hope and belief?

**When we trust in God's wisdom, we see life in a calm confidence.**

## Day 231

*"Blessed are those who mourn, for they will be comforted." Matthew 5:4*

When we go through loss, we cry. That's a natural response and is an outward expression of our grief. Why, then, are we so embarrassed when we cry? We let too many of society's opinions influence us at times. We were told when small not to cry. We were taught how to stifle our tears and stuff our emotions to the back burner. What a disservice to the entire grieving process!

If you feel like crying, then cry. There's no shame in shedding tears. We were given the ability to cry in order to release some of those pent up emotions of sorrow and sadness. For some reason, when tears begin rolling from the corners of our eyes, we think we should turn to a corner and shield others from seeing us be sad and mournful.

Begin to embrace the ability to cry and you will begin to see some changes take place. We feel such relief from releasing those tears, because crying is our body's natural response to holding in too much pain. Tears relieve stress and pain.

When you cry, take a tissue and wipe your tears. No shame is necessary. No guilt is needed. Cry and get some much-needed relief from the pain that you are feeling from your loss. Be assured that there will eventually be a rainbow at the end of your tears, and it's going to be absolutely beautiful!

**God's love can transform our pain to joy and cause our tears to dry.**

## Day 232

*"Those who trust in the Lord are like Mount Zion, which cannot be shaken but endures forever." Psalm 125:1*

It's hard to trust in life when a loss occurs. We prayed for health for our loved one. We prayed for safety for our loved one. We prayed for freedom from addiction for our loved one. We prayed for the release from the grip of depression for our loved one. But, death still happened.

Our mind fills with a thousand questions asking how this could happen. All of them are good questions. All of them are questions that we'd love to have answered. But, there are mysteries in this life, and some questions go without answers—at least for now.

We've hit a crossroads when our questions go unanswered and our faith is shaken. What should we do? It would be easy to throw our hands up in the air and simply walk away carrying our heavy burden of grief. But, that's not what we do. Instead, we trust. We trust in a power that is bigger than we are, more powerful than we are, and more intelligent than we are. We trust because we know that somewhere in this pile of grief there is an answer. We're not going to get that answer today or tomorrow, but if there really is a heaven, we will get our answers there.

We trust because that's the best choice. Really, that's the only choice.

**We can't see electricity, but we trust in it and use it. Why, then, should there be any hesitation in trusting in God?**

## Day 233

*"My grace is sufficient for you, for my power is made perfect in weakness." II Corinthians 12:9*

There's such a mystery found in grief. Many will tell us that when we are weak, we will become strong. That doesn't make much sense at first thought. But, the longer we travel on this road of grief, the more we can understand what is meant.

Let's use trees for an example. Do you know that in order to strengthen a tree, often farmers will leave their young saplings unstaked during the harsh winter months, allowing the trees to be bent and swayed by the winter storms? The trees have a great flexibility to bend with the wind, but not break. When they have survived several harsh winters, the trees are firmly rooted in the ground, the trunks of the trees have grown thicker and can withstand heavier loads, and the branches of the trees are far stronger than they were in the early years of growth.

Maybe this applies to our grief, too. In our early months and years of grief, we cry a lot from the raw pain. We ask question after question. We doubt our faith. But, we somehow continue on. As we grow and develop more in our grief walk, we notice a maturity that wasn't there before. We are able to say that we see life much differently now. We can see more of the whole picture, and there is so much beauty to be seen in spite of our loss.

We have gained new strength when we were weak. Now, years later, it makes perfect sense!

**Choosing life doesn't mean everything is perfect. It simply means you chose the road of hope.**

## Day 234

*"Do not be afraid; do not be discouraged for the Lord your God will be with you wherever you go." Joshua 1:9*

So much fear accompanies loss. We're afraid that we will not be able to pull out of the grief. We're afraid to face each new day without our loved one. We're afraid of changes that must be made because of our loss. We're afraid that life is always going to be lonely. We're afraid that there will be another loss. Our minds are racing with fear day and night.

What if we began to really analyze fear and its purpose in our lives? Would fear be something that we'd keep as helpful in our daily grief walk? When you stop to look fear square in the eye it's safe to say that fear increases our grief and constantly has us on edge. That's the last thing we need when trying to come to grips with what has happened.

Fear thoughts multiply quicker than mice. And, fear thoughts are far more destructive. Every times we listen to a fear thought, our grief inches up a notch higher until soon our bodies, minds, and souls are overflowing in fear.

Every time a fearful thought begins, stop what you're doing and release that thought. You can do it. You can do it by being aware of the fearful thought and then saying aloud that the fear does not hold power over you. Tell yourself you're bigger than your fear. Repeat over and over again that hope holds no fear. Remind yourself to look for the beauty of life that is all around you.

By practicing nipping fear in the early stages you will build a platform of positivity and hope on which to stand. Start building your platform today!

**Fearful thoughts rob a person of all joy. Replace fear with trust, and begin seeing the miracles of life unfolding right before your eyes.**

## Day 235

*"Don't worry about anything; instead, pray about everything; tell God your needs and don't forget to thank Him for His answers." Philippians 4:6*

What are you going through today? Fear? Pain? Doubts? Loss? Sadly, these things touch everyone's lives. You are not unique in your pain, even though your loss is uniquely yours. Every person alive will have their day of reckoning with pain and loss. The big question is really not what are you going through, but rather how are you handling the things that life has thrown at you today?

For a long time following a loss, we don't handle life or the pain of loss at all. The grief binds us up and holds us in a grip of pain, fear, and desolation. Oh, how desperate and lonely we feel! This is when it is good to remember all of the friendships you've made along life's way and recall those survivors you know. Bring them to the forefront of your memory and think about the things they did to walk through the hellish pain of loss.

Guaranteed they sat still for a long time and simply digested what had happened. The reality of loss is always the hardest part. All survivors do something else. They learn how to control their thoughts. When we allow our thoughts to run wild, our thoughts carry us to places we never wanted to go. Train your thoughts to focus on the things that are right and good in life. Teach your eyes to see beauty and your thoughts will follow. Use your mind to visit places of tranquility and peace, and your fear will begin to diminish.

Grief is real and it's so very painful. But, the good news is you don't have to allow your grief to squeeze the life out of you.

**Life's goodness can be seen in every new sunrise.**

## Day 236

*"Cast all your anxiety on Him because He cares for you." I Peter 5:7*

When loss takes place we feel alone. It doesn't matter if we're surrounded by a hundred people, we still feel as though we are standing all alone without a person noticing that we're there. People tell us that they care, but the truth is that it's impossible for them to care as deeply as we care. They didn't know the one we lost as intimately as we did.

So we grieve, and we grieve, and we grieve until we're depleted of all of our energy. It takes us forever, it seems, to move off of the sofa to get to the bathroom. Trying to get ready for bed is such a chore. We can't seem to focus on anything. Our minds lay dormant in a thick fog. We can't process the simplest of things. What has happened?

It would probably be a good idea if doctors explained to us some of the things that we'll experience following a loss. That might take away some of the fear that we're acting far out of the norm for loss. There are times when we feel as though we've had a total breakdown and we're never going to regain our mental ability to think clearly again.

Grief touches every aspect of our lives. One of the first things that happens is the inability to focus or think clearly. It's a good idea to have someone stop in and check on you daily for the first several weeks or months following a loss. Just knowing that someone cares that much can help you to cope with the foggy state of mind that is the result of your grief. Go over shopping lists, doctor's appointments, routes to take to get to work, and even the daily routine of dressing. It might sound silly to some, but a grieving heart is crushed for a while and needs some tender loving care. Don't be so stubborn. Call a friend to help!

**The best friend is the one who will help you get through the messiness of life. That friend is a treasure far greater than gold!**

## Day 237

*"But you, O Lord, are a compassionate and gracious God, slow to anger, abounding in love and faithfulness." Psalm 86:15*

When we suffer a loss, we lose our entire sense of who we once were. Oh, how much we wish we could turn back the clock and have things back to normal. We miss the routines of life that we once took for granted. Just to hear the gentle swooshing of the dishwasher in the background would be welcome.

We feel broken and alone, and we struggle to find our identity. Our old self ended when grief entered the picture.

Why is it we feel like we have to apologize to others? The house is messy because we don't have the energy to move. The garbage can is overflowing with tissues because we've been trying to dry our tears day and night. The bills piled up and didn't get paid because we can't think clearly. The grass needs to be mowed because there's nobody around to take care of it.

Apologize? There's no need! We are living in the reality of our loss and that is one terribly hard place to live. We'll get through, and we are determined to find new hope for the future. But, in the meantime while we struggle facing our daily battles with grief, no apologies needed!

**Imagine a day without the heavy burden of grief. That day is coming sooner than you think.**

## Day 238

*"In the day of my trouble I will call to you, for you will answer me." Psalm 86:7*

Grief is exhausting. It drains us of every ounce of energy. We feel a tiredness that we never knew existed. When we got tired before our loss, there was someone to help with the daily routines of life. Even having someone to carry the groceries up a flight of stairs brought so much relief. But now, we sit in our tiredness and mourn so many different losses. Life has changed in a thousand different ways, and the exhaustion overcomes us.

It's hard to believe, but there really and truly are people who want to help us. All we have to do is call out to them. Let them know how they can help. People don't want to think they are an intrusion in our life that is now so different, so they stay away thinking that is best.

Can you get the courage enough to call one person today and ask for some help? Can you say that you're having trouble finding the strength to get the groceries and give them your list? Can you trust that there is someone who wants to help?

Maybe we just need someone to sit and share a cup of coffee with us for an hour. That person's presence is something that we need to fill up our empty tank. We need them to be our energy for the hour. You will be surprised at how much others want to help. They will come if you get the courage to ask.

**When the world is saying give up, hope whispers hold on. Tomorrow is a brand new day.**

## Day 239

*"Those that sow in tears shall reap in joy." Psalm 126:5*

Today might possibly be the day you've decided to call it quits. You've tried hard to make some kind of comeback after your loss, but the grief continues to be such a heavy weight that you can't breathe. You feel alone, abandoned, and forgotten.

This is written just for you to soak up like a sponge. Never, ever give up! Never listen to the voice of grief that whispers in your ear that you've been forgotten. Never believe that things will always stay hopeless.

You are not just a survivor, but you are a thriver. Believe it. You're here right now because you're far stronger than you think. You feel like giving up, but you're not going to do that. You're battle weary and need a rest. There's no shame in that. The toughest soldiers step out of rank and take time to replenish and rest.

Grab a warm blanket and a pillow. Lay down your weary head. Close your eyes and allow your weary, grief stricken mind and body to let go, rest, and let God. You say you have no faith, but every time you look at the flowers blooming, the stars twinkling in the sky, and the butterfly drinking its daily nectar, you're seeing miracles. You believe in them, and you can believe that God is going to carry you through this.

Believe. Rest. Sit among nature and allow your soul to receive nourishment. Hope is alive and is visiting you right now!

**I don't question the singing of the birds or the rising of the sun every morning. Why should I question anything else of God's wisdom?**

## Day 240

*"Bow down your ear to me, deliver me speedily; be my rock of refuge, a fortress of defense to save me." Psalm 31:2*

When we're deep into grief, we need someone to be our strength. We need someone to help hold us up. We long to have someone to lean on. The hard truth is that most people turn away from us when we're depressed and lonely. It's not because they don't care for us, but it's because they don't know what to do or say that could possibly help. So, in their feelings of inadequacy, they walk away leaving us feeling more alone than ever.

Let's face it. Sometimes we have to be our own best advocate and friend. It's not easy, especially when we're swallowed up in our pain of loss, but there is an inner voice nudging us constantly to hold on and look forward. That inner voice nags us, constantly reminding us that we can do it. It's like the little engine that could. "I think I can. I think I can. I think I can."

And, you will!

**Faith is believing in advance what can only be understood in reverse.**

## Day 241

*"I have called upon You for You will answer me, O God. Incline Your ear to me, hear my speech." Psalm 17:6*

How do people get through really tough times? What is their secret? Why do so many of us struggle with pain and loss, while others seem to keep their faith intact and are able to move forward in life despite the pain?

This is a question that baffles a lot of us. Where do we go and what do we do when tragedy strikes? There's really no set answer to this question. Each and every one of us has our own methods of survival. We might not think of it like that, but it's true. When loss comes into our life, we seem to automatically know how to reach out in our grief for help. We can sense that there is a power bigger than us calling our name. We can feel a presence within us that will not leave us in our pain.

We call this power by different names, but it's the same power that gave us the beauty of nature. It's the same power that can calm the angry seas. It's the same power that sees to it that the sun rises faithfully each morning. Yes, that power is what we instinctively reach for, knowing that in our deepest moments of despair we will be given the hope to hold on!

**It is not the objective proof of God's existence that we want, but rather the experience of God's presence. That is the miracle we are after, and that is the miracle that can be found in all of nature.**

## Day 242

*"May you be given more and more of God's kindness, peace, and love." Jude 1:2*

When we're hurting, we want one thing more than anything else. We want someone to understand and validate our pain. We want someone to listen to us when we call out in pain. We want to know that there is someone that is willing to give undivided attention to us. We want to know that for just a few moments we are someone's most important person in the world.

The reality of life is that this very rarely is the case. People get busy with their own lives. Even our own families tend to forget us very soon after a loss and get back to the work of taking care of their own families and circumstances. We interpret that as rejection, when really it is not. The truth is that life gets busy. People have jobs and bills and sick kids to deal with. People get tired and burned out, and often they have no energy left at the end of a day.

What are we to do then, when we have such great needs? Prayer can work miracles of peace and calm in our lives. Prayer allows us to speak what is on our hearts and minds knowing that we will never be judged for what we say or think. Prayer connects us to a higher power and allows us to feel the mighty presence within.

You might say that you don't believe that. Have you tried it? Sit down for an hour and practice praying. You will be surprised at the peace that washes over you!

**For peace of mind, resign as general manager of the universe.**

## Page 243

*"What is faith? It is the confident assurance that what we hope for is going to happen. It is the evidence of things we cannot yet see." Hebrews 11:1*

For days and weeks on end following a loss we wait for things to change. We wonder when that moment is going to come that will bring joy back into our lives. Will it happen suddenly, or will the joy come back into our lives a little bit at a time?

Discouragement begins to knock at the door of our heart when we're still not feeling joy a year or more after our loss. We lose all hope that things will get better. We've waited and waited, but nothing has happened. We finally throw our hands up in the air shouting that we give up! Do you know that most people give up too soon? People don't hang in there long enough to allow hope to ignite into a flaming fire. They give up while hope is still a flickering light. Discouragement is the greatest killer of faith!

Are you ready to give up today? Do you think that you've been totally forgotten in your pain? Get up early tomorrow morning and step outside to watch the rising of the sun. When you see that sun peeking over the horizon remind yourself that the sun never gives up shining. Even during the most stormy days, the sun is sitting behind the clouds giving light.

Today, this day, just might be the day things change for you. Don't give in to discouragement ever! Keep your light of hope burning and one day soon it will burst into a flame of joy!

**Hope has conspired with God and removed the demons of despair.**

## Day 244

*"In the day of my trouble I will call to you, for you will answer me." Psalm 86:7*

Everyone is told to have a plan for emergencies. We write down the number of the fire company, the police station, our doctor, and most often a family member. We keep this list by our bedside stand or carry it with us knowing that if an emergency arises we might not be able to think straight enough to recall these numbers for help.

Did you use these numbers when loss occurred? Most likely you had moments of total blackout where you couldn't even remember your own name, much less call these numbers. You probably had someone call for help for you. That's just how grief works when it hits the heart without warning. It's terrible and frightening, and it leaves us in a state of being totally numb for a while.

You've probably never seen the name "God" on the emergency call card, yet that is really the one we seek out most often. That's the one who stands by us and gives us that inner strength we need simply to breathe. That's the one who can ingest us with enough power to get is through the troubled days ahead. That's the one who gives us hope!

**God can hear even my faintest cry.**

## Page 245

*"And now, Lord, for what do I wait? My hope is in Thee."*
*Psalm 39:7*

We want so badly to believe in some kind of higher power who really and truly knows us, believes in us, and intervenes in our lives for our well being. Yet, we find it so hard to trust. Some people have said it's too much like a fairy tale where all things have a happy ending, and that's not how real life ends. Real life has too much sorrow and pain. Real life has heartache and loss.

Scientific research has been done that has proven that prayer really does work. People on the east coast can pray for people on the west coast and the prayers can be felt, and changes occur due to the prayer. Yet, we still find it too hard to believe.

When loss occurs, though, we put this to the test right away. One of the first things that we do is call out to this power in prayer. We ask for help. We cry for help. We beg for help. We repeat over and over again that we can't do this alone.

What do we have to lose by believing? Others have gone to their deaths saying it is true. Why not give prayer a try?

**Prayer does not need proof; it needs practice.**

## Page 246

*"Take my yoke upon you and learn from me, for I am gentle and humble in heart, and you will find rest for your souls." Matthew 11:29*

Do you know that grief is the hardest work you will ever do? When you are grieving you're using up all of the stored energy you had. Most times, you don't eat properly or sleep properly to give your body a chance to replenish, so you continue pushing when in grief until you collapse of sheer exhaustion.

Grieving people need rest, but the mind is always racing. We remember every detail of our loss. We go over it a million and one times in our minds and sleep will not come. We can't relax no matter what we do. We try to take a nap, but we do nothing except toss back and forth. We cry buckets of tears and our bodies are so tense that it's difficult to breathe.

Try this simple formula for rest. Stop whatever you're doing, close your eyes, and take in a long, deep, cleansing breath. Hold for a moment then release it slowly. Do this three times, then begin to feel your shoulders relax. Think of something peaceful like the gentle ocean waves quietly lapping against the shore. Take fifteen minutes every day to do this and you will eventually learn how to slow down your anxious thoughts.

**A quiet morning with a loving God brings hope and rest to the weary heart.**

## Page 247

*"The Lord is with me; I will not be afraid." Psalm 118:6*

There are so many things that are scary about loss. We are afraid of facing the future without our loved one. We're afraid we're never going to see our loved one again. We're afraid that we will never stop crying. We are afraid that life will never feel joyful again.

We live in this fear for a long time following a loss, and it's not a fun place to be. We know that we've changed, and our friends and family have taken the time to tell us we've changed. We used to smile and laugh and find joy in everyday things. Now, we are sad and lonely and feel depressed about facing each new day with our heart holding so much sorrow.

One of the very best ways to help us get out of this pit of despair is to begin walking. You don't want to walk because grief has drained you. Force yourself, anyway. Get up and walk even if it's just for five minutes a day at first. After a while, you'll want to increase your walking to fifteen minutes a day because you can notice little changes taking place in you. If you can, find a place to walk where you can enjoy scenes of nature. Trees and flowers and chirping birds are comforting to the soul. Allow some sunshine to be your daily dose of Vitamin D!

In just a couple of months you will notice a big change in the way your view life once again. Your fears will begin to subside, and your heart will begin to smile more often than weep. You will know you are walking towards hope!

**God's gift of the sunshine is a glorious reminder of His presence.**

## Page 248

*"When the cares of my heart are many, Your consolations cheer my soul."*

Sometimes it's just too painful to visit places where you went with your loved one. It doesn't feel the same anymore and all you can do is wish that this loss never happened. Going to the movies is painful. Visiting the same restaurants brings tears. Seeing children playing on the playground is too hard on your heart.

For a while you will stop visiting those places that you once held near and dear. And, that's okay. You'll know when it's time to push forward out of your pain.

One step at a time you can test the waters. Go to your favorite restaurant with a friend and recall happy memories. Sure, you'll probably cry, but your tears are nothing more than an outward pouring of the love you have for the one you miss so much.

Try visiting the park that you enjoyed so much. Allow yourself to feel the very presence of your loved one with you. Get comfortable with that feeling. It takes great courage to do what you're doing, but when you do you will begin to release so much of the sadness and bring to the front of your mind the many, many beautiful memories you shared together.

Isn't that what your loved one wants you to do?

**When the world says give up, hope continues to whisper to try it one more time.**

## Page 249

*"Be men of courage; be strong." I Corinthians 16:13*

Do you know how strong you are? You might not feel like you're strong, but you got out of bed today, didn't you? You managed to get dressed, and you even brushed your teeth. You faced this day even when you didn't want to, and that takes great courage!

Maybe it's time to begin giving yourself some credit. Not everybody has to do what you're doing. Not everyone has had circumstances as difficult as you, yet still gives each new day a try. Face it, you've got an inner strength that is much bigger than what you ever imagined.

Just for today, slowly sip your coffee and remind yourself that you're doing great, because you really are. You didn't quit when life got tough. Instead you toughed it out, and you're going to make it. One day, one step, one breath at a time you're going to make it!

**As sad as I am about my loss, I am thankful that I can still see some hope in each new day.**

## Day 250

*"I trust in your word." Psalm 119:42*

So much of our life changed when loss entered. Some days we wake up and we don't even know who we are. It's like the entire backdrop of our lives has changed. Even the color of the blue in the sky looks different. It's tinted with grey, and there are always rain clouds hovering nearby.

We recall life in different ways, too. Time has changed for us. We talk about the times before our loss and the times since our loss, but loss is always the central theme. We wonder if it's always going to be this way. Will we always have our loss at the very forefront of our heart and mind, or will there be a day when we will place our loss in the center but grow joy all around it?

We don't want to forget, ever, and we won't. We need to reassure ourselves of that. How could we forget that smile? How could we forget the moments we shared? That's impossible to do with a love as strong as we have!

Slowly but steadily we will begin to notice a shift, and it will be evident to us by the way we see the things around us. One day we will wake up and notice that the red rose is really red, and not tinged with black. We will look up to the sky and notice a break in the clouds. We'll be able to look and see that the sky has changed colors, too. The gray hue has disappeared.

Our loss has changed us, and we know that's a fact. But, is it possible that we can see more beauty around us than ever before? Perhaps this is the gift of love given to us in our loss.

**Hidden beneath the barren soil are seeds of hope slowly but surely pushing their way through.**

## Day 251

*"Against all hope, Abraham in hope believed." Romans 4:18*

Do you ever look at some people and wonder how they do it? How do they stay so positive when their lives have been shipwrecked? They cling to their faith. They believe it, and they live it, and it leaves you feeling lacking so much because you have so many questions.

When living through loss, it's normal to have millions of questions. Why did this happen? What purpose does it serve? Why do so many horrible things happen in life? Why do innocent children suffer? Why? Why? Why?

Spending time with faithful people is like spending time with daily food and sunshine. We get nurtured and nourished when in the presence of hope-filled people.

Do you have some friends who are always encouraging you? If not, can you find a book of encouragement to read? When our hearts have been broken by loss, we need to build up the heart again. No, it's foolish to think we can fix the pain that has become part of our lives, but we can rebuild the walls around our heart. We can learn to love again. We can learn to live again. We can learn to hope again.

But, we have to be willing to try. Fill your mind with positive, hopeful thoughts and see what happens. Your sorrow will never leave, but you will see life and beauty again. I guarantee it!

**When you look for the good in the bad, you will find happy in your sad.**

## Day 252

*"The Lord is my portion, therefore I will wait for Him."*
*Lamentations 3:24*

One of our big worries is how we'll ever deal with the things like birthdays, holidays, and vacations without our loved one. Sometimes we surprise ourselves and get through those days relatively okay. The worst part was our own worry.

It's those little things that really take us off guard. The reminders that pop up out of nowhere. We find a stray sock hidden in a dresser drawer and we fall to pieces. We're driving down the highway and our loved one's favorite song comes on the radio, and we have to pull over to the side of the road because we can't see through the flood of tears. We open up a closet and a toy that we haven't seen for years falls off the shelf in front of us, and we go running from the room looking for a place to hide from our grief.

Isn't this how we lived life, though? It was the little things, the little times together that truly were our special moments together. The times we spent in the kitchen rolling out pastry dough together brought so much joy. The hours spent reading story books before bedtime were cherished moments. Taking a walk through the woods on a crisp autumn day and finding colored leaves put a huge smile on our heart.

We're so thankful we had these times together even though there is such an aching to have had more time. Just one more day together; instead we will cling to just one more memory shared.

**Out of every storm eventually springs new hope.**

## Day 253

*"Cast your cares on the Lord and He will sustain you; He will never let the righteous fall." Psalm 55:22*

We can't hide from it, even when we want to hide. The reminders of loss are everywhere. I go to bed thinking tomorrow will be an easier day. Tomorrow there won't be so many reminders. Tomorrow I will stay busier and my mind won't play games with me. Tomorrow I will surround myself with people and won't allow myself to sink down into the depression of loss.

Tomorrow comes, and guess what? Reminders are everywhere of the one I lost. Isn't there ever going to be a day of rest?

Then, I take a deep, long look inside of myself, and I realize that I would be nothing without these reminders. Who would I be if I had never had this one to love? How empty my life would be right now. Who would I have become if my life wasn't touched by this love? I don't even want to think about it.

So, I sit with my grief and embrace it for a while. Yes, I embrace my grief because that is the reminder I have of the time I got to spend with the one I loved with all of my heart. I am blessed, even in my grief.

**In my pain I found the greatest blessing of all—hope.**

## Day 254

*"The Lord gives strength to His people; the Lord blesses His people with peace." Psalm 29:11*

Most of us have some kind of regrets when a loved one has died. These are the hurts that never get resolved. We thoughtlessly hurled an insult in our anger, and we can't forget that occasion. The words sting our heart and fill us with grief. We didn't speak for a long, long time because of a silly grudge that we both held, and that heightens the grief now that our loved one is gone. There are so many things we wish we would have said, but now it's too late.

Regrets place us in a prison of harmful thoughts. We need to find a way to get out of this trap and free ourselves of these thoughts once and for all. Maybe the first important step in doing this is self forgiveness. Can you do that? Can you find it in yourself to forgive you? You've forgiven all others; now it's time to forgive yourself.

Try doing this and see if it doesn't work. Write down on a piece of paper the regrets that you have. Read over that paper a few times, and notice how futile it is to constantly berate yourself. You can't change things now, but you can forgive yourself. The one you love would want you to get rid of this self-inflicted pain.

Why hold on to unresolved pain and guilt? There is nothing you can gain by doing that, and you don't deserve that kind of ongoing punishment. Take that paper of regrets, crumple it up, and throw it away. Gone. Forever it's gone. From this day forward you are forgiven. What a relief to be free from the daily torture put on yourself. This is your new day of forgiveness!

**Hope has a way of erasing past regrets and showing you the beauty of the rising sun.**

## Day 255

*"The Lord is good, a refuge in times of trouble. He cares for those who trust in Him." Nahum 1:7*

Here you are, sitting in your brokenness, wondering how you're ever going to pick up the pieces and rebuild your life. Can it be done after having a hole put right in the center of your heart? Can there really be any kind of joy after such a horrendous loss?

No, you can't rebuild a life like you'd rebuild a house that has been shattered by a storm. But, you can take that most important, courageous first step toward hope again.

What does that first step look like? It's different for everyone. Maybe your first step is going to the kitchen and preparing a meal again. Perhaps your first step is walking out to the garage and building a birdhouse. For some that first step is getting out the vacuum and seeing that the carpet is clean.

First steps are always wobbly, and very small. That's okay. That's exactly how first steps are supposed to be. Can you take a first step today? Do it. You know that you can!

**You can do it when you put your heart and mind to it.**

## Day 256

*"The Lord is upright; He is my Rock, and there is no wickedness in Him." Psalm 92:15*

Grief can make a person feel crazy. Our minds keep spinning and spinning. We can't stop the cycle of horrible thoughts. We keep replaying the death of our loved one over and over again. We want to go crazy. We want to do anything that will make this stop.

Do you know that almost every person who has lost a loved one doubts their sanity at some point during their heavy grief? It helps to talk with others who have grieved a loss because they will tell you that there was a point when they thought they had lost it. They really and truly thought they had gone crazy. It's comforting to know that you're not alone thinking these thoughts.

Thankfully, this frame of thinking doesn't last forever. It usually comes after a day of hard sobbing and uncontrolled thoughts about death. When that starts happening, remind yourself that you are the only one in charge of your thoughts. I know that is hard to believe when you're feeling so vulnerable, but it's true. When you thoughts start getting out of control, step back and remind yourself that this isn't productive grieving. Allowing your imagination to take your thoughts into a deep, dark pit of despair will not help you in any way to reduce the grief you're feeling.

Have a sip of water, grab a tissue to blow your nose, and walk outside to get some fresh air. Take a few slow, deep breaths and have a talk with yourself. Remind yourself that all you need to do right now is get through the next few minutes, and then a few minutes more. You can do it. You will do it. You're not crazy!

**God grants peace to those who ask.**

## Day 257

*"Rest in the Lord and wait patiently for Him." Psalm 37:7*

Our life was so busy that we barely had time to breathe. Then loss entered our life, and now time is standing still. Nothing seems to matter any more. Who cares if we go to work on time? Who cares if we go out to eat with our friends? Who cares if we don't get a shower for three days? Who cares if the bed doesn't get made? Who cares if the dishes are piled a mile high in the sink?

You can relate to this. I know you can, because this is just how the grief of losing a loved one works. Our busy lives that we had come to a screeching halt and we are consumed day and night with the fact that our loved one isn't here any more.

At some point, we know we have to get back to some kind of normal routine in our living. We can't go on like this forever not caring about anything. A good starting point is to begin taking slow daily walks. Try just a few minutes at first, but make those few minutes count. Be sure to soak up everything you see and hear. Can you hear a bird chirping in the distance? Allow it to sing to you. Can you see the buds appearing on the trees? That's a miracle of nature and you're getting to be part of that right now. Do you feel the warm sunshine on your face? Stop and allow the sunbeams to dance on your cheeks.

By taking this walk, you've just been bathed in the newness of hope. Without even knowing it you've been encouraged. And, you did it. You walked out in faith and you began to care again. Nature does it every time.

Nature calms our anxious heart and gives us a glimpse into eternity.

**God sends His love like sunshine in a warm and gentle way.**

## Day 258

*"Depend on the Lord; trust Him, and He will take care of you." Psalm 37:5*

You've had it happen already. Well-meaning people came to visit you after your loss and chided you for worrying about the future. What they don't understand is that this loss took the rug right out from under you and you are worrying. You're worrying about the bills. You're worrying about being alone in the house. You're worrying about things like never having grandchildren, or seeing your child get married. You're worrying that something like this might happen again, and that's the worst worry of all. You're worrying because worry is what you do when you are grieving.

As hard as it is to accept, we needed the talk our friend gave us. It's true. There's no sense in worrying because it doesn't change a thing. Worry never helps us. Instead, worry clouds our thinking, increases our anxiety, and robs us of any shred of joy that we might have.

It helps to keep telling yourself that worry is a waste of time. Worry is futile. Worry serves no real purpose, and you're smarter than worry. Every time a worry thought enters your mind, put a stop to it. How? Have plenty of note cards nearby with positive affirmations and hopeful thoughts written on them. Replace every worry with trust and hope, and watch yourself calm down.

**One small hopeful thought can change the course of your entire day.**

## Day 259

*"God has made me fruitful in the land of my suffering."*
*Genesis 41:52*

You've read books on grief in order to help you as you travel this journey of loss. Most of them say the same thing. They tell you all about the stages of grief that you'll experience. You'll even have numbered charts letting you know the order in which you'll reach these stages. The only problem is, there is very little predictability in grief and there definitely is not a true pattern that fits everyone!

Your grief will be all over the place, and that's something you need to know. Some days you'll cry and scream all day. Then, you might feel numb for a week and have no emotions at all. After that, you might be overtaken with an anger befitting a stampeding bull. You're angry at the one you loved so much for leaving you. You shout terrible things, and you mean it at the time. Two days after this screaming fit, you might go into total withdrawal and not speak a word to anyone, including yourself, for an entire month.

All of this is normal in the abnormal ways of grief. Don't try to follow step 1, step 2, and step 3 because it won't work. Allow your grief to come out as it wants and as it needs. That's the very best way—spontaneous, uninhibited grief. That's how you'll find a cleansing of some of this pain you're carrying inside. As you let out the grief, you'll find yourself feeling a whole lot better! Your grief follows no pattern right now, but that's okay. In time your balance for life will return.

**No matter how bleak the day, hope will find its way into your heart at just the right time.**

## Day 260

*"Shall I not drink from the cup the Father has given me?"*
*John 18:11*

Oh, how exhausting it is to grieve! Our minds seem to go at full tilt ahead and race around and around constantly, but our bodies are drained, and so very tired. We don't even the have energy most days during the early months of loss to pull ourselves out of bed and get dressed.

We need to remind ourselves every single day that our minds, bodies, and souls have been through a terrible shock. Losing a loved one affects every single fiber within us. There is nothing that is untouched from grief. It's like our bodies and minds are moving in slow motion, not fully grasping the depth of what has happened.

This is a time when it's so necessary to take extra good care of ourselves. Make certain we're doing the basics such as keeping hydrated with lots of water. We don't always feel like eating, but how about this? Promise yourself that you'll have a good, old-fashioned cup of chicken noodle soup once a day. Chicken soup is comfort for the body, mind, and soul. Add a brief walk every day, and you'll find you're able to get through the day a bit better.

**When I take care of myself, I'm really investing in my hope for the future.**

## Day 261

*"The nearness of God is my good; I have made the Lord God my refuge." Psalm 73:28*

When loss is part of our lives, we seem to automatically pray. Our prayers might not be the traditional kind, but we talk to God. We bare our souls in prayer letting out all the pain and sorrow we've been dealing with every day. Yes, we even yell at God in our anguish at times. Nobody's really proud to say that. In fact, there is usually a ton of guilt after having a yelling, praying session with God. We don't like to talk about this because we're embarrassed and ashamed. How dare we express ourselves in prayer in such a disrespectful way?

Try to think back on times when others have been in pain and they've opened up both barrels on you. Did you stop loving them because they let out some of their pain? Of course not. In fact, your heart was more in tune to what they were going through, and you wanted to provide even more comfort than you'd already been giving.

God is bigger than us, and He's far bigger than our pain. He can take it when we cry out in pain. Just like you want those you love to come to you in their hour of pain, so does God want us to go to Him in our time of pain—sobs, anger, and even yelling. Pray your heart out. You really and truly do have a God, the Father, who cares!

**God tenderly dries our tears because he cares.**

## Day 262

*"The Lord is a shelter for the oppressed, a refuge in times of trouble." Psalm 9:9*

When someone we love has died because of an illness, often we watched in sadness the daily changing of their appearance. It was heartbreaking to see the body changing from day to day as the illness took away so much life, and try as we might we can't get those images to leave our minds.

What a shame that doctors and nurses don't talk more openly about this when a loss takes place. We're riddled with flashing pictures that come across our mind, and often we have dreams that cause us to cry out in the middle of the night. It's too much for us to bear! We get so afraid that we're going crazy or experiencing something abnormal when we have these visions and dreams, but really this is now part of the grief we carry with us.

How about trying this when you feel strong enough? Find some pictures of your loved one during healthy times. Choose a lovely picture frame and place your favorite picture in it. Look at that picture when your mind becomes overwhelmed with sadness. Give yourself permission to remember happy moments with the one you loved. Study the smile and the vibrancy for life, and feel your grief being comforted. You'll know that you are moving forward in your grief when you are able to remember more vividly your loved one's happy moments rather than the sad ones.

**Hope is being able to see light even when the circumstances of life are emitting only darkness.**

## Day 263

*"The eyes of the Lord search the whole earth in order to strengthen those whose hearts are fully committed to Him." II Chronicles 16:9*

When we're busy living life, we don't often take the time to sit and ponder the possibilities of heaven and an after life. Oh, we think about it some, but not a whole lot until something tragic happens. Immediately after loss, our minds go into overdrive with thousands of questions, and our hearts demand answers.

We read book after book on the afterlife, searching what others have to say because we need to know that our loved one is safe. The problem is we have no real proof until we enter that realm of death ourselves.

Why not cast aside the questions that have no answers and give your mind and soul a break? What have you got to lose by trusting in the promises of God found in the Bible? When we think of a place being prepared for each of us that is beautiful and full of love and peace we can feel the tension and pain begin to leave. Take fifteen minutes every day and look into the big, wide, beautiful sky and picture the one you love sitting in heaven living among God's angels. What a wonderful scene comes to our minds! We can't prove it, but we can believe it!

**You can't see the wind, but you believe in it. Why not believe in heaven, too?**

## Day 264

*"God shall supply all your needs." Philippians 4:19*

It's strange how grief works within us. It enters our lives when loss takes place and it becomes a daily part of our being. We never really thought much about grief until tragedy struck because we didn't have to deal with it. But, now it's here and we wear it like a cloak. It covers us like our skin.

Do you know that your skin is constantly regenerating? Every few weeks you're wearing a new layer of skin. It's fascinating to think of our bodies taking such good care of us! Do you know that grief is much like our skin? Our minds are working very hard to shed the old layer of grief and produce a new, lighter layer of grief. It takes time and it's a daily work in progress, but you can be assured that it's happening.

One day you're going to wake up and realize that your first thought of the day was not your loss. What? Is that possible? Right now it might not seem to be within the realm of possibility, but it will happen just as surely as you'd shedding your skin cells every day.

Your grief will always be a part of you, but you'll continuously be creating new grief thoughts. You'll have better thoughts, stronger thoughts, more hopeful thoughts. You'll wear your new grief but it won't have the weight of your old grief. Believe it because it's happening right now!

**Hope is that persistent flicker of light within the heart that never gives up.**

## Day 265

*"The Lord is gracious and compassionate, slow to anger and rich in love." Psalm 145:8*

Because grief is so tiring, we often excuse ourselves from doing anything related to exercise. If there's an easy way out, we do it. Rather than walk through the store to buy our groceries, we order them online and have our food delivered. Rather than get outside and go to the bank, we use our computer or phone to pay our bills in the convenience of our home. Rather than rake the leaves, we call a neighbor and offer to pay him to do it.

The truth is, if ever there was a time that we need to get up and move our bodies, it's now. We know we're not being lazy. We know why we don't want to move around. We don't want to face people and have to pretend that we're happy when we're not. We don't feel like moving because the grief has exhausted us. We don't want to get up and get dressed because we haven't done the laundry in three weeks, and we don't have any clean clothes to wear. We think of every excuse not to get moving, and the truth is that we have legitimate excuses.

But, if we want to rid ourselves of some of this grief, we must move. We need endorphins now more than ever before, and the only way they will get working in our body is to have movement. As little as five minutes of walking a day will help elevate our mood and put us in a better place emotionally. We can do it! We can do anything for five minutes, including walk!

**Never give up! There is always a blessing waiting right around the corner.**

## Day 266

*"O Lord, you have examined my heart and know everything about me." Psalm 139:1*

Most of us have had some kind of previous experience with death. We understand what death means, and we've had the opportunity to help a friend who has been dealt a blow to the heart and is grieving. We helped for a short time, and then we backed off thinking we were no longer needed. Oh, how differently we think now that we are the one grieving a loss.

We've asked ourselves a thousand times what happened to our friends. They surrounded us with love for a while. Sometimes it felt like too much love and we longed to be able to cry in privacy. We were brought enough food to last a year, and we were so thankful. But, then everything came to a screeching halt.

How can we be angry when we've done the same thing to others? How can we misunderstand when we, too, have left people in their grief thinking that just because they were smiling during our visit they were healed? If only we were more sensitive to the needs of others!

When friends seem to disappear, why not call on the next best thing to help you through the rough times? There is beauty and healing in nature. Sometimes nature speaks to us in ways that people can't. Study the details of a blade of grass or a flower in bloom. Watch a butterfly as it elegantly displays its colors while drinking of the sweet nectar. Lay on your back and watch the clouds floating across the sky. There is no chaos in nature. Everything is precise and orderly. The same one who created the beauty of nature created you and promises to take care of you. Believe it because it's true!

**By remembering the goodness of God our hope is restored.**

## Day 267

*"God is love. There is no fear in love. But perfect love drives out fear." I John 4:18*

Following a loss, the grief we experience is harsh. We never knew there was such mental pain and anguish coupled with so much emptiness. It feels as though our entire life has been emptied of all meaning. When is this going to end? Will it ever get any better? Is there some kind of goodness to follow this torment?

We keep telling ourselves that we want to go back to the time before it happened. If only we could turn back the hands of the clock. We are convinced that life was perfect before death entered the picture of our lives. We don't remember any of the problems and pain we were going through because we don't want to remember. All we know is we want our loved one back and we want this pain to leave.

Eventually reality comes and pays us a visit and talks to us gently but firmly. We know that we can wish forever that this never happened, but this truth is that death did take place. Death is such a hard word to say! We have come to that hard place in life where we have to make a choice. Will we stay paralyzed by this fear and pain all the rest of our days on this earth, or will we make the hard, but right choice, to step outside of our pain?

Grief will always be part of us, but we can learn to appreciate and enjoy life again. Of course it will never be the same. How could it be without the one we loved so much? But, every day miracles are unfolding right before our very eyes, and maybe our grief is telling us it's time to look beyond yesterday and see life as it's happening today. Isn't that what our loved one would want for us?

**Hope only moves in one direction—forward.**

## Day 268

*"Anxiety in the heart of man causes depression, but a good word makes it glad." Proverbs 12:25*

One of the side effects of grief is anxiety. We worry about everything under the sun since the loss took place. Is it any wonder that our hearts have become anxious? Look what a trauma we've been through! It's frightening when someone we love dies. Our minds zig-zag all over the place following a loss until we become wound up as tight as a ball of rubber bands and we can't relax for even a minute.

We worry about the smallest things, yet these things seem so big in our minds. We're nervous and we have that overwhelming feeling that something bad is going to happen again. We're on edge every minute of the day and night!

How do we get this under control? We know that antidepressants are only a temporary fix and alcohol is no fix at all. The last thing we want to do is become dependent on alcohol to calm our nerves. We're smarter than that. We know that alcohol has an opposite effect and raises our level of depression and anxiety. So what do we do?

One thing we can do is to begin filling our minds with hopeful thoughts. At first this is going to be so hard that we might only be able to try for one or two minutes a day. But, as we get better at it, we can increase our time to five or six minutes a day, then work up to ten uninterrupted minutes of feeding our minds only joyful, thankful, peaceful thoughts. Think of it as filling up your well with pure water so that you can drink from it and be healthy. It works! Start filling up your mental well today and see for yourself how the anxiety begins to decrease!

**The valley of bereavement becomes less frightening when we fill our heart with hope.**

## Day 269

*"For great is His love towards us." Psalm 117:1*

When we're grieving there are so many things that bring on tears. We can be walking down the center of an aisle in the grocery store and there it is—the favorite cookies. We stop, stare for a moment, and then go running out of the store. Oh, how much we miss sharing cookies and milk together!

We go home and try to change our attention, so we begin reading a book, and the door slams. We jerk up, pause, and wait. That's the same sound we heard every day when our loved one came rushing through the door. We pull the blanket up over our head, throw down the book and cry for hours.

It doesn't matter what we're doing. This feeling can come over us and send us into a tailspin. Baking a pie. Rearranging the porch furniture. Sipping a cup of coffee. Those memories come rushing in and become too much for us. We crumble to the floor in a pile of tears wishing so much we could relive those moments again.

Once we realize what is happening we can better manage our grief. We're not going crazy or losing it as some would tell us. We're not stuck in our grief. We're just remember moments we shared with the one we loved and we miss those times together. There's nothing crazy or wrong about that.

The tears eventually stop, but the memories will never go away, and we wouldn't want it any other way. Precious memories. How they flood my soul!

**Lift your tear-stained eyes. A rainbow has been placed in the sky just for you.**

## Day 270

*"The Lord will guide you always, He will satisfy your needs. You will be like a well-watered garden, like a spring whose waters never fail." Isaiah 58:11*

It's been said that no two people will ever grieve the same loss the same way, and that's true. We can see it between friends and family members. The way we grieve, and the level of pain we have is different for each one. These differences can be both a blessing and a curse. It's hard when others don't feel your same level of loss and pain, and that can be misinterpreted as others don't care as much as you do. Of course intellectually we know this isn't true. It's a matter of differences in the way each one grieves.

These differences can also become one of our greatest blessings because when one is being hit hard with the stormy seas of grief, another might be having a better day and can help hold you up. Grief, while it is common among all people, is also different and that makes grief both unique and personal. We can view our grief through the lens of our own eyes and see so differently from others. That's why we need to allow each person space to grieve in his or her own way. No judgments. No criticisms. Grief is hard enough to deal with without being told we're doing it the wrong way!

Today, remember that you're perfectly fine to grieve in your special way, but you're also perfectly fine to give that same freedom those around you. That's the only way we're going to make it through this valley of despair.

**I'm not competing with anyone. I wish all the gift of hope.**

## Day 271

*"How precious it is, Lord, to realize that you are thinking about me constantly! Were I to count them they would outnumber the grains of sand. When I awake, I am still with you." Psalm 139:17*

Oh, how much we wish to remember what it was like to feel happy! It's been months since we've smiled. It's been years since we've really allowed ourselves to laugh. Why do we do this? Why do we withhold joy like this? The answer is simple. We are too afraid that if we begin to step out of our grief even for a moment we will forget our loved one. We are plagued day and night by that ongoing fear of forgetting the one we loved so much so we have stopped ourselves short of learning how to enjoy life again.

Just for today, it would be so nice to sit our grief on a chair beside us and simply breathe without its stronghold around our neck. Just for today it would be so freeing to visit with friends and not worry about laughing aloud when someone says something funny. Why do we fear the judgment of friends? We've forgotten that they want us to be happy.

Just for today, it would be wonderful to not feel guilt for the death of our loved one. Why do we think we could have prevented it? We can't prevent accidents or cancer or tragedy from striking. We can't, and we must begin believing that we did our best, because we did.

Just for today, we will step away from our grief for an hour and take a long, deep breath, look at the world around us and smile. We owe that much to ourselves.

**Hope is alive and is unfolding right before my very eyes.**

## Day 272

*"The Lord replied, 'My presence will go with you, and I will give you rest.'" Exodus 33:14*

We look in mirror and some days we don't even recognize ourselves. Grief has taken its toll. Our shoulders are slumped. We have bags under our eyes. Our hair hasn't been styled in months. Our clothes don't fit because we've put on so much weight from sitting around worrying so much. We've become someone we never wanted to be.

Our personality has changed, too. We're short-tempered, lashing out at the drop of a pin. We cry constantly. We have an inner anger that we're afraid to let loose. Every conversation we have is laced with fear and negativity. Oh, how much we dislike the person we've become!

Loss is a joy robber, but we don't have to live like this forever. That's what friends keep saying, but it's so hard to believe that our lives could ever get back on some kind of an even keel again. Everything feels so mixed up, messed up, and out of place.

Trying to activate some healing isn't easy, but we have to at least give it a try. What have we got to lose? It's miserable living this way, and we know our loved one wouldn't want this life for us. What if today was the day to make a hair appointment? What if next week we began eating more nutritious meals and added ten minutes of walking among nature every day? Could we do it?

If we can survive this many months after the death of the one we loved so much, we can do anything. Today is the day to start feeling better. Today is the day to take that first step outside of grief. It takes lots of courage, but today is the day! Let's do it!

**With hope, life is one endless stream of possibilities.**

## Day 273

*"The Lord gives strength to His people; the Lord blesses His people with peace." Psalm 29:11*

After a while, we shut down and don't talk about our loss anymore. Why is that? It seems like nobody really cares and we don't want to constantly burden others with our sadness. We put on our happy face mask and become the world's greatest pretenders. We get really good at it, except for one thing. Grief cannot be suppressed for long or it will build up inside until it explodes!

Suppressed grief can cause all kinds of problems, from sleep disorders to panic attacks to high blood pressure to anxiety. It's so much better to let out some of the pain we're holding inside.

Do you have a friend of two who will listen? You don't know until you try. Tell your friends how you're feeling. If that doesn't work, tell your doctor, your pastor, or your neighbor who you've been avoiding. Talking about your grief will help you. The loss you experienced was real. There is a story that you have to tell. It's an important part of your life, and right now it's the *most* important part of your life. Don't keep bottling up your grief!

Telling your story will be sad, but every time you tell your story it will become more real, and also the sharp edges of pain will not be as sharp as they once were. A good friend will encourage you to talk. A good friend will listen. A good friend will always be interested in your story because it's part of who you are.

**God sees your tears and will tenderly hold you until every heartache disappears.**

## Day 274

*"The Lord hears when I call to him." Psalm 4:3*

We never thought it would happen, but it did. We went about the entire day without crying. Yes, we thought of our loss, but we didn't have the usual melt down. As we sat in the chair looking at the evening newspaper, we actually focused on what we were reading and we wondered what was happening to us. Is it possible that we're beginning to see life in a new way?

We recall yesterday's walk and remember whispering how beautiful the flowers were in the neighbor's garden. We also walked slower, taking in the beauty of the sky. We sat for a while on the porch and watched the sun slowly disappear behind the horizon.

Is this how it happens? Is this how hope returns? If so, it's wonderful. It's really wonderful to have a much-needed day of unexpected beauty.

**Hope leaves behind the sweet smell of summer.**

## Day 275

*"My hope comes from him." Psalm 62:5*

Do you know that nothing can totally snuff out hope? That's really hard to believe during the early days of grief when our loss is so raw and full of pain. We can't see anything good or hopeful for months. We don't know how we're going to get through the day, much less think about future plans. That's totally out of the question.

We struggle with our grief daily. We're fighting hard to live within this brokenness of loss, but we feel like we're on sinking ground. We're doing all of the things we've been told to do that might help. We're reading positive stories. We're talking long walks among nature. We're journaling our thoughts. We're getting out with friends a little bit more. But, the grief is still a lingering dark cloud, hovering above us, that won't go away.

There's something important going on inside of us, though. There's an unrest that we can't explain. It's bubbling up inside and it's causing us to feel strangely uncomfortable. And, then one day everything comes to light.

Hope has been growing deep inside of our soul. The kind of hope that keeps us going. The hope that tells us to never give up. The hope that carries us through the storm and gets us safely to the other side.

**Hope is the anchor of the soul.**

## Day 276

*"Lord God, all powerful, who is like you? Lord, you are powerful and completely trustworthy." Psalm 89:8*

It's tough coming to grips with death. We deny death is part of life until it happens to someone we love and then death is all we can think about. We can't move our thoughts to anything else.

Death was that hushed topic that we never mentioned, but since loss has touched our life, that's all we talk about. We don't understand death, but we long to learn more about it. Our loved one is there—wherever there is. How can we know for sure? It's important for us to know that the one we love is free from pain. It's important to know that our loved one is not cold or hungry or afraid. We need to know that everything is okay.

We don't have much choice in this matter when you get right down to it. We either believe what has been written by the teachers and prophets of old, or we reject the teachings. If we believe that life continues on in a spiritual sense, we gain a sense of peace, and that's what we're really searching for in our quest to know more about death.

Is it so hard to believe? When we look at the precision and details of nature, it's not hard to believe. When we study all of the intricacies of the universe it's not at all hard to believe in some kind of eternal higher power. Nature seems to be the glue that connects the dots between a higher power, a spiritual world, and God. Death is that bridge we must all cross over to get to our true, lasting destiny. The proof is here. We simply have to have the faith to believe, and that brings us peace.

**Allow the brightness of the stars to shine down on you. God's power can be seen everywhere, even in the darkest night.**

## Day 277

*"Blessed be the Lord, who daily bears our burdens." Psalm 68:19*

In our grief we feel as though we've been singled out among all people. It really feels that personal. We cry out to God in our pain asking why He chose us? Why our child? Why our loved one? Why now? Why did it happen in the tragic way it happened? Why? Why? Why?

We can ask a million times why and never get an answer. Oh, how frustrating that is! We go round and round full circle, and we're left sitting in the ashes of our pain. As our grief continues on, we're able to see life more clearly, and we come to realize that maybe we weren't singled out. Maybe death and loss do come to others. It's hard to admit this at first because we want to have a reason to blame God for choosing us.

The hard truth is that we are part of this universe, and in this thing called life there is also loss. Eventually, loss will touch every family, and death will come to every person. While my story of loss is unique to only me, it has similarities to many others. I'm not the only person grieving at this moment, and in some small way, there is comfort in knowing that I am not alone.

**Life's circumstances can embitter us, but if we allow God's grace to touch us, we can travel through even the hardest of times with hope.**

## Day 278

*"I was crying to the Lord with my voice and he answered me from His holy mountain." Psalm 3:4*

One of the things we never, ever want to hear when we're grieving is that something good can come from this. People who are trying to help us will remind us of this constantly but we close our ears to it. How can anything good come from the loss of someone I love? We don't want to hear accolades about the bright side of life when our heart is crushed by the pain of loss.

As the months go on following our loss, we gain a new way of looking at life. I'm not sure what you'd call it, but we look at life through a lens of tears and pain, and somehow we begin to see so much beauty in the small moments of life that we never saw before.

A child picks up a wiggly worm while playing in the park and we weep. We never felt compassion for the tiniest of God's creations before. We see the colors of wild flowers intermingled together, forming a palette of colors that create a true masterpiece. We study the pattern on the wings of a butterfly and tears flow down our cheeks, because we know we are looking at a miracle and a blessing.

Can any good come from so much pain and loss? If the good is measured in how we view the world through eyes of hope and beauty, then the answer is yes. Yes, it is possible to have some good come from our loss and pain if we allow our heart to be opened to it.

**When it is darkest, only then can you clearly see the stars.**

## Day 279

*"The Lord is my Shepherd; I lack nothing." Psalm 23:1*

Grief comes in waves and the waves are totally unpredictable. People have written book after book describing the stages of grief that we can expect. While it's true there are stages of grief, there's no hard and fast rule about the order in which these stages appear to us.

The one thing we know for certain is that grief is real, and there is no predictable pattern as to how it appears. The emotions we experience sometimes make us feel like we're on a wild roller coaster ride and we never know where the dips and turns are, nor do we know the speed of this racing ride. It's both exhausting and frightening.

The only thing we can say with certainty is that this ride eventually levels out. I'm not saying the ride is ever smooth sailing, but it does get more manageable. In time, the reality of our loss becomes part of daily life for us, and somehow we learn to live within this brokenness.

Our minds calm down, and our pain eases enough that we are finally able to say with assurance that we know we're going to make it. And, we will!

**Right when you feel like you can't hold on any longer, the sun begins to shine, letting you know the storm has moved on**.

## Day 280

*"I have told you these things, so that in me you may have peace. In this world you will have trouble. But take heart! I have overcome the world." John 16:33*

What a shame that we are our own worst enemies when it comes to grief. We're forever putting ourselves down telling those around us that we deserve what we're getting. We spew out all of our imperfections remembering every little detail of what we did or said that we feel deserves punishment.

We just can't seem to let go of the guilt. Others try to help us get past this, but we hold on and continue to beat ourselves up over and over again.

Nobody expects us to be perfect, and we know that. We can't be perfect when it comes to grief. That's an impossibility for everyone. We do the best we can each day, and often we fall way short of where we'd like to be. But, we pick ourselves up and try again tomorrow. How much we need to hear the words, "You're forgiven. You are loved just as you are."

Today, let's try practicing the necessity of letting go. Take a long, deep breath, and as you exhale let go of all of the baggage that you're carrying around once and for all. It does you no good except to constantly drag you down in your grief.

**What a relief to know that we can begin new each day**.

## Day 281

*"He is my defender. I will not be defeated." Psalm 62:6*

Why do people think it's good to tell a person suffering from a great loss to toughen up? "Pull yourself up by the bootstraps and go on." How many times we've heard that and how many times we feel like screaming that if we could do that we would. If only this grief was that simple!

Grief is messy, and it's complicated, and it touches everyone in a different and unique way. Losing someone we love leaves our heart with an open, gaping wound subject to all kinds of extra pain. Words can be said so carelessly to us. Sure, they're meant to help, but so often people just don't think through what they tell us. They want to see us looking well and happy, so they get impatient and try to push us through grief at break-neck speed. It cannot be done.

We are tough—much tougher than anyone really knows. Anybody who can get up out of bed following a loss is full of courage. The circumstances of some deaths are too painful to say, yet many have to live with the memories of these tragedies day after day. Murder. Suicide. Drug overdoses. Car accidents. Drownings. It takes the courage of a mountain lion to face each new day, yet it's being done.

Don't let others try to get you to race through your grief. Take it one day at a time. There's no rush. Your mind has a lot to process and you're doing great. You're a survivor, and you're going to make it. One day, one step, one breath at a time and you'll make it.

**Never, ever give up! The beginning is always the hardest.**

## Day 282

*"But God will never forget the needy; the hope of the afflicted will never perish." Psalm 9:18*

Never in a million years would we wish the pain of loss on anyone, yet the harsh truth is that many suffer this pain every day. Oh, how wonderful it is when we can sit in a corner of the room with another fellow griever and share the innermost sorrows of our heart. Nobody can understand this pain like a person who has already traveled this road and has come out on the other side.

There seems to be a natural bond made immediately when we find someone who truly understands. We form warm friendships, and we find it so easy to talk about our loss. We don't feel embarrassed or ashamed when talking to another fellow griever because we know that they will love us and accept us unconditionally.

Finally we've found something that gives us hope for the future. We see someone genuinely smiling and telling us that the journey is hard and the journey is long, but we can make it. Yes, those are the words we've been longing to hear for such a long, long time!

**God is no stranger; He's as close as the wind and as mighty as the stars that cover the sky. He is the one Friend that time cannot end.**

## Day 283

*"Know that wisdom is such to your soul; if you find it, there will be a future, and your hope will not be cut off."*
*Proverbs 24:14*

Whenever you get so despondent about this grief you are living with, take time to stop and think how different your life would have been if you had never had that loved one in your life. That's a lonely, frightening thought. Can you imagine how lonely life would have been?

It's hard to think of any blessings when we're so focused on loss, but the truth is that we have been blessed with a life to love. Some of us had only a brief time together while others of us had many years together. Either way, we got to experience the miracle of loving someone so much that now our heart is breaking without them.

There will be a day when your thinking changes and you will be able to see how much your life was blessed because of love. Grief teaches us so many important, lasting life lessons. The most lasting lesson of all is knowing how fortunate we are to have a reason to grieve. Our grief is an outward expression of the love that lives within our heart.

**Our inner happiness depends not on what we experience but on the degree of our gratitude to God, no matter the circumstance.**

## Day 284

*"Rejoice in hope, be patient in tribulation, be constant in prayer." Romans 12:12*

Some people believe that if you're a person of faith, you will not grieve. Oh, how wrong this thinking is and how much guilt it throws onto a believer grieving the loss of a loved one! All people grieve, and it doesn't matter how much faith they have, their hearts still weep for the one that is no longer here.

People of faith might have an easier time working through the really hard parts of grief, but it's not uncommon for followers of God to question their faith for a while during the early months of loss. Many believers grow upset with God, even angry with God, for a time. There's an unreasonable expectation placed on people of faith that makes grieving extra hard.

It's more fair to say that loss places everyone on level ground. No exceptions. The pain is there, and it's so real. No matter what level of faith we have or don't have, we still feel the brokenness with our heart and it hurts so much to not be near the one we love.

How wonderful for the ones who can cling to their faith holding fast to their beliefs. There is a peace with belief. One has only to look at the morning sunrise or the portrait of the rainbow in the sky following a storm to understand the power of belief!

**The stormy seas may get rough, but they will never overpower you when you are firmly anchored to God.**

## Day 285

*"May the God of hope fill you with all joy and peace in believing, so that by the power of the Holy Spirit you may abound in hope." Romans 15:13*

Loss is heavy on the heart, and there are times when we need a break from the pressing heartache and grief. It's hard to do this, though, without feeling like we're being a deserter leaving our loved one behind. For a long, long time we feel like we absolutely must grieve day and night or our love is weakening.

When grief weighs so heavy upon your heart that you feel like you can't breathe, it's time to take a much-needed grief break. Thankfully, there are ways to replenish your depleted mind and soul by connecting with the beauty and serenity found in nature.

Can you think of one thing that helps ease your troubled mind? Walk outside, lift your head up, and look at that big, beautiful sky. Remember the wonder found in the heavens above. Sit under the shade of a tree and feel the coolness of the soft breeze brushing against your face. Study the delicate grass that is touching your bare feet and allow memories of those carefree summer days of your childhood return. Can you see the sunbeams dancing just for you? Oh, how wondrous is the beauty found in all of nature.

These mini grief breaks are necessary to your health. It's good for your body, mind, and soul to step away from your grief for a few moments and allow peace to flow through your veins. Grief is hard work. It's the hardest work you will ever do. After your break, you will return to your grief just a bit stronger. That is a blessing for you!

**God whispers to us during the calm as well as the storm. He is always there caring for our soul.**

## Day 286

*"He remembered us when we were in trouble. His love continues forever." Psalm 136:23*

It's so frightening to say it aloud, but the truth is that when our loved one left us, we wanted to leave, too. We're so lost and alone, and the thought swirls through our mind time and time again. We're thinking out of desperation.

As time moves on, and we begin to face reality more clearly and honestly, we know that joining our loved one isn't an option. In fact, it never was an option. It was only a thought pouring forth from a broken heart. We're so lost that we don't know what to do or where to go. We don't know how to get past this hurt, or worse yet, we don't know if the day will come when we'll ever move beyond this hurt.

This is a good time to remind yourself that nothing lasts forever. There is no pain that lasts forever. There is no sorrow that lasts forever. There is no brokenness that lasts forever. We were born with a special inner strength called hope and there is absolutely nothing that can snuff out the flicker of hope that dwells within us.

Do you remember watching the embers of a fire softly glowing until a gust of wind came along and fueled that fire? That's how hope works within you. Those embers of hope are always there softly burning in the chambers of our soul. Then one day when you least expect it, something happens to fan those embers and you'll find yourself feeling the hope you've had all along giving you new strength and new reasons to go on!

**I have always been delighted at the prospect of a new day, a fresh try, one more start waiting somewhere behind a new morning.**

## Day 287

*"God has said never will I leave you or forsake you."*
*Hebrews 13:5*

There are days when the grief is too much and you feel like throwing in the towel and calling it quits. Life has been unfair, there's no doubt about that. You've had months and months of sorrow and anguish, and it's not getting any better. Your head is throbbing from crying. Your body aches from being exhausted. Your mind is in a constant state of panic and fear. What's the use of going on?

And, then it happens. You look out the window and there's a big, bright beautiful sun shining just for you. You try to get up off of the couch but the kitty is all snuggled up next to your purring her happy song. The phone rings and it's a friend calling to check on you.

What's happening? Do you know that hope is never late arriving? Do you know that just when you're at wits end a sunbeam appears and ushers hope back into the door of your life? Hang in there, and don't give up! Tomorrow is a brand new day. You're going to feel better!

**Every day the world is born anew just for you.**

## Day 288

*"For I know the plans I have for you," declares the Lord, "plans for welfare and not for evil, plans to give you a future and a hope." Jeremiah 29:11*

Of course we want to do it. We want to move forward since our loss, but we don't know how. We understand that our loved one wouldn't want us living in daily sorrow like this, but moving out of this deep pit of despair is much easier said than done. Nobody can really tell us exactly how to do it. Grief is far too complicated and individual for that.

So, we learn that the best thing we can do is to take it a step at a time. Sometimes it's one breath at a time. But, we get discouraged because it feels like this pain is never going to end and we're just so tired of dealing with it day in and day out.

Let's try this. Each day choose one step of faith that you will take and then do it. It doesn't have to be big to be a step of faith. How about making today the day you pick up the phone and call a friend? You initiate some friendship instead of waiting for your phone to ring. Tomorrow, how about cooking a small meal. You don't feel like doing it, but that's okay. Do it anyway. Make a simple salad and bake a potato. You can do it!

Buy a notebook, and number it from one to thirty. Choose a step of faith for each day of the month. Promise yourself that you'll do it! Do you know that Mt. Everest was climbed one step at a time?

**The path may be rocky and twisted, but the Shepherd remains by my side every step of the way.**

## Day 289

*"But the fruit of the Spirit is love, joy, peace, patience, kindness, goodness, faithfulness." Galatians 5:22*

How will you know when you're getting stronger in this grief? That's a valid question and one that every person grieving wants to know.

Do you remember when you were really sick with the flu? For several days you were down and out. Your eyes were blurred from fever. Your body ached. You couldn't eat. You were coughing and sneezing. Your felt horrible! Then, you began taking your medication and drinking lots of hot tea. Each day you had some reassuring signs that you were on the mend. Your fever broke, and your body aches left. Your nose stopped dripping and your cough quieted down. You sat up in bed and ate some chicken soup. You were slowly regaining your strength.

That's just how it is when walking this journey of loss. Your strength will return, but it's a slow process. You'll notice little changes every now and then. One week you'll notice the buds appearing on the trees. In a few weeks you notice the days are getting longer. A few weeks later you sit with a cup of coffee on the porch and see the robin searching for its worm. These may be little things, but they are great reminders that you're going through a rebirth. You're walking this journey of loss into a place where you will find new hope!

**No winter lasts forever; no spring skips its turn.**

## Day 290

*"In God I have put my trust, I shall not be afraid." Psalm 56:11*

For a long time following a loss, the only thing on the calendar for the day is grieving. That's not how we planned it, and that's certainly not how we want it, but that's how it is. When living with a broken heart, the pain of loss supersedes everything else in life.

We walk around the house not knowing what to do or how to act. Every thought is consumed with our loss. How did this happen? Why did it happen? I can't really be true. This is all a very bad dream and tomorrow things will be back to normal.

Normal never comes, though. And, this isn't a bad dream. This grieving needs our constant attention. Every part of our life hurts, and we just keep spinning in circles not knowing what to do to get through this pain.

Years ago there was a popular children's book called *There's a Cricket in the Library.* The visuals in this book are very appropriate for grief. After being scolded for disturbing the peace and quiet too many times, the cricket ends up packing his little suitcase and leaving for a while. That's just what we need to do with this grief, as hard and as impossible as it seems. We need to pack it up and send it away for a while. Start by packing it away for fifteen minutes every day. After a while, pack it up for thirty minutes, and keep doing that until you finally find yourself in a place where you and the grief can live together in your own special places in the room.

There really will be a day when you can remember more vividly that your loved one lived, rather than focusing only on the death. Keep reminding yourself of that!

**What a relief to know that life always outshines loss.**

## Day 291

*"Taste and see that the Lord is good; blessed is the one who takes refuge in him." Psalm 34:8*

We try so hard to explain our loss to others using descriptive words, but the words fall so short of the true meaning and depth of our pain. It's like having a hole right in the center of our heart, and every time our heart beats, the pain reminds us that the hole is there. We say it feels like having an arm or leg cut off. It's like trying to walk around, but we don't have all of our body to help us, and the pain is excruciating. We think others understand what we're trying to say, but do they really?

Do they know what it's like to set one extra plate at the dinner table only to have our loved one not show up? Do they know what it's like to make reservations for two to see the play, and then suddenly burst into tears when we realize what we just did. Do they understand what it's like to see all of the children playing on the playground at school and we stop and stare thinking, hoping, and praying that the one we saw really was our child?

The loss is the pain. That's what makes it hurt so much. It's the place that nobody can fill that drives us crazy with anguish and suffering. Of course nobody can understand this pain, because this is our pain and not their pain. How foolish of us to think that we could possibly get others to feel what's inside of our heart and our head.

For today, it's okay that others don't understand. They didn't love the one like we do. That's something that nobody will understand. And, it's okay. It's really okay.

**How much faith is needed to get us through our grief? Just enough—that's all. Just enough.**

## Day 292

*"The name of the Lord is a fortified tower; the righteous run to it and are safe." Proverbs 18:10*

Anger is a word that we don't want to talk about. It's embarrassing to say that we're angry with the world, but honestly isn't that how grief makes us feel sometimes? We're not proud of our anger. Not hardly! We try so hard to subdue our anger, but it's there inside. Every now and then it comes bubbling to the surface, and it isn't pretty.

We're angry at the doctor for making the wrong diagnosis. We're angry with the driver of the other car for speeding. We're angry for the pain our loved one had to endure. We're angry at cancer and diabetes and heart attacks. We're angry at depression and suicide. Oh, how angry we are at those!

We're angry at the unfairness of life, and there's not a thing we can do except be angry. We cry into our pillow every night knowing that this anger is not doing us a bit of good.

Rather than being ashamed of how we're feeling, we need to give ourselves permission to express our emotions, including our anger. What we're feeling is normal, and in time this anger will get more in control. The anger will begin to soften as peace and hope begin to creep ever so quietly into the cracks of our broken heart.

We notice a rainbow and we stare, not in anger, but in thankfulness for a sign from heaven. We look at the brightest star shining in the evening sky, and we're filled with hope that our loved one is shining just for us.

Could this be our sign of hope coming to visit? Could hope be bringing some much-needed peace along with it? For today, let's set our anger aside, and allow the sunshine to touch our cheeks. Oh, how much we needed this gift today!

**Just when you think all hope is gone, the tiny sparrow appears as a reminder that God is near.**

## Day 293

*"Your word is a lamp for my feet, a light on my path."*
*Psalm 119:105*

Some people seem to see invisible signs that say it's okay to cry here, but it's not okay to cry there. The last thing in the world we need is for people to tell us when and where we're allowed to cry! The odd thing about crying is that we don't want to cry in public places. For some reason, it makes us feel weak, and heaven knows we're already feeling weak enough!

We need to step back and think about this. Do we think any less of people for crying when they are struggling or hurt or in pain? Of course we don't! In fact, we have often shed tears right along with them because we are so moved by their painful circumstances.

We don't have to hide our tears. We don't have to be ashamed because we're crying in grief. We certainly shouldn't feel embarrassed for opening the corners of our heart and letting out some of the pain.

Tears are a natural response to the pain of loss and grief. We'll soon notice that when we allow others to see our tears, they will be more willing to sit down and share what's on their heart, too. Fellow grievers. Yes, that's what we are. Fellow grievers who are strong enough to say it's okay to cry.

**A teardrop on earth calls the Creator of the universe to stand by our side.**

## Day 294

*"Cast your cares on the Lord and he will sustain you; he will never let the righteous be shaken." Psalm 55:22*

One of the biggest things we grieve about is the future that has been taken away from us since our loss. In the blink of an eye it's like the slate called "future" was wiped clean. Oh, how much it hurts to know that we'll never dance at our child's wedding. We'll never celebrate another anniversary. We'll never again have a family vacation that can be called complete.

Days, months, and sometimes years are spent in this agonizing state of grieving the loss of the future we dreamed would be ours. One day, though, a lightbulb goes off and we are stopped in our tracks.

We never have the promise of a future. The future is unknown to every one of us. That hurts so much to say, but it's the truth. This one revelation can help us tremendously in our grief walk. Just this one insight about our unknown future can be a critical turning point in our grief if we allow it to be. Our grief often sends us clear messages, and this one is very easily heard.

Live in the moment of today, because that is all any of us is promised. Just today. We don't have control or predications about tomorrow, but we can learn to treasure those small but wonderful miracle moments of today.

**Don't wait any longer. Today is your day. Seize it!**

## Day 295

*"Commit to the Lord whatever you do, and he will establish your plans." Proverbs 16:3*

Ahh, the ocean is so lovely and gives so much peace when sorrow floods the soul. Should you be so lucky to live near the ocean visit it often, cry your tears of grief, and watch the waves carry your pain out to sea.

You might not have the blessing of the ocean, but everyone has the beauty of the infinite blue sky! Have you ever stood under the vast blue heavens and simply let go? Breathe in deeply, exhale slowly while staring at this beautiful creation, and feel the pain you're carrying in your heart begin to ease. The sky is limitless and helps us put our pain and loss into perspective.

Volumes of books have been written about the beauty of the sky. Painters delight in the moods of the sky with the clouds sailing by. You, too, can enjoy a bit of freedom from this heavy weight of grief you've been carrying around when you soak up the beauty of nature found around you.

Do you believe in a higher power? Can you for just a few moments believe? There is such mystery found in nature that it's hard to take it all in. What if your loved one is part of this beauty right now? Can you imagine the bliss? Allow nature to take you to a place of ultimate imagination and break away from the sorrow that is bearing down on you. Allow yourself to feel the peace that surrounds you and believe—really believe—that the one you love is part of all of the beauty and peace right now!

**Every rainbow adorns the sky with a message of God's love.**

## Day 296

*"Cast all your anxiety on him because he cares for you." I Peter 5:7*

Who knows why, but we all do it. All of us who grieve put on a mask and hide behind it. Perhaps we don't want to feel vulnerable in front of others. Maybe we don't always like to share our pain. Or, maybe it's because we're tired of others not understanding what we're going through, so we disguise our sorrow.

The mask is something we learn to use early on in our grief. "How are you?" "I'm okay." Really? Is that really how you're feeling? Inside there is screaming and sobbing and retching. We hold it in until we're alone, and as soon as the mask comes off we turn into another person. We become the person who intimately walks with pain and loss every day.

Maybe there's a reason other than wanting to hide that we wear the mask. Maybe deep down we want to feel normal again. Maybe we need to feel something other than pain. Maybe the mask has become a coping mechanism for us so we don't completely fall apart to the point we're never able to get up again.

We need to learn to be okay for a while with the mask. We've been through a trauma that many will never know, and we have found something that works for us. We've found something that helps us get up in the morning and navigate through the day. That's not so bad, is it? When we feel like we're dying inside, we do what we have to do to keep the flickering flame of hope alive, even if it means wearing the mask.

**God's voice is a constant whisper of hope.**

## Day 297

*"Because he himself suffered when he was tempted, he is able to help those who are being tempted." Hebrews 2:18*

It's to stop beating yourself up over the past. Today is the day to begin letting go of those things that continue to haunt you in your grief and make the burden of guilt a thousand times heavier than it should be.

Do you know that everybody alive has regrets? No one is perfect, including you. There are things you did and said before this loss that you regret. You weren't kind enough. Your words came out sounding harsh and judgmental, but you meant them to help. You lashed out in anger and never said you were sorry. You didn't spend enough time with your loved one. We could go on and on for hours about all of the regrets we have.

When someone we love dies, our regrets become bigger than a mountain and they sit right in front of us staring us in the eyes. It's hard to get past these regrets. There's no doubt about that. But, you have to keep chiseling away at the guilt and knock down that regret list or it will knock you down hard.

It's easier said than done, and it will take a lot of hard work. But, until you forgive yourself, your grief will continue to swallow you up and keep you in a dark lonely pit. You've freely forgiven others, and now it's time to search deep into your heart and forgive yourself!

**Forgiveness is life's way of dealing with unfairness.**

## Day 298

*"May the favor of the Lord our God rest on us; establish the work of our hands for us—yes, establish the work of our hands." Psalm 90: 17*

Today is a good day in our grief and we breathe a long sigh of relief. We go outside, take a long, meandering walk, stop and talk to our neighbor on the way home, and we can say with truth that it feels good to be alive. What a blessed relief to be feeling this good!

All of this wonderfulness takes a wild turn tomorrow when we wake up and feel our emotions jumping wild. What is wrong? Didn't we just have a day of relief and joy yesterday? What went wrong?

We need to remember that the journey of grief following loss isn't an easy one. It's often two steps forward and five back. We think we've made great progress and then grief rears its ugly head and throws us a curveball that we didn't see coming.

Don't let this wavering path get you discouraged. You're doing great. You're out of bed, and you're moving. Maybe you're moving slower today than yesterday, and maybe your tears are flowing like a river, but you're here. You're going to be okay. This is a temporary setback and you're going to be alright. This is all part of this journey. Tomorrow is a brand new day. You're on the track of life and you're moving. That's good enough for now.

**Joy follows sorrow just as surely as spring follows winter. Believe it and you will soon live it.**

## Day 299

*"The righteous person may have many troubles, but the Lord delivers him from them all." Psalm 34:19*

Grief from loss makes us feel kind of crazy for a while. Our minds go every which way, and often we make no sense at all. Of course we don't! Look at all of the pain we've been through!

It's almost like our minds have to begin over again. We doubt so much of what we once believed. We question who we are and what our purpose on earth is. We thought we believed in heaven, but now we're not sure. We were absolute in our faith before our loss, but everything seems all wrong now, including those principles of belief that we once held so near to our heart.

There's something that seems to help and that comes from connecting with nature. It sounds perhaps too easy a solution for so much doubt and disbelief, but the recurring themes in nature create a picture of absolutes that we need right now. The rising and setting of the sun are steadfast and sure. Oh, how much we need to believe and trust in something! The stars that twinkle in the sky are there to guide us through the darkness of the night. What a blessing! The raindrops falling softly from the sky are reminders that God provides for all things.

Yes, there is the word God. Can it be possible that underneath all of these doubts there is still a belief? Maybe. Maybe nature has been the catalyst to begin my belief again!

**Faith is the inborn capacity to see God behind and in everything.**

## Day 300

*"For I know the thoughts that I think toward you, says the Lord, thoughts of peace and not of evil, to give you a future and a hope." Jeremiah 29:11*

Today is the day you've decided you will hum a tune and actually sing along to the words to your favorite song. You've always loved music, and you miss hearing it and singing along. You try, you really, really try, but the sound just won't come. You're blank. You open your mouth and nothing is there.

What has happened? Did grief really take everything away from you? You can't even hum along to the song, much less sing, and your heart saddens once again. You promise yourself you will keep trying until there is a song that comes from your mouth. So, tomorrow you try again, and the next day, and the next day, until finally it happens.

You've reached a mountaintop in your grief. For the first time since your loved one left you're able to hum along to the tune of a song, and it feels like pure victory! You did it. You worked so hard, but you did it. You conquered this goal in your grief, and you proved that there is still some kind of joy in your soul.

Tomorrow you will meet life right where you are and you will try again. You're doing great. Keep humming to that song. You're really doing great!

**You have to fight hard through some really bad days to place a song on your heart.**

## Day 301

*"And God will wipe away every tear from their eyes; there shall be no more death, nor sorrow, nor crying. There shall be no more pain, for the former things have passed away." Revelation 21:4*

There are times when we simply don't want to share our grief. We retreat from everyone knowing we need some alone time. We're not having a pity party. We just feel too tired to tell our story one more time. It takes too much energy to try to explain what we're going through.

Sitting in the quiet of ourselves, we almost feel like an empty shell. So much of our life as we once knew it is gone. We cry tears of sorrow for hours on end because we feel so alone in this grief. If only we knew how to regain some of our zest for living again!

These mood swings are so hard to deal with each day. How can we begin to explain to others how we feel when we don't understand ourselves? For every one step forward we take it feels like we take five steps back.

A day alone is often all it takes to remind us how much we need our friends to help us. So, we call on a friend, we tell our story again, and we cry. Only this time when we cry, we have a friend nearby to lean on! Oh, how much we've come to depend on the strength of those around us to get us through!

**When it rains it pours, but the storm isn't as frightening when sitting under the umbrella with a friend.**

## Day 302

*"Come to me, all you who are weary and burdened, and I will give you rest." Matthew 11:28*

It's never good to move somewhere new immediately after a loss. Why? Because there is great comfort in the familiar. We fool ourselves into thinking that moving will give us a fresh, new beginning. Maybe it will do that in time, but not right away.

Have you ever paid attention to a wounded puppy? Where does it go to find comfort? It stays home, in the familiar, where it knows it will receive lots of love and care. The same is true for us when we are wounded from our grief. If we pack our bags, move out of our home, and go to new surroundings we will find that we are all alone, and that's the last thing we need right now.

Give grief time to settle while you remain in the comfort of the familiar. Too much change too fast will only add to your pain. Grab a cup of tea, sit in your favorite chair, and just be. Breathe slowly. Lean into your grief, and you will find that you are much stronger than you thought you were. Allow that old chair to hold you tight while you cry. That chair knows you and has given you lots of comfort before, and it knows how to take care of you now. In time you'll be able to step outside into the unfamiliar, but right now your grief is plenty enough uncharted territory to live with. There's no reason to add one more burden to your heavy heart!

**There is hope within the face of the familiar.**

## Day 303

*"Have I not commanded you? Be strong and courageous. Do not be afraid; do not be discouraged, for the Lord your God will be with you wherever you go." Joshua 1:9*

When the grief of loss first hits us it's like a ton of bricks. We feel smashed and battered and weak and torn. We feel like we don't have one ounce of energy or strength left within us. During these first weeks of grief our friends are such a blessing to us. They come to visit. They call us often to check in with us. They bring us food. They even come sit with us through the lonely hours of the night.

Then, something happens. Everyone seems to get back to their normal way of life, and the support we once had becomes less and less. We no longer get daily calls. Our visits are less frequent. And, the food stops altogether. Suddenly it dawns on us that we're left to take care of ourselves.

How are we supposed to do that? We feel so lonely and so lost. Do we look for ways to stay extra busy? Do we read books on grief and hope to find answers there? Do we seek the help of a professional counselor? Do we take long, frequent walks in nature? Do we take up a new hobby?

Whatever we do, we need to make certain that it is something that is refreshing and replenishing to the soul. We need to find something that feels good deep down inside of us. How will we know what that is? Just keep experimenting. Little by little we'll find something that suits us. We'll find that special thing that encourages us, lifts our spirits, and helps us feel less alone and a bit more alive! It's up to us to keep that flame of hope burning within as it rekindles the life within our soul!

**Hope is a choice that is always the best choice!**

## Day 304

*"Be strong and take heart, all you who hope in the Lord."*
*Psalm 31:24*

Oh, how much the memories hurt! Memories are a double-edged sword. We want to remember everything we possibly can about the one we loved with all of our heart, but it pains us to much to recall the times we once had. Knowing that never again will we have a birthday, vacation, Christmas, or meal together is heartbreaking.

We reminisce because these memories remind us of the love we once shared. But, these same memories have a way of making our grief feel so raw all over again.

We need to find a balance of remembering the past and living in the present. That's so much easier said than done! When our hurts are aching for the one we love, we revert back to the past because that's where we want to be. Oh, how we long for those days when we had our loved one by our side!

It helps so much if we have someone to remember with us. On those special days like birthdays and holidays why not invite some friends over? The last thing we want to do is be all alone with only our memories. That will only make our grief swell within us and fill our hearts to overflowing sorrow. When memories are shared, so is our grief. We will get through these hard days. But, it's so much better to get through them with a friend!

**What a Friend we have who daily bears our grief!**

## Day 305

*"Trust in the Lord with all of your heart and lean not on your own understanding; in all your ways submit to him, and he will make your paths straight." Proverbs 3:5-6*

It's so discouraging when someone tells us that it takes years and years to work through the grief of loss. Worse yet is when we're told that this pain lasts a lifetime. Where's the hope in that? We know that we'll never feel the same again, but we are hopeful that it won't always feel terrible like we're feeling right now.

We need to be patient and forgiving with ourselves and give lots of room for setbacks. We already know that some days are going to throw us a curveball and we'll end up right back on first base with our grief again. But, for now we know that each day we make it through we've accomplished a lot.

The goal is to make it through just one day at a time. One day, one step, one breath. Then, we repeat that all over again. One day, one step, one breath. As the weeks move on, we begin to notice that every now and then we can throw in one more step, and another and another until we realize that we've actually moved forward in our grief and we can spend several hours without being all-consumed by our loss.

Every day is a new challenge, but every day in grief also gives us a day of new hope!

**Hope always produces the courage to go on!**

## Day 306

*"The Lord himself goes before you and will be with you; he will never leave you nor forsake you. Do not be afraid; do not be discouraged." Deuteronomy 31:8*

It happens every time we walk in nature. We get encouraged. We look at all of the tiniest of details, and we are in awe of creation. Nature is one thing that seals the deal with our belief in a higher power. Everything in nature is so precise and ordered that it's impossible to believe this all came together by mere happenstance.

There's something about loss that creates doubts within us, and that's to be expected. When loss occurred all our our core beliefs came into question. Why did this happen? Is this a punishment of some kind? Why did my loved one die in this way? Why now?

We question. We doubt. We cry out in anguish. Then we take a much-needed walk through the woods, or we go sit in the park and feed the birds. We do a lot of looking and thinking, and the only conclusion we can make is there is a higher power. There is life after death. There is something more.

My doubts fly out the window as I realize that the same God that created the universe created me. The same one who created the beauty found in nature created my loved one. My doubts subside and I feel more calm in my grief. My hope is restored.

**A walk in nature renews our hope.**

## Day 307

*"Therefore encourage one another and build each other up, just as in fact you are doing." I Thessalonians 5:11*

It's so easy to get discouraged when wading through a sea of grief. We feel so overcome with sadness, loneliness, and the feeling that we've somehow let down the one we loved. We struggle with these feelings day after day, trying so hard to move forward, but it's not easy. The thoughts of worry for the future plague us, and we grow tired and feel so weak.

After a while, though, we realize we're still here, still trying hard to work through this loss, and we're actually doing it. We didn't give up along the way like we thought we would. We didn't cave in to discouragement. We're still plodding along in life, making small steps toward stepping outside of our grief. And we realize maybe we're actually much stronger than we initially thought.

The months keep passing, and slowly we notice a growing strength within us. It feels so good to get through a few days without tears. Then, we find ourselves beginning to smile more about everyday life. We begin noticing the sunshine and flowers. We can hear the birds singing in the background. We see the swaying of the trees during a gentle breeze. And, we know that something wonderful has happened. We're going to make it! Yes, we are learning to live within our grief and we're going to make it!

**Hope is what keeps you going when all reason within says to give up.**

## Day 308

*"Eye has not seen, nor ear heard, nor have entered into the heart of man the things which God has prepared for those who love Him." I Corinthians 2:9*

We all do it because that's how grief works. We sit our loved one on a pedestal of perfection. Why do we do this? Because that's how a grieving heart works. We only remember the kind, wonderful, and good things about the one we loved, and that's such a blessing.

Every so often, though, when stories of remembrances are being told to us by others, they'll remind us of our loved one's imperfections. We recoil in hurt and we don't want to hear anything negative at all. It's so hard to hear that the one we loved wasn't perfect. Oh, we know it, but we don't want anything except accolades repeated. We feel bound by some kind of griever's code of love to protect our loved one's name forever and ever.

As hard as it is, every now and then it's good to have a small bit of a reality check. It helps us to stop from digressing into a deep pit of regret over things not said or done. Self-blame is a terrible thing to live with, and we don't deserve to punish ourselves over and over for not being the perfect parent, child, sibling, spouse, or friend. Nobody's perfect—not even the one we loved so dearly!

Today practice some much-needed forgiveness and acceptance of yourself. You've shown unconditional love for the one who died. Now it's time to show the same unconditional love to yourself while you're alive.

You've been through a lot, and a bit of self-acceptance will go a long way in your journey through grief.

**God pours His love on us constantly and unconditionally even when we feel we don't deserve it.**

## Day 309

*"Do not be anxious about anything, but in every situation, by prayer and petition, with thanksgiving, present your requests to God. The peace of God, which transcends all understanding, will guard your hearts and your minds in Christ Jesus." Philippians 4:6-7*

Most often grievers are also worriers. Our hearts worry about so much of the future. We can't handle thinking about how things are going to be a day from now, much less a year from now. We worry about what the holidays without our loved one will be like. We worry about our family's response to this loss. We worry about future birthdays and anniversary dates. We worry about how we will keep our loved one's memory alive. We worry about every future unknown that there is.

Worry is a form of fear, and it's no wonder that we've become filled with worry. Look at all we've been through! But, there comes a time when we must stop, step away from our grief and do some honest looking at this thing called worry.

Worry doesn't help us in any way at all. In fact, it wears us down, depletes our energy and takes up our precious time. Worry never solves anything, nor does it change anything. We're anxious about things that most often never happen. Worry consumes us day and night and drives away any carefree thoughts we might possibly have.

Let's make a promise to ourselves that today we will worry about one less thing. Let's practice non-worrying. We can do this for a day at a time. If that's too much, let's try to spend one hour a day without any kind of worry. Instead, let's fill our minds with pictures of beautiful, tranquil seas. Let's breathe in slowly and feel the warm sunshine on our face. As we close our eyes, let's picture a green meadow with soft grass sprinkled with daisies bending ever so gently in the summer breeze.

When we practice leaving our worries behind, we will begin to feel true healing in our grief!

**Anxious thoughts rob us of God's intended joy.**

## Day 310

*"When you pass through the waters, I will be with you; and when you pass through the rivers, they will not sweep over you. When you walk through the fires, you will not be burned; the flames will not set you ablaze." Isaiah 43:2*

The roller coaster ride of grief is rough. We never quite know what turns lie ahead, nor do we know how many hills and fast slides down we're going to encounter while on this ride. When loss takes place, something very strange happens to us. We no longer see our world in colors, but rather we see our world as gray. The sun stops shining for us. Night turns into day without much change. We fail to see the flowers blooming, or to hear the birds chirping. Our world has suddenly become different and so very unpredictable.

After months on this whirlwind ride of emotions, we begin to have a bit more control. At times we can even put on the brakes and slow down. But, we never give ourselves permission to jump off of this ride and take a walk among the quiet places in life. We seem to think that our world consists only of grief and anything else has ceased to exist.

We're braver than this. We know that we are, but it takes courage to stop the grief train and step off. We're so afraid of what we'll see in the world without our loved one. We allow fear to keep us trapped on the roller coaster until one day we make a decision. This is it. I'm pulling the brake and stopping to explore this land of new normal.

Ever so slowly we begin looking around us and, much to our surprise, there is color in our world once again. No, the colors aren't brilliant purple and red, but there are subtle, soft colors of sky blue, aqua, and sunshine yellow. We look all around our new world and we see warmth and a welcome mat that lets us know there is a place for us here. We were so afraid that there was never going to be a place where we could see beauty again. This new world is far different than the world we once knew, but it is now ours, and there are blessings to enjoy as we gently step outside of grief. We are slowly learning how to breathe in the fresh air of new hope and it feels so good!

**Can you see it? No day is so dark that there is not at least some light.**

## Day 311

*"What, then, shall we say in response to these things? If God is for us, who can be against us?" Romans 8:31*

Not everyone will understand this, but those who have lost a loved one will. There is a longing inside of us to write our loved one a letter. We didn't get to say all that was in our heart before this untimely departure, and the words are yearning to be told. So, we must follow our grieving heart.

We share all of the things we never could say before. We lavish our loved one with words of compassion. We don't hold back saying how proud we are, and how appreciative we've been for all of the ways their life has blessed us. We shed tears of sorrow in our letter. Tears of sadness and regret for all of the moments we missed to spend precious time together. We ask for forgiveness for those times when we spoke unkindly and for when we lost our temper and spoke harsh words in anger.

Our letter is an outpouring of love from our heart. It is by far the most honest, open, beautiful love letter we've ever written. We wonder how we've found just the right words to express how we feel. We take this letter and hold it close to our heart while soaking it with our tears.

Can our loved one really hear what we've said? Can this love letter reach the one who has gone? We will never know for certain, but what would be wrong with believing that these words have reached the one we love? For the sake of quieting some of our grief, we believe that this love letter of honesty and beauty has served its purpose of mending any wrongs, and keeping our relationship bound in love throughout all of eternity. Now we are free to grieve in peace.

**Pain always leads us to a place of new hope.**

## Day 312

*"The name of the Lord is a fortified tower; the righteous run to it and are safe." Proverbs 18:10*

Have you ever been caught in a drenching rain when the thunder began to roar and the lightning flashed across the sky? Probably the very first thought that hit you was to run as fast as you possibly could to find safety from the storm. The same is true for us when we are caught in the middle of a life storm such as loss. We want to run for shelter but we don't know where to go.

Seeking shelter from the storms of life has always been difficult, but it doesn't have to be that way. Slow down and think for a moment about all of the ways we are protected during storms. We have friends and family who will listen to us. If need be, they will feed us a warm meal, give us a comfortable bed to sleep in, and provide words of encouragement until the storm passes.

We also have the blessing of the written word. We live in a time when the written word can be accessed in just a matter of seconds in the form of e-books. If we want to seek shelter by surrounding ourselves with words of encouragement, we can do that so easily.

What about prayer? Is it possible that prayer is the one source that has the most powerful effect on us, yet we don't use it often enough? Today, let's tap into this power found in prayer. Let's pray to our higher power and ask for shelter from this most difficult storm of loss. Let's ask and believe that we will receive shelter.

Let's close our eyes and ask for the strength we need from deep within our soul to be protected as we are tossed to and fro in the eye of this storm. Let's pray and believe and allow prayer to have its way with us.

**There is no such thing as an unanswered prayer. Believe it. Receive it. Give thanks for it.**

## Day 313

*"Are not five sparrows sold for two pennies? Yet not one of them is forgotten by God. Indeed, the very hairs of your head are all numbered. Don't be afraid; you are worth more than many sparrows." Luke 12:6-7*

There's not a person around who doesn't feel the pain of loneliness when going through a loss. The support is there in the first months following the loss, but slowly the phone stops ringing, the doorbell remains quiet, and friends stop asking how we're doing. It feels so lonely inside of this skin of grief.

It would be easy to have a full-blown pity party and be safe in saying we deserve it. But, we know that's not what we want to do. We need simple validation for our loss. We need someone to be there when the ache of grief becomes overwhelming. We don't want to be alone in our brokenness because it's too frightening.

Since our loss, we've slipped out of touch with a lot of reality. We can't remember what it's like to be so busy that we barely have time to brush our teeth. Grief has a way of making time stand still for us, and we mistakenly think that the same is true for all of our friends. The hard truth is that life moves on for others. It has to. They're not being hurtful to us. Moving on is just a fact of life.

Rather than sit in our loneliness, why not invite a friend over for some tea and a piece of pie? Use that time together to freely talk and share. You'll be surprised how much this time together will help!

**A cup of tea and a friend always produces new hope.**

## Day 314

*"Where does my help come from? My help comes from the Lord, the Maker of heaven and earth." Psalm 121:1-2*

We have this grief, this loss, on our minds night and day. There is never a moment when we're free from thinking about it. We might consciously choose to think of other moments in time, but we know with full certainty that buried in the subconscious it's still there. Why then do our friends think that by mentioning the name of our loved one they will bring up old sadness?

Oh, how much we wish others knew the healing we receive when we hear the mention of our loved one's name. Old grief? How can this be old grief when we wear it with us all of the time? We never bury grief the way one can bury a lie. A lie can be forgiven and forgotten, but a grief will always remain with us. It is now part of our entire being. That's not to say that our grief will define who we are, but our grief is part of us and we will carry it within our heart all the days of our lives.

The next time someone apologizes for bringing up the sadness of loss, we will respond with a thank you for remembering. Remembering not only brings to mind the sadness, but also the joy. Never does one want to forget those details that made the one we love so special!

**The greater the happiness, the greater could be the sadness. That is the price one pays for love.**

## Day 315

*"I have told you these things so that in me you may have peace. In this world you will have trouble. But take heart! I have overcome the world!" John 16:33*

There are so many things to consider when a loss occurs. The future as we once had hoped is wiped away. How can we possibly accept so much loss?

Life seems so bleak for a while until we stop and sit quietly and take stock of all of the precious moments we had to share. Life was so beautiful at one time, and not everyone gets to enjoy blessings like that. We miss those times. We miss the one who has now left us so very much. But our heart swells with memories that take us to a place when life was sweet beyond compare. Only we can enjoy those memories because they are uniquely ours. It hurts so much to know that we can never make more of those memories, but it helps so much to know how full our heart is of those times spent together.

Nature teaches us so much about life and loss. Hold a beautiful blooming flower in your hand. Study all of the details of color and design that make that flower stunning beyond compare. We enjoy the fragrance left behind by that flower, and we treasure the peaceful moments that the flower in bloom gives us. But, we know that flower will not be here forever. The same is true for our lives. We are never promised tomorrow. That's why these memories are held so dear. They help us to recall the good and precious times we were given to enjoy.

**A precious memory can be the best friend of all.**

## Day 316

*"Cast your cares on the Lord and He will sustain you. He will never let the righteous be shaken." Psalm 55:22*

Life can be rolling along okay when suddenly, out of nowhere, the tears begin streaming down our face. A song has just come on the radio that brings back a surge of new grief. Oh, how much it hurts! It's so raw and hits us hard. It feels like we're starting this grief walk all over again. We fill with doubt and fear wondering if we've made any progress at all.

Why do we put so much pressure on ourselves? We have had our loved one with us for a long time—long enough to fill our entire heart with joy and love. When loss took place, a huge hole was left right in the center of our heart, and now we have no clue how to fill it.

Tending to a broken heart takes time and lots of hard work. Every day we feel the hole and every day we try to live within this brokenness. Some days we do well; other days are terribly difficult. One thing is for certain, for each day that we get up out of bed, get dressed and look for the sunrise welcoming a new day, we're showing great courage. We are slowly filling that space in our heart with renewed hope one step, one hour, one breath at a time.

**Sometimes I don't see the big picture because I can't. There are too many tears. God tenderly asks me to trust.**

## Day 317

*"You are my refuge and shield; I have put my hope in your word." Psalm 119:114*

Sometimes we're in so much pain that we can't see the effects this grief is having on us. Friends tell us we look tired, and we get our feelings hurt. Our family tells us we seem on edge all of the time and we snap back at them. Our co-workers become concerned because we can't get through a day without crying, and we tell them that we'll be just fine.

It's often difficult to see how deeply we've fallen into the pit of despair unless those close to us gently point it out to us. Self-care is something we don't always think about when grieving a loss, but it's so necessary. We know that we're not feeling well, and we realize we're exhausted from all of this grief, but it's so difficult to admit that we need to stop and simply be still for a while.

Why do we feel such a need to prove to others that we're so strong that we don't need any help? When we are working our way through grief we need others to lean on. They're willing to help us, but it's difficult if we continue to push them away.

Wouldn't it feel refreshing to sit under the shade of a tree and collect our thoughts while taking in the sights and sounds of nature? We weren't meant to carry heavy burdens of pain all of the time. In fact, we know that we can't keep going like this. It's time to say I surrender. I need help. This is our time to rest and allow this pain to be shared. It's our turn to graciously and thankfully accept some help.

**Sometimes hope comes in the form of a friend.**

## Day 318

*The is my rock and my fortress and my deliverer, my God, my rock, in whom I take refuge, my shield, and the horn of my salvation, my stronghold. Psalm 18:2*

Working our way through grief isn't easy. We know we need to find something that serves as an outlet for our pain. Not everyone was meant to write a book or to sit down in front of a easel and paint a lovely picture in order to work our way through grief. We can, however, write down some thoughts from time-to-time.

Grief is a journey and it's wise to chart this journey if only with a few words. "Today was dark and gloomy. Yesterday it rained all day and I stayed in my bedroom. I slept through the night for the first time in six months. I took a walk around the block and finally was able to hear the birds chirping. Yesterday I set my alarm and made it outside to the edge of the field to watch the gorgeous sunrise."

Our words tell the story of the progression of our grief journey from heartbreak to hope. When we have it written down, even though the words are few, we can be encouraged to see the progress we've made.

If writing isn't your cup of tea, maybe you'd find some peace in putting together puzzles. Start with something easy and work your way up to putting together a picture of a thousand pieces. How healing that would be to see the finished product!

Find some way to let the grief flow through you. Choose something that you enjoy doing, and allow it to be your grief guide. You'll be amazed at the progress you're making!

**There is no burden so heavy that God cannot lift it.**

# Day 319

*"But those who hope in the Lord will renew their strength. They will soar on wings like eagles; they will run and not grow weary, they will walk and not be faint."*
*Isaiah 40:31*

There are days when we want to throw our hands up in the air and give up. We want to walk away and never come back. We drop so low in our grief that we can't see anything except the dark clouds hanging overhead. We've all been there. We feel flat inside. Empty. Devoid of all emotion.

We feel like there will never be another day worth living. We have fallen into the pit of depression and we don't know how we're ever going to get free from this mess. Worse yet, we don't even care. We've given up all hope.

And, then it happens. It's like a miracle taking place. We can't explain it, but we know how it feels. We've cried until there are no more tears left in us. We've screamed until we have no voice left. But, this feeling comes over us and we feel some strange kind of peaceful knowing that we're going to get through this.

Right at that moment, the phone rings, and we get enough voice back that we can talk. We gain our composure and we realize that our friend needs us. We no longer feel powerless and unwanted. In an instant we're given some purpose again, and that's all it takes to get us in a better frame of mind.

We can feel the energy of hope returning to us, and we give a big sigh of relief knowing we've just passed through one more stormy day of grief and made it ashore.

**When life seems so dark and empty, remember that it is filled with the presence of Angels. We are never left to struggle in this life alone!**

## Day 320

*"Be strong and take heart, all you who hope in the Lord."*
*Psalm 31:24*

Losing a loved one is a trauma not to be taken lightly. Not everyone understands this until it happens to them. For a long time it feels like all life for us has stopped. We can't figure out where we are or what we're supposed to do in the world of unknowns.

It's as though we're in a daze, frozen in an ice block with nothing to help thaw us out. This grief is too much for us to handle all at once. Strangely helpful is how life seems to pull us along whether or not we want to participate. At first we get aggravated and even a bit angry that the rest of the world hasn't shut down because of our loss. Thankfully, though, the world is pressing on and is tugging at us to step out in faith and wet our feet to this thing called life again.

It's frightening to think about, but we know we that at some point we have to begin living again. It will be different, and we know that. But, we also know that shutting down all purpose for living isn't helpful, and it is certainly not what our loved one would want us to do.

We begin to emerge from our cocoon much like the butterfly. We take it very slowly at first. It's odd how learning to live again happens for us. We thought we were totally withdrawn from life when the truth is that we've been growing through our pain all along! Finally we realize that we have more courage than we ever dreamed possible. We're alive. We finally realize we're alive!

**Your hope is much stronger than your fear; you can do this!**

## Day 321

*"When you pass through the waters, I will be with you; and when you pass through the rivers, they will not sweep over you. When you walk through the fire, you will not be burned; the flames will not set you ablaze." Isaiah 43:2*

It feels like too much! All of this grief that is swallowing us up each day is just too much for our heart to handle. The message around us to give up is loud and clear.

But, we don't give up. We persevere for one more day. And, then another. And, another. Finally we begin to notice some little things about us. When we're working we are also humming the tune of a favorite song. We ask ourselves how that happened. How is this possible? We are awake early enough in the mornings to take a brisk walk to begin the day. Again we ask ourselves when this happened? Wasn't it just last week that we didn't have enough energy to get up off of the couch?

We pass by the bakery, and the aroma of freshly baked bread catches us off guard. We stop and go back into the bakery and stand still for a long, long time just experiencing the different smells of the pastries and pies baking. Is this possible? Are we really able to smell again without crying?

It's the little things that have been happening that have pointed us into the arena living life once again. We were so consumed with our grief that we didn't notice that we were taking baby steps back to life again, and it feels so good. It feels so very, very good!

**It is God to whom and with whom we travel. While He is the end of our journey, He is also at every stopping point along the way.**

## Day 322

*"Never will I leave you; never will I forsake you." Hebrews 13:5*

Our faith was so strong before this loss happened, but then it went right out the window. We're so detached from our faith now that it's hard to remember we had any faith at all. Grief tugs and pulls at our faith and throws all kinds of hard, unanswerable questions in our face. We're all mixed up and the truth is right now it's easier not to believe than to pretend to be a person of faith.

Something's wrong, though. Something doesn't feel right deep down in the core of our being. We're never at peace. Never. Not only have we lost our faith, but we've lost our joy. Life has become meaningless.

We wonder aloud. Can we possibly believe that there is a God and that this God is near to us even within our deepest, darkest sorrow? We know it's impossible to see what's lying ahead around the corner, but is it possible that we can have faith for one day?

We brush off our wounded selves and look up to the expanse of the big, blue sky and we tremble in awe. Yes, we can believe. We can believe that the heavens above are big enough to hold our loved one until we meet again.

**When at a critical crossroads in life, always choose hope.**

## Day 323

*"May the favor of the Lord our God rest on us; establish the work of our hands for us. Yes, establish the work of our hands." Psalm 90:17*

Probably the hardest part about this grief work is knowing that there is nobody who can do it for us. We can get tons of support, and we should do that. We can attend seminars and workshops and educate ourselves on grief, but at the end of the day we will still be the one that has to work through our own grief.

That's frightening, to say the least. Knowing that nobody can do this except ourselves is terrifying! There comes that critical moment when we can no longer hide from our grief, but we must face it head-on. What will happen? Will we be able to do this? What's it going to be like?

Most times we don't even realize when that turning point moment occurs in our grief. We've been working towards this moment of having a face-off with grief all along, but we didn't realize it. We thought we were making no progress at all when all along we were taking steps forward—courageous steps forward.

We drove alone to the grocery store. We spent an entire day alone. We took a walk to the end of the driveway, paused and took in the sights and sounds of nature. We slept through the night. We watched the sunset in complete amazement at its beauty. We cooked a meal. We extended an invitation to a friend to go see a movie together.

All along we've been having our face-to-face moments with grief, and we've been showing our courage. Quietly, persistently, and hopefully we've been facing our grief.

**Hope keeps on going when all reason says to stop.**

## Day 324

*"Depend on the Lord; trust Him, and He will take care of you." Psalm 37:5*

It's difficult for others to see us grieving. That's probably one of the biggest reasons they leave us in our grief. It's too hard for them to see us crying so much. It's too hard for them to hear our constant questions. It's too hard for them to see us in so much pain knowing that it can't be fixed.

It would be better for others to leave us stranded in our grief than to tell us to hurry up with our grieving. That's almost like telling a newborn baby to stand up and start jogging. It can't be done. Grief is a journey and for most of us this journey lasts a lifetime. Yes, we will eventually learn how to predict our bad days and prepare for them. We know that we are a changed person and our old self will never return. We know that grief takes a lot of time, and that's exactly what we're doing. We're giving our grief time to bring about some healing.

How much time is needed for the griever? If only there was a definite answer! The only right answer is enough time to find a place of hope. That's as individual as our fingerprint and as important as our heartbeat. Giving ourselves permission to grieve in our own way and in our own time is one of the most precious gifts we can give!

**When life gives us a hundred reasons to cry, hope gives us a thousand reasons to smile.**

## Day 325

*"Continue praying, keeping alert, and always thanking God." Colossians 4:2*

Following a loss people often ask us how we're feeling. It's really difficult to know just how to answer that question. We don't know how we're feeling because our emotions vary from day to day, sometimes from hour to hour. What's worse is we don't know how to compare our feelings any more. We don't remember when we felt good since grief entered our lives. We simply know we're not feeling right.

In order to answer the question, most often we simply say we're okay. What a vague answer to such a complex question! There is some good in answering that way, though. Our subconscious behaves according to the thoughts we feed it. What if we constantly said we feel miserable or terrible or hopeless? Our minds would begin believing that these are the only feelings we have, and it would be terribly difficult to persuade our minds otherwise.

What if just for today we said we felt stronger? What if we said we felt more hopeful? What if we said we believe we're moving along slowly but surely in our grief? Today let's arm ourselves with words of power and hope. Let's keep repeating these words over and over again to ourselves until we begin believing them. How are we today? Better. Courageous. Hopeful. Positive. Thankful. Guaranteed we're going to have a better day in our grief when these words are part of our vocabulary!

**I am in charge of how I feel and today I am filled with hope.**

## Day 326

*"Therefore encourage one another and build each other up, just as in fact you are doing." I Thessalonians 5:11*

People mean well when they try to encourage us in our grief, but sometimes it doesn't come out that way. It would be a lot better if they came up beside us and gave us a hug rather than rattled off some words that leave a biting sting with us for weeks to come.

"Your husband is so much better off. At least he's out of pain."

"God needed one more little angel to brighten up heaven."

"God chooses the best to go first."

"You can always have another baby."

"At least she's now in peace."

"He lived a good life. You can be thankful for that."

"I know exactly how you feel."

When we are grieving, we're extra sensitive to every word that is spoken to us. What normally wouldn't hurt us deeply, not only hurts us, but the words linger with us and play over and over again in our heads like an unending echo.

We need listening ears. We have our story to tell, and right now it's the most important story we know. We need caring people who will listen. The next time some well meaning person tries to help by saying words that really hurt, we will be brave enough to ask them to stop talking and listen. Just listen. That is the best help of all.

**A quiet morning with a loving God puts the events of the upcoming day into proper perspective.**

## Day 327

*"All you who put your hope in the Lord be strong and brave." Psalm 31:24*

Dealing with today's sorrows is difficult. We feel lost and alone and terrified at the idea of facing a new day without knowing what is to come. Loss has a way of leaving us dangling by a thread. We feel as though all control has flown out the window, and we are left to blow with the wind. Deep down we know that isn't true, but that's how we're feeling at the moment. We feel so vulnerable now that we've suffered a loss.

Our mind can begin to work overtime if we allow it. We begin recounting all of our errors of the past, and all of the ways we could have been better. We fret and worry as we remember more and more regrets. Then, we switch into forward gear and start thinking of all of the special events and moments we will miss because of our loss. Our mind goes in circles filling more and more of its susceptible places with fear, doubt, regret, and sorrow.

When this kind of nonproductive thinking begins we need to put a halt to it, or these thoughts will eventually destroy us. Let's face it. We can't go back and change one thing in the past. We can't make events of our life turn out differently. We can't take back words that were already said. This is senseless worry and an extra burden of guilt that will weigh us down.

The same is true of the future. We can't predict the future, so why spend endless nights awake worrying about it? Let's try really hard to keep focused on one thing—today. Let's try our best to get through today one hour, one thought, one breath at a time. This will help us to stay on track and to chunk down our grief into sizeable amounts that we're able to handle!

**It takes a focused vision to see God in the painful storms of life.**

## Day 328

*"Now may the God of hope fill you with all joy and peace in believing, that you may abound in hope by the power of the Holy Spirit." Romans 15:13*

Signs of the holiday season are everywhere. Twinkling lights. Decorated houses and streets. Christmas carols playing on the radio. Glittering decorations in store windows. Candy canes
and Santa Claus. Stockings hung by the chimney. Churches with nativity scenes, and Christmas plays performed by the children. Merriment is everywhere...at least it is supposed to be the happiest season of all!

For many, the holiday season is a time of sad reflection, loneliness, and a reminder of pain and loss. Holiday depression is a very real thing. A person touched by illness, broken relationships, addiction, job loss, or the death of a loved one finds it hard, if not impossible, to sing Christmas carols and really mean it.

When you are struggling with heartache due to loss, it's important to remind yourself many times over that your pain will not last forever. You have an inner strength, hope, that will help carry you through the dark times. Just as a Christmas cactus knows when to bloom, your inner strength knows exactly when to bloom for you.

Be calmed by the peace of the holiday season, and allow hope to fill your heart with new courage. You are much stronger than you think! Because we have a Savior, we can claim this day as a miraculous gift to enjoy!

**Inner peace grows in proportion to our hope.**

## Day 329

*"The wisdom that comes from God is first of all pure, then peaceful, gentle, and easy to please." James 3:17*

We've entered a land of grief and it isn't a good fit. It feels painfully uncomfortable and we wish we could take it off like a heavy coat and lay it aside once and for all. But, grief doesn't work like that. It has become part of us. It has infiltrated through our pores into the very depths of our soul and there it abides. Forever.

What we do with our grief becomes a very personal thing. Others will try to tell us how to rid ourselves of grief, pull ourselves up by the bootstraps and move on, but we know better. Grief can't be shoved away once it has entered our core. We do have choices, though.

We can choose to let our grief multiply day after day until it runs amuck causing havoc within our body, mind, and soul, or we can choose to learn how to live within our grief and allow it to have a corner in which to dwell. Easier said than done, but it is possible!

Every day grief presents itself in a new and different way. Once we understand that, we can begin to see our grief as a bit more manageable. It's not as overpowering as it once seemed. When we face our grief daily and have a heart-to-heart talk with it, we can be more aware of its presence within and we can meet our grief head-on with hope. When grief says quit, we say keep on. When grief says we can't do it, we say we can persevere. When grief says life will be never be worth living again, we say we will find new miracles of hope and joy. And, the more we practice this, the more we will learn how to live within our grief rather than be controlled by our grief!

**There is no medicine like hope, no incentive so great, and no tonic so powerful as the expectation of a coming miracle.**

## Day 330

*"Come to me all you who are weary and burdened, and I will give you rest." Matthew 11:28*

One of the worst things we have to deal with during our hardest days of grief is the sheer exhaustion we feel every day. Grieving a loss is hard, endless work, and it's ever so tiring! There isn't even a good descriptive word to use for this kind of tired. It's being tired from the inside out. It's a kind of tired that makes us feel heavy, foggy, and unspirited. We muddle through our days without much emotion other than sadness.

We know this is no way to live, but we don't know what to do about it. If only there was a clear cut plan, a ten-step road that leads to the abandonment of grief, but there isn't. This grief walk is different for everyone, and we know that. Just thinking about it is exhausting. It's like being on a journey that has no end in sight.

There is hope, though. When we look at others who have traveled similar journeys of loss, we see them smiling. They seem to have energy for the day. They even have a look that says to us that they're actually able to be somewhat happy about a few years on this road of grief.

Today, rather than think of the exhaustion and hopelessness of grief, I will focus on the people I know who are further down the road than I am in this journey, and I will picture their smile. I will allow this smile to give me some energy. I can do this. I can make it through today because I know others who have done the same!

**Sometimes the best thing you can do is not wonder, not imagine, not obsess. Just breathe. Breathe and have faith that everything will work out because it will.**

## Day 331

*"Peace I leave with you; my peace I give you. I do not give to you as the world gives. Do not let your hearts be troubled and do not be afraid." John 14:27*

Our minds can drive us half crazy with worry when we're grieving a loss. We think of every imaginable thing that can go wrong in life now that we've experienced the worst—the death of the one we loved so very much. To experience a loss is to go through a major trauma, and trauma leaves us wounded in ways we never felt before.

Life feels shaky following a loss. What bad thing will happen today? Will this be the day I get another horrible phone call? Can we make it through this year without another loss? It's almost as though grief is holding a carrot and dangling it in front of us saying, "Follow me. Come on, follow me into the valley of despair."

We realize our thoughts need to take a major turnaround, but it sure is easier said than done. Creating a new thought pattern during grief is going to take some time and some major focusing.

We know that we have to do it if we're going to survive this trauma and attempt to live life joyfully again.

How about if we begin one thought at a time? One positive thought for each day is something that we can do. Today I will take a half-hour walk and focus on the beauty of nature. I will look for birds, squirrels, and chipmunks. I will stop along the way to smell the flowers. I will stand under the big, blue sky, and I will remind myself that a power much greater than I is in control. I don't have to worry today, so I won't. Today I will feel the relief in letting go of my worry. Today I will simply breathe and let it be.

**God has given us many promises for hope and joy. Take a promise today and make it yours.**

## Day 332

*"Anyone who is having troubles should pray. Anyone who is happy should sing praises."*

It's been used since the beginning of time, and it has been debated for as long. This thing called prayer is difficult to understand. It's especially hard to trust in prayer when grieving a loss. We pray for peace, but instead our hearts are troubled. We pray for healing and each day feels worse than the day before. We pray for strength for the day, but instead our body is weak from exhaustion.

We prayed for healing for our loved one, but it didn't happen.

We wrestle day and night with this thing called prayer. Should we or shouldn't we pray? Does it matter at all if we pray? Are our prayers really heard and answered? Some people have gone to their deaths defending prayer. They have told story after story about how prayer brought them relief during times of deep inner pain and struggles. They are able to forgive because of prayer. They are able to find peace in the midst of life's greatest pain and sorrow.

Why not give it a try? We have nothing to lose, and this thing called prayer just might work. Grief is a joy robber and a sleep thief. If we can get relief enough to sleep and peace enough to smile, then prayer is definitely worth trying. Today we will say a simple prayer. "Lord, give me peace within, for you know how much I need help. Amen."

**Deep in the heart of every person lies a seed of hope wrapped in a prayer.**

## Day 333

*You will be secure, because there is hope; you will look about you and take your rest in safety. Job 11: 18*

If only we could get rid of this pain. How many times we've said these words since our loss. We're so tired of feeling constant pain. We wish we could take off this pain like we'd take off a coat and set it in a corner for a while. But, we know we can't do that.

Sometimes we turn to things to numb our pain like alcohol or pills. We need to be really careful that we don't get sucked into the false assumption that a temporary numbing will help us. An antidepressant or a glass of wine before bed might be what the doctor ordered, but we need to use caution that we don't overdo it. We need to be careful not to do anything harmful to our minds or bodies.

Remember that it takes time to get through the hard parts of this suffering. That time is going to be different for each and every one. But, eventually we will feel stronger. We will never feel just like we did before our loss, but in time we can be happy again. That's why we must take special care. We have not stopped living life yet. There's a lot left to see, and dare we say there's a lot left to enjoy.

**When the world says to give up, the voice of God continues to whisper "hold on."**

## Day 334

*"Very truly, I tell you, you will weep and mourn...you will have pain, but your pain will turn into joy." John 16:20*

Why do we have to have holidays after a loss? Doesn't the world understand our pain? When we are grieving we wish so much that those around us understood how hard it is to see all of the glitter and tinsel and hustle and bustle of family holidays when our lives have changed so drastically. We feel terrible inside, and we face these holidays with dread, rather than any kind of anticipated joy. Grief is especially hard around any holiday or special anniversary date.

As time goes on something happens, though. Our grief shifts from raw pain to a more subdued ache. And, that ache eventually softens into something that we carry deep within our heart. We know it's there, but it doesn't have the same sharp, stabbing pain as it once did. Oh, how thankful we are for that!

During this time of the shifting of our pain, something else happens. We no longer dread the memories that emerge as we once did. Our memories fall softer on our hearts and give us a calming comfort. We remember with love how blessed we are to have this part of our loved one remain with us. Precious memories, oh how they comfort our soul!

**As long as we have memories yesterday remains, and as long as we have hope there will be the gift of tomorrow.**

## Day 335

*"Nothing in the world will ever be able to separate us from the love of God." Romans 8:39*

Reminders are everywhere it seems. We open a closet door and a jacket appears to jump out at us. We pull open the dryer, and there is that sock that has been missing for over a year. We go outside and look for the rake, and out of nowhere appears the hat that holds a million and one memories. Coincidence? Maybe. We'd rather think that these pieces of our loved one have come as a reminder that all is well.

Can we ever prove that the feather floating through the air at just the right time was a message from heaven? Did the shiny penny that was found heads up have any real meaning? What about the cardinal that appeared out of nowhere and sat upon the windowsill?

We cherish these treasures. We hold them close to our heart, because this is the only communication we have between the now and the forevermore with our loved one. Grief brings us to a whole new level of spiritual awareness. At first it was a bit frightening, but now we've grown accustomed to looking for treasures.

Call it what you may, but we'll simply say that our loved one paid a visit. We get great comfort in these visits and sometimes this is all we have to keep us going until the next time.

**There is no death; only a change of worlds.**

## Day 336

*"The name of the Lord is a strong tower; the righteous run to it and are safe." Proverbs 18:10*

We remember every single detail of that day. At first it was just a fog, but little by little when the numbness wore off everything became acutely clear. We don't want to remember. We don't try to remember. But, it happens often. We wake up at night remembering details. We go to bed promising we won't think about it, but it's there. The moment our loved one left us our world changed.

We know that this isn't healthy to keep recounting every detail. But, the mind is so tricky. We have to work daily to keep tabs on our thoughts, or they will run away with us to a place where we don't want to go.

What a gift we have in the beauty of nature! When our world is crashing in and we can't deal with this pain any more, we can escape to the beauty of a world that has been created just for times like these. If we're unable to visit the ocean and walk along the peaceful shore, technology can take care of that for us. All we have to do is watch a video and we can be placed anywhere in the world we'd like to be in the matter of seconds. We can look off of the peak of the Swiss Alps, or we can peer across the Grand Canyon. We can take a siesta under a palm tree.

Everyone needs a mental break from the heaviness of grief. Today take fifteen minutes and allow your mind to take you to a far away place where you can only see and feel peace and tranquility. You deserve this and a whole lot more!

**Our valleys may be filled with sorrows and tears; but we can lift our eyes to the hills to see God and the angels constantly watching over us.**

## Day 337

*"Pray and ask God for everything you need, always giving thanks." Philippians 4:6*

Some of us are just plain stubborn. We foolishly think that we can handle anything in this life alone, including our grief. However, this is one time we're going to need some help. There's nothing valiant about trying to prove how strong we are when inside the pain is squeezing the life right out of us.

Grief is terribly hard work. When we are grieving the loss of someone we loved with all of our heart, our insides have been turned upside down. Life is messy and hard to maneuver through. Our energy is zapped. We question all of our beliefs. We lose trust in people and in life. Many times our faith momentarily flies right out the window. Our anchors are gone and we're left floating around in a state of confusion.

There is a story that has been around for years, and we can learn a lot from it. As it's told, a little girl was visiting her friend and got home later than expected. Her mother asked why she was so late getting home. "I was helping Elizabeth. Her doll broke." The mother asked, "Did you help Elizabeth fix it?" The child said, "No. I stayed and helped her cry."

**A friend strengthens you with prayers, blesses you with love, and fills you with hope.**

## Day 338

*"O Lord my God, in Thee I have taken refuge." Psalm 7:1*

After several months, or maybe even a year or two, our grief begins to change. We feel a bit better, and we definitely feel stronger than we did when it first happened. Something odd happens when we enter this new stage of grief. We begin to experience a new range of emotions, and one of them is guilt. We feel so guilty for moving ahead with our lives. It feels as though we're betraying our loved one in some strange way. When we're caught off guard smiling, that same wave of guilt washes over us. How can we smile when the one we love isn't here with us?

We realize that this is the first day we've experienced without thinking hundreds of times about our loved one. We were busy working and enjoying time with family, and now we feel like a traitor. We feel so ashamed because we are beginning to rebuild a life that includes joy.

This is a time to be very gentle with ourselves. It is all part of the process of grief. We're going to feel terrible for a while about moving forward. In time we'll grow to a place where we'll realize this shift is part of our healing. We'll be faced with one of the hardest, yet most necessary, decisions of all—giving ourselves permission to feel joy. That day is coming. We might not want it to, but we were not designed to carry the heavy weight of grief all of the days of our life. With our permission, our heart will begin to heal and will slowly allow room for a world of new joy.

**Keep your heart open to hope. As long as there is hope, there is joy.**

## Day 339

*"Trust in the Lord forever, for in God the Lord, we have an everlasting rock." Isaiah 26:4*

We never really thought much about dreams until now. Grief dreams are definitely ones we remember vividly. When we dream of our loved one it seems so real. We talk to each other. We smile and we laugh. It's just like old times. In fact, our dreams seem so real that when we wake up it takes us several moments to grasp that this was just a dream.

Upon realizing that what we just experienced was just a dream, our heart plummets. For just a brief moment we experienced our life as we once knew it. We were so happy in that dream. We fall into our pillow sobbing because we never want to let loose of that happy, whole feeling again. Oh, how much we miss our loved one!

Sometimes it helps to shift our thinking just a bit. Instead of feeling sorrowful about our dreams, we can think of them as a visit from our loved one. We can close our eyes and remember that dream over and over again a thousand times, each time experiencing the joy of our visit. It's okay if it was only a dream. If thinking of our dream as a visit helps us in our grief, then that's just what we'll do. Besides, who's to say it wasn't really a visit?

**Most people are stronger than they know; they just forget to believe it sometimes.**

## Day 340

*In my trouble I cried to the Lord, and He answered me.*
*Psalm 120:1*

We go through such times of turmoil when we're grieving a loss. We are so anxious that our minds whirl around and around until it's almost impossible to calm down. We try every known calming technique we can think of, including drinking chamomile tea, walking during the day, thinking positive thoughts, and some days these things really work well. But, nighttime is another story altogether.

We go to bed feeling exhausted from fighting all day long with our grief. We lay our head down on a comfortable pillow determined to get some sleep. And, then it starts all over again. We toss and turn with our minds running a mile a minute. No matter how hard we try, we can't stop those thoughts of missing the one who is gone.

The tears soak our pillow night after night and we wonder when this is all going to end. When morning finally comes, things somehow seem different. Even though our hearts are still so heavy with sorrow and sadness, things are just a bit better. Maybe it's seeing the dawning of a new day. Maybe it's the comforting smell of coffee brewing. Maybe it's simply knowing that we're one more day closer to finding a place of hope.

**At my lowest God is my hope. At my darkest God is my light. At my weakest God is my strength. At my saddest God is my comforter. How glad I am that God is always near.**

## Day 341

*"Weeping may endure for a night, but joy comes in the morning." Psalm 30:5*

When we were little children, we had no trouble believing our parents when they told us that things would get better in the morning. If we were sick, we believed our fever would leave and we'd soon be outside playing. If we were sad because we had a fight with our friend, we believed that tomorrow would be a happy day of friendship again.

When struggling with our companion of grief, no matter what anybody tells us, it's hard to believe that there will ever be a day when life will seem joyful again. All we can understand is the pain we're experiencing right at this moment. We know this hurts worse than anything we've ever felt, and we cannot perceive this heavy weight leaving us any time soon.

Maybe it wouldn't be a such a bad idea to believe just for one day in the things our friends are telling us. Maybe things will get better for us. Maybe as we travel further along on this journey, life will regain meaning and actually begin to blossom into some new meaning for us.

This is a good time to remind ourselves of the trust we had as a child. We believed—*really believed*—that every day was going to be an even better day than the day before. That's not a bad idea to hold onto during this walk through grief!

**Hope is the breakfast of champions.**

## Day 342

*"The Lord will also be a stronghold for the oppressed, a stronghold in times of trouble." Psalm 9:9*

We have done all that we can do living within this grief. We have worked hard to move forward to a place where we can be productive again. We've worked hard to understand that life isn't always fair, and we know that many innocent people do suffer great injustices. We push through each day and manage not only to smile, but also to show others that we have an inner courage that keeps us going.

We feel stronger each day except for one thing. We've not been able to forgive ourselves. We've somehow managed to recall all of the wrongs we've done in our life. Now we store those wrongs in a place within our minds where they are like a flashing neon sign that reminds us every hour of the day of our many flaws. We remember every harsh word we've ever said. We remember the time when we spoke out of turn and hurt the heart of the very one we loved so much. We remember times when we were neglectful.

Why is it easier to forgive others than to forgive ourselves? We weep inwardly so hard and so long when what we really need is to once and for all let go of this pain and forgive ourselves. How? We ask ourselves that question over and over each day. How can I forgive myself?

We forgive ourselves by extending love to ourselves and accepting the fact that we are imperfect beings trying to do our very best. Forgiveness of self is necessary to shed that last heavy weight of guilt that accompanies grief and to be able to smile at the sunshine once again. Just for today, can we be a little kinder, a little more understanding of ourselves? Forgiveness will come when we love ourselves enough to say we're not perfect and neither was the one for whom we grieve. When we forgive we are honoring love. When we forgive ourselves we are also honoring the one we loved.

**Hope grows within the forgiveness of oneself.**

## Day 343

*"Preserve me, O God, for I take refuge in Thee." Psalm 16:1*

Ever so slowly we get through yet another day of grief. Then, we get through another. And, another. Maybe, just maybe, this pain is going away much like the aches and pains of the flu. We hope upon all hope that the worst of it is behind us. Then, it happens. We smell an all-too-familiar smell and it sends us reeling to our knees. We see someone passing along the sidewalk that looks just like her. We walk into the store and bump into his best friend.

We are overcome with grief all over again. It's fresh and raw. It's as though it just happened and we wonder how we will ever press on when every time we take a few steps forward we're knocked back ten.

We step back and think amid our falling tears. We knew this would happen. We were warned by others who have walked this path before us that this is just how grief acts. So, we brace our shoulders back, take a long deep breath, and dry our tears knowing we will get back up and keep on trying. We're not going to give up. Our loved one wouldn't want to see us stop living.

Things will get better. We know they will, but it's going to take time. Lots and lots of time. This grief that has come back to revisit us will soon go into hiding for a while and we will be able to see the blue skies once again.

**Be wise enough to hold onto the hope that burns within you.**

## Day 344

*"But Thou, O Lord, art a shield about me, my glory and the One who lifts my head." Psalm 3:3*

We wonder if anyone else has ever felt such pain as we do. This grief is too much to bear and we feel so alone as we're walking this long, difficult journey of loss. For a long time we don't want much to do with others because we don't want to be told how to grieve. We want someone to listen to us tell our story of loss over and over again. We want someone to share in sympathy with us. But, we don't want anyone telling us how to handle this pain that is uniquely ours.

Over time we realize that we really do want to talk to others in a more open way about our grief, so we seek out local or online grief support. We openly talk of our woundedness, and we are amazed at how many others quietly give a nod of the head letting us know that they really do understand. Maybe we aren't the only ones suffering in this way. Maybe there are countless others who are feeling alone, lost, and like they are the only one carrying so much pain.

We realize finally that there is much good to be found in sharing. We are on level playing ground. We understand one another. We know the language without speaking a word. Our tears tell the story. To receive a hug of comfort from another grieving one is to receive the most valued validation of all. Someone else knows. Someone understands. Someone has the capacity to truly and sincerely sympathize. And that is all we ever need.

**The greatest gift of courage is to bear the pain of loss and not lose hope.**

## Day 345

*"Behold, God is my helper; the Lord is the sustainer of my soul." Psalm 54:4*

It's impossible to believe that life will get better when our grief is new. Our world looks so dark and nothing makes sense. We are confused and angry at life for taking the one we loved. The anger wells up inside of us. It's more hurt than anger, but who can separate such deeply grieving emotions? Every emotion runs together, forming one huge tidal wave of pain that washes over us day and night.

It doesn't happen all at once. The grief doesn't suddenly become subdued leaving us at peace. No, it's not like that at all. It's more like the slow unveiling of spring following the harsh, cold winter. The snow begins to melt. The temperatures slowly rise to slightly above freezing. The sun begins to shine more. The ground begins a slow, continuous thaw. Then what we've been waiting for appears! The first spring crocuses and early daffodils peek up from the once frozen ground, and we know with absolute certainty that there will be springtime blooms to follow.

This same thing will happen to us in our grief walk. For months we don't see any hint of spring in our lives, then little by little a flash of light illuminates us with a smile.

We can finally hear the sound of birds chirping in the background. We notice that we are beginning to see the sunbeams dancing and the butterflies circling around their favorite flowers. Our spring is finally arriving, and we are so ready to experience the beauty once again!

**Hope is the fuel that keeps you going even when you think you're running on empty.**

## Day 346

*"My soul wait in silence for God only, for my hope is from Him. He alone is my rock and my salvation, my stronghold; I shall not be shaken." Psalm 62:5-6*

So many people tell us to keep busy after loss and we'll feel better. Keep busy and we'll forget some of the pain. Keep busy and we'll sleep better at night. Keep busy and we'll feel good because we're accomplishing something.

So we do just that. We go half crazy taking on projects. We work extra hours on our job. We even do some volunteer work thinking of all of the inner benefits we'll receive by busying ourselves in a helpful way.

But, this technique fails us miserably. Keeping busy doesn't take care of our grief. It doesn't take care of us. It doesn't take care of our desperation and loneliness. Keeping busy simply exhausts us physically and emotionally to the point of collapse.

Nature teaches us so many lessons about life and healing. When we look at nature, we never see it rushing to and fro. The sunrise and sunset take place precisely at the right time every day. Flowers know when to bloom, and trees know when to burst forth in leaves. The ground knows when to prepare for the hard winter ahead, and the birds know the exact time to fly south.

The source of our well-being comes from centering our thoughts on all that is hopeful. No, it's not easy to focus on hope when we are grieving, but with practice we will soon find out that we can do it! The calmer we stay, the more we remember that this pain is not always going to be raw, the more we will gather hope-filled thoughts within our minds and begin to see a difference. One step, one thought at a time, we will walk into a place of newfound strength and comfort.

**Never lose hope. When the sun goes down the stars come out.**

## Day 347

*"Restore to me the joy of Thy salvation and sustain me with a willing spirit." Psalm 51:12*

When we were kids all of life was a fun, exciting adventure. Every day was new and filled with hundreds of surprises. We explored every insect, every flower, every toy, and every crack and crevice that we found. Our appetites for life could not be filled. At the end of the day we fell into our beds tired from such a great day and already filled with enthusiasm for the new day coming.

When loss entered our lives, time stood still. Those first days and weeks of grief seemed like they'd never end. One day ran into the next, and the beauty of life seemed to be sucked right out of us. We lost our purpose, and every day was filled with darkness and drudgery.

Thankfully this slowing down of time does not last forever. Little by little we begin to adjust to living life again. The raw pain subdues and we are able to manage our days more easily. In fact, there are times when we catch ourselves staring out of the kitchen window and thinking how beautiful the earth looks adorned in flowers and trees and sunshine. We pause from what we're doing, but it's a good kind of pause. It's a pause that we have chosen for the benefit of replenishing ourselves from this sorrow and grief.

Time no longer stands still as a brutal enemy. Rather we choose to rest from the busyness of the day so that we can soak up some of the blessings that have come our way. Hope has a wonderful way of coming alive and we are so thankful!

**I don't know all of the mystery that surrounds grief and loss, but I do know that hope always prevails.**

## Day 348

*"Be strong, and let your heart take courage, all you who hope in the Lord." Psalm 31:24*

Dealing with grief within a family is so hard to do. Communication gets all tangled up, and we don't know what to say or when to say it. We don't even know if we should say anything. If only there was a tried and true one size fits all guide book to follow! But, we know that grief is as individual as our fingerprint, and that makes it even more difficult to know how to act within a family when everyone is on a different page in their grief.

The best way to approach any kind of communication is to begin with sincere honesty and admit we don't know what to say. Then ask if anyone wants to talk about their feelings with this loss. Little children often have great fears and questions they want answered, but they don't know how to bring up the subject. We need to give lots and lots of room for emotional differences and be careful not to voice any judgments on how another is acting in their grief. The moods within a family will be all over the place! We seem to let our guard down when we're among family members and out pours all that we've been holding in! That's okay. That's the beginning of talking, and that's also the beginning walking forward in our grief.

Remember that we need each other more now than ever before. When emotions run high, take a slow, deep breath, count to ten and remind yourself that everyone will express their pain differently. When we validate each other's grief, we've made a big stride in moving forward with learning how to communicate and live within this terrible brokenness. One day, one thought at a time, we will do it.

**Always remember that no matter how broken you feel, you are someone's reason to smile.**

## Day 349

*"The Lord is near to the brokenhearted and saves those who are crushed in spirit." Psalm 34:18*

Following a loss we seem to think that if we fill every waking moment with something to do, we will escape pain. We busy ourselves doing everything we can think of to fill up each day so that at the end of the day we can fall into our beds exhausted.

This busy lifestyle works for a short while until we realize that we're getting burned out. We don't feel right. We know something is wrong but we can't quite put a name to what it is. It's called grief burnout. We've been on the run for days and weeks on end without stopping long enough to catch our breath, and now we've reached a point of mental, physical, and emotional exhaustion.

Our bodies let us know when it's time to stop. Everything seems to shut down at once. We feel sick. We struggle with headaches. We have backaches, leg aches, panic attacks, extreme anxiety, and we cry buckets of tears. Everything is out of whack and something has to give.

This is the time for us to simply be still. Find a quiet place at home and sit. Rest. Allow our thoughts to float. We don't have to think about anything specifically. We just need some good old fashioned rest. We need time to regroup and learn to love being within our home again. It takes time to understand the meaning of all that has happened and to learn how to love being in our own skin again. It takes lots and lots of time. Rest.

Replenish. Love ourselves. We can do it. We must do it, and we will!

**Be strong enough to let go and patient enough to allow hope to arrive.**

## Day 350

*"For in the day of trouble He will conceal me in His tabernacle; in the secret place of His tent He will hide me; He will lift me up on a rock." Psalm 27:5*

When life is rolling along in a routine way, we have a tendency to worry about the future. It's normal to think ahead with a bit of fear. There is always fear with the unknown. After a loss something happens inside of us that turns the volume up on our propensity to worry. We begin worrying about what will happen ten years from now, twenty years from now, and beyond. We don't just worry, we plan out the worst possible scenarios in our minds and, with each different scene we imagine, we are doomed.

It takes a lot of effort to put the brakes on this kind of thinking, but we must! Fearful worry will take away any bit of joy we might have and will put us in an emotional funk that will take years to overcome.

We've been through a lot. Loss is never easy, and the lingering grief deserves our every attention. But, one thing we must keep foremost in our minds is the fact that when we worry incessantly over the future, we are robbing ourselves of any joy we might have today.

Try to lift your eyes up beyond your grief and look to the sunbeams dancing in front of you. Allow one of those sunbeams to enter your heart, and notice the difference in the way your day goes. With each sunbeam, one worry is erased and a seed of joy is planted. Your grief will always be a part of you, but make certain that hope lives on in you, too!

**Hope dances in the rain until the sun comes out again.**

## Day 351

*"But as for me, I trust in Thee, O Lord. I say, 'Thou art my God.'" Psalm 31:14*

It's hard to trust in anyone or anything once our hearts have been broken by loss. We were so innocent in our thinking about life. We believed with all of our hearts that good things happen to good people. We never thought that a devastating illness, tragic accident, drug overdose, or suicide could be responsible for the loss of someone we loved with all of our heart. Yet, we learned that tragedies do happen to good people. Tragedies happen to innocent people. Tragedies happen to those we love, and our hearts feel raw and shattered. How can we ever trust again?

When walking this journey of grief, we need someone or something to trust in—something to anchor to—to hold us upright. But, we battle within ourselves wondering if we could ever trust again. Our friends and family remind us of the beliefs that held us together during other painful situations in life. We see others holding fast to their faith in a higher power and we crave to have some of the strength that we see in them.

Maybe, just for now, you can find it within yourself to trust for just one day that you will gain the strength to move forward in this grief. Maybe you can get through today with some trust, and try it again tomorrow. After all, what have you got to lose? Give trust a try, if only for today!

**Pain is real, but so is hope. I will place my trust in hope.**

## Day 352

*"In Thee, O Lord, I have taken refuge." Psalm 31:1*

Months ago when our grief was raw and overpowering, we never thought it was going to be possible to experience even a hint of joy in our lives again. In fact, we got angry and hurt when anyone suggested the possibility. Our hearts were so broken and torn that we were certain we would feel this level of intense pain forever.

Slowly life has been evolving into something new, though. We realize that we have changed since our loss. We don't like all of the changes that have happened, but we notice that some of the changes that are taking place are actually blessings. It almost feels like a betrayal to say that any kind of blessing could result from a loss, but we are living proof that blessings are happening.

Before our loss, we rushed through life hardly ever noticing the sound of the birds chirping their morning songs, but now we stop whatever we're doing and listen with delight. We set our alarm an hour early just so that we can walk outside to savor our morning cup of coffee and take in the miracle of a sunrise. We cherish the background noise of people gathered together talking and enjoying one another's company.

Is it possible that we're beginning to feel life once again? Is it possible that we are more aware of the everyday blessings found in the small moments in life? Maybe—just maybe—we're beginning to trust in life once again, and it feels so very good!

**Hope and trust are companions that arrive dressed in the familiar moments of life.**

## Day 353

*"Though I walk in the midst of trouble, Thou wilt revive me." Psalm 138:7*

When walking the path of grief and loss, it's normal to feel all alone. Our thoughts deceive us into thinking that nobody has ever experienced pain on the same level as ours. While it is true that each person's pain is unique and very personal, it helps to know that there are others who have had similar pain, and they can help us on this journey.

There is an instant feeling of kindred hearts when we meet someone who has carried this pain of loss. They understand our feelings, and they can truly sympathize with our pain. Sometimes we meet these friends by accident when telling our story of loss. Other times we seek them out by going to grief support meetings or events.

Whatever way we meet, this blessing of friendship is one to cherish and hold dear. When a fellow sufferer walks alongside of us, the load we're carrying is so much easier to bear.

Why not take a chance and expose your pain enough to let a friend come into your circle of grief? Chances are, there are others looking for fellow grievers to join them on this journey, too!

**To help a friend in need is easy, but to give him your time is to give a piece of your heart.**

## Day 354

*"My soul weeps because of grief; Strengthen me according to Thy word." Psalm 119:28*

For months we have been consumed with every aspect of grief that is known to mankind. We've cried for days on end. We've fallen into bed at the end of each day exhausted from the energy it takes to grieve. We've secluded ourselves from friends because we haven't been able to enjoy things like going out for dinner or to the movie theater. We found a certain safety in doing these things. We knew that they were within the normal realm of loss, and that gave us a certain level of comfort.

But now we're feeling different. We have moved along in our grief almost without realizing it. We now can enjoy things like long walks among nature. We are beginning to enjoy doing some activities with friends, if only on a limited basis. We even benefit in a little bit of alone time. We're not afraid of being alone with our thoughts like we were during the early weeks of our loss.

We have a desire to do something, and we're not quite sure what that something is yet. We know we're ready to take one more step forward and experiment with life once again. Maybe we'll try a new hobby. Or maybe we'll volunteer at the local library reading stories to children for an after school program. The desire to do something meaningful is there and that is a wonderful feeling. We're beginning to find purpose in life once again!

**Never allow the waves of grief wash away your hope.**

## Day 355

*"For I am the Lord your God, who upholds your right hand, Who says to you, 'Do not fear, I will help you.'"*
*Isaiah 41:13*

When a loved one dies, we begin to think more spiritually. We're not afraid to talk about heaven and what it means to us. We're not at all hesitant to talk about eternity and the idea that each of us has a soul. In fact, we find great comfort in talking with others about the possibility of our spirits living on forever.

We often paint a picture of heaven in our minds, and it's such a beautiful one. We envision our loved one being surrounded by angels in a place that knows no pain or sorrow, and our hearts find great peace in this. For a while we experienced an internal tug-of-war. We wrestled with the idea of how wonderful it would be to leave this earth and sit forever with our loved one.

When reality settles into our hearts and minds, we realize that we still have a purpose and a place on this earth. We are free to experience a relationship with our loved one that only those who know loss can experience. We have an eternal hope living within us that lets us know our loved one is at peace and one day we will be, too.

Finally we have come to a place of softer grief knowing that there is more to life than meets the eye. We have had that wonderful awakening to knowing that we are spiritual beings and the only way to pass over to this place we call heaven is death. We finally used the word death in a way that gave us hope!

**Walk with me along the pathway of grief and I will help you find the hope of heaven.**

## Day 356

*"In quietness and trust is your strength." Isaiah 30:15*

After walking this journey of grief for months, we find something happening deep inside of us. There seems to be a quieting of our pain. At first we don't realize it, but we are given little glimpses of hope that help to awaken our senses that have been pressed under the weight of our grief for so long.

Morning comes and we begin our day by thinking about our to do list rather than the fact that our loved one isn't here. We run several of our daily errands and notice that we made it through the car ride without tears streaming down our face. We run into friends we haven't seen in a long time, and we can say with a small bit of confidence that we're doing better. These are such little things, but they let us know that we are finally beginning to feel again.

Finding our way back to life after loss is a slow process, but every step along the way is a reminder that we're going to make it. One day, one step, one breath at a time we're going to make it!

**Hope is not a dream. It's a way of bringing us back to experience life again.**

## Day 357

*"Do not fear, for I am with you; do not anxiously look about you, for I am your God. I will strengthen you, surely I will help you. Surely I will uphold you with My righteous right hand." Isaiah 41:10*

One of our biggest fears is that if we move on in our grief we will forget our loved one. We feel as though we are in some way being disrespectful and showing dishonor to the one we loved with all of our heart. It helps to establish early on in our grief walk that we will never forget the one we loved. The pain will become less raw, but that doesn't in any way mean that we are forgetting. Our love won't allow us to do that.

Early on in our grief we weren't able to look at pictures. It was too painful. Now is perhaps the time to create a beautiful album of pictures and place it where you can look at it whenever you'd like. You can also make a place for items that hold special meaning just to you. You can use these as reminders of certain events that meant so much to you because they were shared with the one you loved. You don't have to create a shrine, but it helps to have an area of the room to hold that special picture, mug, blanket, or pressed flower that represents beautiful memories.

You might not be there yet, but there will come a time when you will remember more vividly that your loved one lived instead of only remembering the sorrow that came with death. How wonderful to know that we have these choices in our grief!

**Grief never ends, but with time and hope it does change shape.**

## Day 358

*"Thy word is a lamp to my feet, and a light to my path."*
*Psalm 119:105*

Holidays are so hard when walking through the valley of loss. We wonder how we'll ever get through the day without our loved one. We fret and worry for weeks on end about what the day will look like. We picture ourselves totally falling apart in front of our family and friends. We imagine a hysterical crying fit or moments of lashing out in anger. We close our eyes and let the tears stream down our face as we cry out that we just can't do this.

The truth is we will do this, and we will do it on our terms. Holidays are a lot easier if you come up with some kind of a plan. Inwardly you know your limits. If you're not at a place to be around a crowd of cheering, celebratory people, then there is no reason to put yourself through that kind of misery. Instead, plan whatever best fits your mood. Maybe you want to go out of town for the holiday and not spend it with family. Perhaps McDonald's sounds better than turkey this year. If you're not in a gift-giving mood, then there is no need for apologies or guilt. This is a hard time in life, and you have every right to do what you feel you can do and nothing more.

The hardest part is coming up with a plan and sticking to it. This is the time you must do what you feel is best for yourself, not what others say you should do. There will be other holidays. It's up to you to follow your heart. Remember, you are the one trying to live within this brokenness. You have every right to skip a holiday when you feel the need.

**Never give up. Your day of hope is on the way.**

## Day 359

*"Hear my prayer, O Lord. Give ear to my supplications!"*
*Psalm 143:1*

The memory of our loss will always be part of us. We will always remember the way it felt when we got the news. We will recall those first agonizing months following loss. Maybe we won't remember all of the details, but we will remember the hard time we had fumbling through life without meaning or purpose. We will remember, and that's okay. We wouldn't want it any other way because these memories help to remind us of how far we've come. These memories help to remind us of our inner strength and the will we had to go on.

We have traveled a difficult road and we know that there is no ending to this thing called grief. But, there is a place where the road becomes less rocky and the storms are less frequent. The journey becomes a bit easier, and we can even experience the sun shining on fields of flowers along the way.

We will always slip in and out of grief. That's a fact that is now part of our lives. But, the good news is we understand a bit better how to brace for the grief storms, seek shelter, and then emerge back into the sunlight of hope. Even better is knowing that we have choices along the way!

**Grieving is a journey that teaches us how to love in a new way.**

## Day 360

*"Let me hear Thy lovingkindness in the morning; For I trust in Thee; Teach me the way I should walk; For to Thee I lift up my soul." Psalm 143:8*

We form a picture in our minds of how it must be for our loved ones who have left us. These images are based mostly on what we learned as a child in Sunday school and also from our life experiences growing up. If we remember being cradled in the arms of a loving mother or father a gentle image of love comes to mind. We imagine our loved one being held close, cradled in the arms of a mighty one who is both tender and strong. We picture a place called heaven that is filled with brightness, illumined by a light that is blinding to the human eye. We envision a place where everyone has a smile and feels only peace and love.

Can we really know if this is true? No, not until we pass into the place of the eternal. But, we've been given descriptions, and some claim to have visited there for a brief while and returned to tell us of this magnificent place. We will never know for sure until we pass over, but we get such a calm that washes over us when thinking about these scenes of heaven that it does no harm at all to guide our minds there.

What a wonderful thought to imagine our loved one enjoying peace and love and beauty. These thoughts become our saving grace in this walk through grief. We can imagine no greater scene than this of perfect love. Today we will allow this peace to dwell within us and we will be comforted.

**Hope diminishes the power fear holds over us and gives us a glimpse of the beauty of heaven.**

## Day 361

*"Wait for the Lord; Be strong, and let your heart take courage; Yes, wait for the Lord." Psalm 27:14*

We desperately want our relationship to continue with our loved one after death. Parent and child, husband and wife, brother and sister. We can't stand the thought of this relationship ending with death. So, we look for clues that our loved one is still near us in spirit. We hear others talking about the rainbow that forms a beautiful arc reaching across the sky every year on the date of the death. And, we feel a bit jealous.

Why haven't we seen a sign like this? Another talks about the cardinal that sits on the windowsill and stares as if to say, "This is me. I'm here and I'm okay." Why haven't we seen such a miracle? Others talk of seeing shadows in the night, blooming flowers in the middle of winter, and even going so far as to say they heard their loved one's voice.

Why haven't we seen a sign? Our heart pleads for some kind of message to let us know we still have a relationship with the one we love. And, then it hits us like a bolt of lightning! There is nothing, not even death, that can sever the ties of love. Maybe our sign will never be bold and forthright, but deep within our heart love lives on, and that is good enough. There can never be an end to this kind of enduring love. We will keep our loved one's memory alive in our conversation every day, and by doing this we keep our relationship alive, too.

**One day I caught myself smiling for no reason, and I realized my heart was filled with hope.**

## Day 362

*"Those who know Your name trust in You, for You, Lord, have never forsaken those who seek You." Psalm 9:10*

It's almost been a year, and some days we feel so much better. How welcome are those days when grief lifts and allows the sun to shine for us. Then, without warning, we are thrust into the darkest night, left struggling and wondering what to do. The darkness overtakes us and we feel such fear. It's almost as if our grief has returned full force with a vengeance.

It helps to understand that grief will always be a part of us. Some days will be good. Some will be better. And, other days will be not so good. Grief is a path that we are traveling, and it has many bends and curves. Many hills are steep and treacherous. We will slide back down the slope and have to start climbing all over, time and time again. Anniversary dates, birthdays and holidays always send us back into that darkness for a while. Is it any wonder? It's hard trying to celebrate when our hearts have been deeply wounded and are carrying around constant pain.

Don't be discouraged. These special days on the calendar only last for twenty-four hours. You can do this. You can make it through one day. Others have done it, and you will, too!

**Never let a stumble in the road be the end of your journey.**

## Day 363

*"The Lord is my strength and my shield; My heart trusts in Him, and I am helped." Psalm 28:7*

It would be so great if we could say that soon this journey of grief will end. Lots of well-meaning people tell us that within six months to a year our pain will be gone. We know better than to believe that, because we're living within this grief. We know that this pain never ends. It will change, just as we will change, but it never ends.

Change is such a scary word. We didn't want to change. We were so happy before this loss, and now we have been pushed into a place called our new normal. Just hearing those words creates a stir within us that brings us to a level of anxiety. We want normal, not *new* normal. But, the truth is we are now living in a new place within our brokenness. We can't be fixed, and we understand that. Countless others expect us to be "good as new" in a few months, but we know that simply can't be.

The best way to find a place within this new normal is to tell your story. Tell it over and over again until you're comfortable telling it. Then tell it some more. Why? Because this story, your story of loss and grief, will eventually evolve into your new story of how you learned to live within your brokenness. Your story is one of hope and strength and courage. It needs to be told.

**You are stronger than you think, more courageous than you know, and filled with enough hope to move mountains.**

## Day 364

*"You have turned my mourning into joyful dancing; you have removed my sackcloth and clothed me with joy."*
*Psalm 30:11*

There will come that defining moment in your grief journey when you absolutely know that you are going to make it. You know that so much in your life has changed, and not all of the changes are as bad as you once thought they would be. You have learned how to live on a higher plane—a spiritual plateau where you can see beyond the horizon of this earth into a land that stretches into all of eternity. You realize that death has been your deepest sorrow, but you have also learned how to pull an even deeper joy from within this pain.

You understand grief and it no longer controls you. You have learned the art of living within your grief. You have learned how to find a deep, meaningful blessing in each day. You have learned the value of capturing life's small moments and allowing those moments to bring you to a place of peace and calmness that can't be explained to others who have not walked this path.

You have learned that from the depth of deep sorrow comes a joy that is spiritual. Not everyone knows how to reach this place of joy, but you do. You know what it is to have your heart broken and also to have your heart touched by mercy. You know you have an unending inner strength that will not give in to this pain.

You know you are a person of hope and courage. You know because you got up this morning. You watched the sunrise. You felt the grand beginning of a new day. You experienced the most genuine form of hope and joy. You are a survivor!

**God takes my pain and graces me with hope and courage for the day.**

## Day 365

*"Turn your ear to me, come quickly to my rescue; be my rock of refuge, a strong fortress to save me."* Psalm 31:2

Sometimes we simply need to hear the words, "I'm with you. I'll never leave you. You can tell me anything, and I'll listen." There is no greater healing balm to the soul of the grieved and broken than to know that we are not alone in our pain.

How blessed is the one who has a friend that stands by through the thick and thin of life, never judging or criticizing weaknesses or shortcomings. In this journey of grief we will have many slips and falls and blunders along the way. We'll never get it completely right. But, when we have someone in our corner listening and allowing us to draw strength when we are weak, we know that we're going to be okay.

Not everybody has a physical friend like this, but we each have the blessing of a higher power. Some call this power God. Others simply say the creator of all things. When we fall weary on this journey and need help, we know all we have to do is sit under the stars at night and see the mighty power of light shining on us letting us know we are not alone. We can watch the rising of the sun in its perfection and understand that there is a power mightier than us, and we take great comfort in knowing that same power is watching over us in our grief. We have not been left alone—not for one minute!

The same power that made the sun, the moon, and the stars and set them in motion, made us and cares for us in a way that provides strength for the weary of heart, hope for the hopeless and new beginnings for the lost. May we rest in the peace of knowing we have not been left alone on this journey of grief, but rather we have a companion who gives us an indwelling of hope that stays forever ignited. We will walk the remainder of this journey in quietness and peace!

**A strong person is the one who has learned how to rest in the quiet strength of hope.**

# ABOUT THE AUTHOR

Clara Hinton is best known for her writings on grief associated with child loss. Her first book, *Silent Grief: Finding Your Way Through the Darkness,* was published over twenty years ago and continues to provide encouragement for thousands of bereaved parents. In early 2016 Hinton released *Child Loss: The Heartbreak and the Hope* following the unexpected death of her adult son. This book is finding its way into the heart of thousands of parents of child loss and has become a sustaining source of hope.

Throughout the years, Hinton has written several short essays on hope and healing. Recently she decided to put many of these writings into a daily meditation book for those grieving a loss and finding themselves in need of hope. It is Hinton's prayer that *Hope 365: Daily Meditations for the Grieving Heart* will bring hope and healing to those struggling with the profound grief brought on by loss.

Hinton is an international speaker, certified bereavement facilitator, workshop leader, author, blogger, and grief coach. She has led workshops coast-to-coast over the past twenty years, bringing hope and encouragement to thousands of families suffering through the grief of child loss.

You can find Hinton on Facebook at Silent Grief —Child Loss Support, where her daily posts encourage hundreds of thousands every week. Visit her on the web at ClaraHinton.com, SilentGrief.com, and SilentGriefSupport.com. For booking, contact Hinton at clarahintonspeaker@gmail.com.

Look for Clara Hinton's next book coming out soon, *Carmella: The Brown Eyed Girl Who Won the Hearts of Thousands.*

# ABOUT CHURCH PROTECT, INC.

Jimmy Hinton, Church Protect, Inc.
Co-founder and CEO

Thank you for your purchase of *Hope 365: Daily Meditations for the Grieving Heart.* Ten percent of the proceeds of every book sold is donated to the nonprofit organization Church Protect, Inc.

Church Protect, Inc. is a ministry dedicated to providing the best resources for churches to prevent child sexual abuse and minister to survivors of abuse. Their mission is *Protecting, Equipping, and Supporting churches to prevent and report abuse while meaningfully helping those who have been impacted by the trauma of sexual abuse.*

Co-founder and CEO Jimmy Hinton preaches for a church in rural Pennsylvania. After hearing an allegation of abuse against his father, Hinton and his mother reported his father to authorities. Hinton's father subsequently confessed to molesting over 20 very young children and is now serving a 30-60 year prison sentence.

Church Protect Co-founder Jon Uhler is a licensed therapist who had worked at a prison for nearly a decade and had logged thousands of hours counseling several thousand sex offenders. Uhler also has extensive experience counseling survivors of child sexual abuse, has conducted unique research into the family dynamics of compulsive and/or emotional overeaters, worked with trauma survivors who suffer with dissociative identity disorder, and has seminary training. Church Protect was a natural transition of Uhler and Hinton's meeting one another and sharing their stories.

The uniquely combined pastoral and clinical experiences, expansive knowledge of what pedophiles look like both in prison and on "the outside," their love for the Scriptures, and their hearts for survivors of abuse, all give Church Protect directors an emergence of well-rounded resources to keep children safe from predators. From online consultations for church leaders, to extensive seminars, to their survivors' support forum, Church Protect offers plenty of help for people of all backgrounds.

Perhaps their proudest accomplishment is their survivors' support forum, directed by Alex Howlett. This unique resource is a members-only, completely free and private support group for survivors, led by a survivor. It's an encouraging, hopeful, and healing environment for survivors to share their struggles and hope with one another in a setting where anonymity is protected. Because Church Protect cares for survivors, who are often mistreated or ignored by churches, they have vowed to offer their survivor support services free of charge. The only way this is possible is through the generosity of others who, frankly, have a heart for survivors of abuse.

For more information about Church Protect, Inc. visit churchprotect.org or contact churchprotect@gmail.com.